10953

KT-130-574
Tel: 01962 624760

THE DEAD SEA SCROLLS IN ENGLISH

Geza Vermes was born in Hungary in 1924. He attended the University of Budapest and subsequently studied at Louvain where he read Oriental history and philology, and obtained a doctorate in theology. In 1957 he was appointed to a lectureship in biblical studies at the University of Newcastle upon Tyne, and in 1965 was elected to the readership in Jewish Studies at the University of Oxford. He is a Professorial Fellow of Wolfson College and the editor of the *Journal of Jewish Studies*. He was the first president of the British Association for Jewish Studies (1975) and of the European Association for Jewish Studies (1981–84). He is a Fellow of the British Academy.

Geza Vermes is a pioneer of Qumran research. His first book, *Les manuscrits du désert de Juda*, appeared in 1953. He is also the author of *Scripture and Tradition in Judaism* (1961, 1973, 1983); *Jesus the Jew* (1973, 1976, 1981, 1983); *The Dead Sea Scrolls: Qumran in Perspective* (1977, 1981, 1982); and *Jesus and the World of Judaism* (1983). He has played a substantial part in the rewriting of Emil Schürer's classic work, *The History of the Jewish People in the Age of Jesus Christ*. One of its volumes (III/1, 1986) includes a detailed introduction to the non-biblical Dead Sea Scrolls.

He is married to Pamela Vermes, an expert on the thought of Martin Buber, and pursues his writing in close collaboration with her.

DIOCESE OF
THOROLD & LYTTELTON
LIBRARY
WINCHESTER

THE
DEAD SEA SCROLLS
IN ENGLISH

∽o∾

G. VERMES

THIRD EDITION

PENGUIN BOOKS

Penguin Books Ltd, 27 Wrights Lane, London w8 5tz (Publishing and Editorial)
and Harmondsworth, Middlesex, England (Distribution and Warehouse)
Viking Penguin Inc., 40 West 23rd Street, New York, New York 10010, USA
Penguin Books Australia Ltd, Ringwood, Victoria, Australia
Penguin Books Canada Ltd, 2801 John Street, Markham, Ontario, Canada l3r 1b4
Penguin Books (NZ) Ltd, 182–190 Wairau Road, Auckland 10, New Zealand

First published 1962
Reprinted (with revisions) 1965
Reprinted 1966
Reprinted (with revisions) 1968
Reprinted 1970, 1972, 1973, 1974
Second edition 1975
Reprinted 1976, 1978, 1979, 1980, 1981, 1982, 1983, 1984, 1985, 1986
Third edition 1987

Copyright © G. Vermes 1962, 1965, 1968, 1975, 1987
All rights reserved

Filmset in Linotron 202 Baskerville

Filmset, printed and bound in Great Britain by
Hazell Watson & Viney Limited,
Member of the BPCC Group,
Aylesbury, Bucks

Except in the United States of America, this book is sold
subject to the condition that it shall not, by way of trade or otherwise
be lent, re-sold, hired out, or otherwise circulated without the publisher's
prior consent in any form of binding or cover other than that in which it is
published and without a similar condition including this condition
being imposed on the subsequent purchaser

CONTENTS

❧

TO THE MEMORY OF
THE GREAT QUMRAN SCHOLARS
OF THE FIRST GENERATION

E. L. Sukenik (1889–1953)
H. H. Rowley (1890–1969)
W. F. Albright (1891–1971)
R. de Vaux (1903–1971)
A. Dupont-Sommer (1900–1983)
Y. Yadin (1917–1984)

and

FOR PAM
The fruits of our common labour

ABBREVIATIONS

CD   Cairo Damascus Rule
DJD   *Discoveries in the Judaean Desert* (Clarendon Press, Oxford)
DSS   Dead Sea Scrolls
En.   Enoch
Fr.   Fragment
H   *Hodayoth* = Hymns
M   *Milḥamah* = War Rule
Melch Melchizedek
p   *pesher* = sectarian Bible commentary
Ps^a Psalms Scroll a = 11QPs^a
Q   Qumran cave (1Q, 2Q, etc. = Qumran cave 1, 2, etc.)
S   *Serekh* = Community Rule = 1QS
Sa   *Serekh*: Appendix a = Messianic Rule = 1QSa
Sb   *Serekh*: Appendix b = Blessings = 1QSb
TS   Temple Scroll = 11QTS

PREFACE

❧

Forty years have elapsed since the spring of 1947 when, in a well-nigh inaccessible cave close to the shore of the Dead Sea, a Bedouin shepherd boy accidentally discovered very ancient Hebrew and Aramaic manuscripts. That year has proved to mark a turn of eras, the dividing line between the pre-Qumran and post-Qumran age, in the field of biblical and Jewish studies and even in New Testament research. No one concerned with these disciplines can now traverse safely the paths of the inter-Testamental world without being well acquainted with the Dead Sea Scrolls. This book is intended to assist the reader to acquire the minimum necessary familiarity with the literature from Qumran.

I myself first learned about the Judaean discoveries in 1948, when I was still an undergraduate in Louvain. In 1949 I published a rather naïve article on the subject, and in 1952 completed a doctoral dissertation on the historical framework of the Scrolls, which appeared in book form the following year under the title, *Les manuscrits du désert de Juda.* Though my interests have since grown and extended to other domains, in some sense I have always remained faithful to my first academic love.

The original version of this book, issued in 1962, itself now celebrates its silver jubilee. In writing it, I sought primarily to address the general reader. However, over the years it has become clear that *The Dead Sea Scrolls in English* has been turned also into a textbook for Qumran courses and used as such by an increasing number of college and university students. I have therefore decided to profit from the opportunity afforded by this first major revision to pay particular attention to their needs by providing more bibliographical data.

Compared to its predecessors, the present edition contains two further novelties. To begin with, it has been considerably enlarged through the inclusion of the Temple Scroll and other material published during the last dozen years. In addition, the three introductory essays, composed before 1962, have been replaced by an abridged version of the corresponding chapters, reproduced by kind permission of SCM Press from my book, *The Dead Sea Scrolls: Qumran in Perspective*. Written in 1977, revised in 1982 and again before going to print this time, they represent a reasonably up-to-date statement on the Qumran sect, its history and religious outlook. Readers needing more introductory information are advised to consult that volume.

I must regretfully confess that this third edition of *The Dead Sea Scrolls in English*, although more comprehensive than the 254 pages of the 1962 original, or even the 281 pages of the 1975 second edition, still falls far short of being all-inclusive. The guilt lies elsewhere, in the slackness of those responsible since the early 1950s for the publication of the many fragments found in Qumran Cave 4. They now firmly promise speedier progress. Let us give them the benefit of the doubt and hope that, come the golden jubilee in 1997 (may we all live to see it!), they will have actually repaid the heavy debt owed for so long to the world of learning.

INTRODUCTION

❦

On the western shore of the Dead Sea, about eight miles south of Jericho, is Khirbet Qumran. It lies in one of the lowest parts of the earth, on the fringe of the hot and arid wastes of the Wilderness of Judaea, and is today silent, empty, and in ruins. But from that place, members of an ancient Jewish sect whose centre it was, hurried out one day and in haste and secrecy climbed the nearby cliffs in order to hide away in caves their precious writings. And there they remained for some two thousand years.

This, briefly, is the story of their discovery.

The first lot of documents, consisting of several biblical and non-biblical scrolls, was found accidentally by an Arab shepherd in the spring of 1947. In 1949, the place was identified and explored by archaeologists, and the authenticity and antiquity of the find were established. Then, between February 1952 and January 1956, ten more caves were located. For two of them (3 and 5), the archaeologists were responsible; workmen on the site discovered four others (7, 8, 9 and 10); and the indefatigable Ta'amireh tribesmen, who most of the time succeeded in outwitting their professional rivals, were able to uncover four more (2, 4, 6 and 11), two of them (4 and 11) containing extremely rich manuscript deposits. Finally, in 1967, the giant Temple Scroll emerged from clandestinity and joined the other documents in the Shrine of the Book in Jerusalem.

Also, between 1951 and 1956, the archaeologists, after an initial blunder when they failed to recognize the connexion between the scrolls and the nearby ruins, were occupied with the excavation of the Qumran community settlement itself and, in 1958, with its dependence at Ain Feshkha, two miles or so farther south.

Altogether, the eleven more or less complete Dead Sea Scrolls and the thousands of fragments belonging originally to almost six hundred manuscripts, amount to a substantial body of literature covering the Hebrew Bible, other religious compositions, and works proper to a particular Jewish sect.

The books and articles written on the subject would fill a large library, but in the main they have been highly technical and therefore accessible only to the specialist. The present work gives the actual text of the non-biblical religious writings, so to a large extent the reader will now be able to judge them for himself. It may nevertheless be useful if I first do what I can to dispel confusion by defining the nature of their contribution to scholarship and to a fuller appreciation of Judaism and Christianity.

The Qumran biblical documents cover the whole Hebrew Bible, with the exception of the book of Esther, and are about a thousand years older than the most ancient codices previously extant. With this newly discovered material at their disposal, experts concerned with the study of the text and transmission of the Scriptures are now able to achieve far greater accuracy in their deductions and can trace the process by which the text of the Bible attained its final shape. Moreover, they are in a position to prove that it has remained virtually unchanged for the last two thousand years.

The Qumran fragments of the Pseudepigrapha (non-biblical religious compositions) and Apocrypha (considered non-biblical by Jews and some Christian bodies, but accepted as secondarily or fully canonical by other Churches) have also been of vast benefit to learning. Preserved by the early Church, these books had been handed down in translation – in Greek, Latin, Syriac, Ethiopian, etc. – but had inevitably suffered some degree of interference at the hands of interpreters and copyists. Now that several of them (Ecclesiasticus, Tobit, Jubilees, Enoch, the Testament of Levi, etc.) are available in their original Hebrew or Aramaic in manuscripts which are *circa* 2,000 years old, it is for the first time possible to assess the fidelity of the translated texts.

It goes without saying, however, that beside the profit to specialists in textual criticism, palaeography, linguistics, and so on, the major gain has fallen to the student of the history and religion of Palestinian Judaism in the inter-Testamental period (150 B.C. to A.D. 70). For him, the sectarian writings, which form the bulk of the Dead Sea literature and were formerly quite unknown, have opened new avenues of exploration into the shadowy era of the birth of Christianity and of the establishment of Rabbinic Judaism. Previously, very little of it was known. First- and second-century rabbis had not permitted religious writings of that epoch to go down to Jewish posterity unless they fully conformed to orthodoxy, and although, as I have said, some of them were preserved by Christians, the fact that they had been used as a vehicle for Church apologetics caused their textual reliability to be suspect. But the Scrolls are unaffected by either Christian or Rabbinic censorship, and once their evidence is complete – a great deal still remains to be published – the historian will be thoroughly acquainted, not with just another aspect of Jewish beliefs or customs, but with the whole organization, teaching, and aspirations of an inter-Testamental religious community.

In the following pages I assume, in the company of the majority of scholars, that the ancient Jewish sect of the Essenes and the Qumran Community were probably one and the same. The first-century Jewish philosopher Philo of Alexandria, the historian Flavius Josephus, and the geographer and naturalist Pliny the Elder have all discoursed on this sect of ascetics whose common life and severe discipline they seem greatly to have admired, and any profound study of the Community as a religious group demands careful scrutiny, not only of its own compositions, but also of these classical reports. For a full discussion of the problem of the sect's historical identity, readers are referred to my book, *The Dead Sea Scrolls: Qumran in Perspective* (SCM Press, 1982), pp. 116–36.

The foregoing remarks will, I hope, give some idea of the reason why the Scrolls have awakened such intense interest in the academic world. But why have they appealed so strongly to the imagination of the non-specialist? After all, other manuscripts of biblical significance have been discovered in recent years, such as the Coptic documents from Chenoboskion, including the *Gospel according to Thomas*; yet these have raised comparatively little stir.

The outstanding characteristic of our age appears to be a desire to reach back to the greatest attainable purity, to the basic truth. Affecting the whole of our outlook, it has necessarily included the domain of religious thought and behaviour, and with it the whole subject of Judeo-Christian culture and spirituality. A search is being made for the original meaning of issues with which we have become almost too familiar and which with the passing of the centuries have tended to become choked with inessentials, and it has led not only to a renewed preoccupation with the primitive but fully developed expression of these issues in the Scriptures, but also to a desire for knowledge and understanding of their prehistory.

The Rules, Hymns, biblical Commentaries, and other liturgical works of the Qumran Community respond to this need in that they add substance and depth to the historical period in which Christianity and Rabbinic Judaism originated. They reveal one facet of the spiritual ferment at work among the various parties of Palestinian Judaism at that time, a ferment which culminated in a thorough examination and reinterpretation of the fundamentals of the Jewish faith. By dwelling in such detail on the intimate organization of their society, on their interpretation of Scripture and history, on the role attributed to their Teacher, and on their ultimate hopes and expectations, the sect of the Scrolls has exposed its own resulting doctrinal synthesis. This in its turn has thrown into relief and added a new dimension to its dissenting contemporaries. Thus, compared with the ultra-conservatism and rigidity of the Essene Rule, orthodox Judaism appears progressive and flexible, and beside Essenism and Rabbinic orthodoxy the Christian revolution stands out invested with religious actuality. Yet at the same time, the common ground from which they all sprang, and their affinities and borrowings, emerge more clearly than ever before. The faith of each of these three religious movements was, in fact, a separate and distinct commentary on the one body of traditional Jewish teaching and – this is a point which is slowly being realized – neither of them can properly be understood independently of the others.

Essenism is dead. The brittle structure of its stiff and exclusive organization was unable to withstand the national catastrophe which struck Palestinian Judaism in A.D. 70. Animated by the loftiest ideals and devoted to the observance of 'perfect holiness', it yet lacked the pliant strength which enabled Rabbinic Judaism to survive and flourish. And although its Teacher of Righteousness clearly sensed the deeper obligations implicit in the Mosaic Law, he was without the genius of Jesus who laid bare the inner core of spiritual truth and exposed the essence of religion as an existential relationship between man and man, and between man and God.

I. THE COMMUNITY

~◦~◦~

In the course of the last four decades, the information garnered from the Scrolls and from Qumran's archaeological remains has been combined by experts to form a persuasive portrait of the people to which they allude. Yet for all the advances made in knowledge and understanding, the enigma of the sect is by no means definitely solved. After all this time, we are still not certain that we have interpreted the whole evidence correctly or collated it properly. Questions continue to arise in the mind and there is still no way to be sure of the answers.

Our perplexity is mainly due to an absence in the documents, singly or together, of any systematic exposition of the sect's constitution and laws. The Community Rule legislates for a kind of monastic society, the statutes of the Damascus Rule for an ordinary lay existence; and the War Rule and Messianic Rule in their turn, while associated with the other two, and no doubt reflecting to some extent a contemporary state of affairs, plan for a future age.

Taken together, however, it is clear from this literature that the sectaries regarded themselves as the true Israel, the repository of the authentic traditions of the religious body from which they had seceded. Accordingly, they organized their movement so that it corresponded faithfully to that of Israel itself, dividing it into priests and laity, the priests being described as the 'sons of Zadok' – Zadok was High Priest in David's time – and the laity grouped after the biblical model into twelve tribes. This structure is described in the War Rule's account of Temple worship as it was expected to be at the end of time:

The twelve chief priests shall minister at the daily sacrifice before God . . . Below them shall be the chiefs of the Levites to the number of twelve, one for each tribe . . . Below them shall be the chiefs of the tribes (IQM II, 1–3).

Still following the biblical pattern, sectarian society (apart from the tribe of Levi) was further distinguished into units of Thousands, Hundreds, Fifties and Tens (1QS II, 21; CD XIII, 1–2). To what extent these figures are symbolical, we do not know, but it is improbable that 'Thousands' amounted to anything more than a figure of speech. It is not irrelevant, in this connection, to note that the archaeologists have deduced from the fact that the cemetery contained eleven hundred graves, dug over the course of roughly two hundred years, that the population of Qumran, an establishment of undoubted importance, can never have numbered more than 150 to 200 souls at a time. Also, it should be borne in mind that the total membership of the Essene sect in the first century A.D. only slightly exceeded 'four thousand' (Josephus, *Antiquities* XVIII, 21).

To consider now the two types separately, the monastic brotherhood at Qumran alludes to itself in the Community Rule as 'the men of holiness' and 'the men of perfect holiness', and to the sect as 'the Community' and 'Council of the Community'. The establishment was devoted exclusively to religion. Work must have formed a necessary part of their existence; it is obvious from the remains discovered at Qumran that they farmed, made pots, cured hides and reproduced manuscripts. But no indication of this appears in the documents. It is said only that they were to 'eat in common, pray in common and deliberate in common' (1QS VI, 2–3), living in such a way as to 'seek God with a whole heart and soul' (1QS I, 1–2). Perfectly obedient to each and every one of the laws of Moses and to all that was commanded by the prophets, they were to love one another and to share with one another their 'knowledge, powers and possessions' (1QS I, 11). They were to be scrupulous in their observance of the times appointed for prayer, and for every other event of a liturgical existence conducted apart from the Temple of Jerusalem and its official cult. 'Separate from the habitation of ungodly men' (1QS VIII, 13), they were to study the Torah in the wilderness and thereby 'atone for the Land' (1QS VIII, 6, 10) and its wicked men, for whom they were to nourish an 'everlasting hatred' (1QS IX, 21), though this went together with a firm conviction that their fate was in God's hands alone. At the poet proclaims in the Hymn with which the Community Rule ends:

I will pay to no man the reward of evil;
I will pursue him with goodness,
For judgement of all the living is with God
And it is He who will render to man his reward.

(1QS x, 17–18)

They were to be truthful, humble, just, upright, charitable and modest. They were to

watch in community for a third of every night of the year, to read the Book and study the law and to pray together (1QS vi, 7–8).

These are, as may be seen, mostly the sort of recommendations to be expected of men devoting themselves to contemplation. A point to bear in mind, however, is that the contemplative life is not a regular feature of Judaism. An additional distinctive trait of these sectaries is that another qualification was required of them besides holiness: they were expected to become proficient in the knowledge of the 'two spirits' in which all men 'walk', the spirits of truth and falsehood, and to learn how to discriminate between them. They were taught, in other words, how to recognize a 'son of Light' or potential 'son of Light', and how to distinguish a 'son of Darkness' belonging to the lot of Belial (1QS iii, 13–iv, 25; cf. below pp. 64–7).

The hierarchy at Qumran was strict and formal, from the highest level to the lowest. Every sectary was inscribed in 'the order of his rank' (1QS vi, 22) – the term 'order' recurs constantly – and was obliged to keep to it in all the community meetings and at table. But the 'sons of Zadok, the priests' came first in the order of precedence. Although nothing to this effect is mentioned specifically in the Community Rule, the superior, the so-called *mebaqqer* or Guardian, was undoubtedly one of their number, as was the Bursar of the Congregation entrusted with handling the material affairs of the Community. In their hands lay the ultimate responsibility for decisions on matters of doctrine, discipline, purity and impurity, and in particular matters pertaining to 'justice and property' (1QS ix, 7). It was also a basic rule of the order that a priest was required to be present at any gathering of ten or more meeting for debate, Bible study or prayer. A priest was to recite the grace before the common meals and to pronounce blessings (1QS vi, 3–8). He was no doubt the man whose duty it was to study the Law continually (1QS vi, 7; viii, 11–12). One interesting feature of the priesthood at Qumran is that their precedence was absolute. In Judaism as represented by the Mishnah, the priest is superior to the Levite, the Levite to the Israelite, and the Israelite to the 'bastard' (Horayoth iii: 8). But the priestly precedence is conditional. If the 'bastard' is a man of learning, we are told, and the High Priest a 'boor', 'the bastard . . . precedes the High Priest'.

The highest office was vested in the person of the Guardian, known also as the 'Master' (*maskil*). The Community was to be taught by him how to live in conformity with the 'Book of the Community Rule' (1QS I, 1), and to be instructed by him in the doctrine of the 'two spirits'. He was to preside over assemblies, giving leave to speak to those wishing to do so (1QS VI, 11–13). He was to assess, in concert with the brethren, the spiritual progress of the men in his charge and rank them accordingly (1QS VI, 21–2). And negatively, he was not to dispute with 'the men of the Pit' and not to transmit to them the sect's teachings (1QS IX, 16–17).

Of the sect's institutions, the most significant appears to have been the Council of the Community, or assembly of the Congregation. From a passage ordering all the members to sit in their correct places – 'The priests shall sit first, and the elders second, and all the rest of the people according to their rank' (1QS VI, 8–9) – it would seem to have been a gathering of the whole community, under the priests and men of importance, with the Guardian at the head. But in another text the rule is as follows:

In the Council of the Community there shall be twelve men and three Priests, perfectly versed in all that is revealed of the Law, whose works shall be truth, righteousness, justice, loving-kindness and humility. They shall preserve the faith in the Land with steadfastness and meekness and shall atone for sin by the practice of justice and by suffering the sorrows of affliction. They shall walk with all men according to the standard of truth and the rule of the time (1QS VIII, 1–4).

These three priests and twelve men are referred to nowhere else, so we cannot be sure of their place in the Qumran order. Their presence was obviously essential: the Rule states that when 'these are in Israel, the Council of the Community shall be established in truth' (1QS VIII, 4–5). But whether they formed the nucleus of the sect as a whole, or the minimum quorum of the sect's leadership symbolizing the twelve tribes and the three Levitical clans, or a special elite within the Council designated elsewhere 'the Foundations of the Community', must be left open to question. The purpose of the meetings is in any case clear. It was to debate the Law, to discuss their current business, to select or reject new-comers under the guidance of the Guardian, to hear charges against offenders, and to conduct a yearly inquiry into the progress of every sectary, promoting or demoting them in rank, again under the Guardian's supervision (1QS v, 23–4; vi, 13–23). During their sessions, order and quiet was to prevail: a person wishing to offer his opinion or ask a question was to crave permission in a prescribed way. He was to rise and tell the Guardian and the Congregation, 'I have something to say to the Congregation' and then wait for their consent before going ahead (1QS vi, 8–13).

The procedure followed in enquiries into infringements of the Law and the sect's rule has been preserved, and the list of faults with their corresponding sentences tells us more about the mentality of the Dead Sea ascetics than any isolated exposition of their doctrine and principles can do.

Beginning with the blackest sins: any transgression, by commission or omission, of 'one word of the Law of Moses, on any point whatever' earned outright expulsion. No former companion might from then on associate with the sinner in any way at all (1QS viii, 21–24).

Expulsion followed, secondly, the pronouncement for any reason whatever of the divine Name:

If any man has uttered the [Most] Venerable Name, even though frivolously, or as a result of shock, or for any other reason whatever, while reading the Book or praying, he shall be dismissed and shall return no more (1QS vi, 27–vii, 2).

Thirdly, a sectary was expelled for slandering the Congregation (1QS vii, 16). Fourthly, he was sent away for rebelling against the 'Foundations' of the Community:

Whoever has murmured against the Foundations of the Community shall be expelled and shall not return (1QS vii, 17).

Lastly, where a man had been a member of the Council for at least ten years and had then defected to 'walk in the stubbornness of his heart', not only was he to be expelled, but the same judgement was extended to any of his former colleagues who might take pity on him and share with him their food or money (1QS vii, 22–23).

The remaining offences are of a kind that might be confessed and censured in any Christian monastic chapter of today, though one cannot perhaps say the same of the penances imposed for them.

In a descending order of gravity: a man who 'betrayed the truth and walked in the stubbornness of his heart' (1QS VII, 18–21), or transgressed the Mosaic Law inadvertently (1QS VIII, 24–9:1), was visited with two years of penance. He was to lose his rank and during the first year be separated from the 'purity' of the Congregation, and during the second year, from its 'drink'. Both notions will be developed presently. He was then to be re-examined by the Congregation and subsequently returned to his place in the order.

Lying in matters of property, in all probability, the partial concealment of personal possessions, earned exclusion from 'purity' for a year and a cut by one quarter in the food ration (1QS VI, 25–27). Disrespect to a companion of higher rank, rudeness and anger towards a priest, slander and deliberate insult, all earned one year of penance and exclusion from 'purity' (1QS VI, 25–27; VII, 2–5). After this, the sentences decrease to six months, three months, thirty days and ten days of penance.

For lying deliberately and similarly deceiving by word or deed, for bearing malice unjustly, for taking revenge, for murmuring against a companion unjustly, and also for going 'naked before his companion without having been obliged to do so' – a curious proviso – the sectary was to atone for six months. For failing to care for a companion and for speaking foolishly: three months. For falling asleep during a meeting of the Council, for leaving the Council while members were standing (in prayer?), for spitting in Council, for 'guffawing foolishly', for being 'so poorly dressed that when drawing his hand' – 'hand' being a euphemism – 'from beneath his garment his nakedness was seen': thirty days. And for leaving an assembly three times without reason, for interrupting another while speaking, for gesticulating with the left hand: ten days (1QS VII).

That the common table was of high importance to Qumran daily life is evident from the fact that only the fully professed and the faultless, that is to say those who were 'inscribed . . . for purity' and not subsequently disqualified, were allowed to sit at it. There is no explicit mention of a ritual bath preceding the meals, but from various references to purification by water, as well as the presence of at least two bathing installations at Qumran, it is likely that the sectaries immersed themselves before eating. But little more is learnt of the meal itself from the Community Rule than that when the table had been 'prepared for eating and the new wine for drinking', the priest was to be the first to bless the food and drink (1QS VI, 4–5). The implication would be that after him the others did the same, an inference supported by the Messianic Rule, where a similar meal is described attended by two Messiahs (1QSa II, 17–21). Some uncertainty surrounds the meaning of 'new wine', but it would seem from the use in the Scrolls, with the exception of the Temple Scroll, of the alternative Hebrew words for wine – *tirosh* and *yayin* – that the latter has pejorative connotations. More likely than not, the 'wine' drunk by the sectaries, 'the drink of the Congregation', was unfermented grape-juice.

Another topic to be considered under the heading of the sect's life and institutions is the crucial one of induction into the sect. And if it should seem strange to place it towards the end rather than at the beginning, the explanation is that with an idea, however sketchy, of what was entailed by adherence to the movement, the process by which it admitted a Jew into its company becomes easier to follow.

According to the regime followed at Qumran, a person desiring to join the sect remained on probation, certainly for two years and possibly for three or more. His first move was to appear before the Guardian 'at the head of the Congregation', meaning no doubt during a session of the Congregation, who enquired into his principles to discover if he was a suitable postulant. If they were satisfied, he 'entered the Covenant' (1QS VI, 13–15). That is to say, he solemnly swore there and then to adhere to the Torah as the sect interpreted it, vowing

by a binding oath to return with all his heart and soul to every commandment of the Law of Moses in accordance with all that has been revealed of it to the sons of Zadok, the Keepers of the Covenant (1QS v, 7–11).

After a further period of unspecified length, during which he received instruction from the Guardian 'in all the rules of the Community', he appeared once more before the Congregation, who confirmed him as a novice or dismissed him. But although he was now accepted into the Council of the Community, he was nevertheless still not admitted to 'purity' for another full year.

This concept of pure things (*tohorah, taharah* or *tohoroth*, literally 'purity' or 'purities') needs some comment. In rabbinic literature, *tohoroth* signifies in general ritually pure food as well as the vessels and utensils in which it is contained or cooked. It includes also garments. The *tohoroth*, moreover, are distinguished by the rabbis from *mashqin*, liquids, the latter being considered much more susceptible to contract impurity than solid comestibles. Hence, in ordering the novice not to touch the pure things of the Congregation, the Community forbade him all contact with its pots, plates, bowls, and necessarily the food that they held. He was not, in effect, to attend the common table. Although the context is very different, a parallel rule figures in the Temple Scroll (LXIII, 13–14), prohibiting a Gentile woman married to her Jewish captor to touch his *tohorah* for seven years.

During this first year of the novitiate, the newcomer to the sect could not share the sect's property. At a third community inquiry, he was examined for 'his understanding and observance of the Law' and, if his progress was judged to be acceptable, he handed over his money and belongings to the 'Bursar of the Congregation', but they were set aside and not yet absorbed into community ownership. During this second year, furthermore, the ban on touching the pure things was relaxed, but he could still not touch liquids, the 'drink of the Congregation'. Finally, the second year over, the novice had once more to undergo an examination, after which, 'in accordance with the judgement of the Congregation', he was at last inscribed among the brethren in the order of his rank 'for the Law and for justice and for purity'. Also, his property was amalgamated with theirs and he possessed the right from then on to speak his mind in the Council of the Community (1QS VI, 13–23).

In sum, this strict and extended curriculum falls into two stages. The postulant is first brought into the Covenant, swearing total fidelity to the Mosaic Law as interpreted by the sect's priesthood, and to 'separate from all the men of falsehood who walk in the way of wickedness' (1QS V, 10–11). He then secondly embarks on a course of training as a preliminary to joining the 'holy Congregation' (1QS V, 20). In other words, entering the Covenant and entering the Community was not one act, but two.

It has long been debated whether the Qumran sectaries were married or celibate. From the image of their life projected so far, few will probably disagree that the idea of the presence of women among them appears incongruous. The impression received is that of a wholly masculine society: indeed, they were actually enjoined 'not to follow a sinful heart and lustful eyes, committing all manner of evil' (1QS I, 6). Moreover, in support of the argument for celibacy, the word *ishah*, woman, occurs nowhere in the Community Rule. Or rather, to be more exact, it is encountered once in the final Hymn, in the cliché, 'one born of woman' (1QS XI, 21). Yet the fact cannot be overlooked that although in the graveyard itself the twenty-six tombs so far opened at random (out of eleven hundred) have all contained adult male skeletons, the archaeologists have uncovered on the peripheries of the cemetery the bones of a few women and children.

The Damascus Rule and the Temple Scroll, as well as the Messianic Rule and occasionally the War Rule, are concerned with a style of religious existence quite at variance from that at Qumran. In the 'towns' or 'camps', as the Damascus Rule terms them (CD XII, 19, 23), adherents of the sect lived an urban or village life side by side, yet apart from, their fellow-Jews and Gentile neighbours. Rearing children, employing servants, engaging in commerce and trade (even with Gentiles), tending cattle, growing vines and corn in the surrounding fields, discharging their duties to the Temple by way of offerings and sacrifice, they were obliged like their brothers in the desert to show absolute obedience to the Law and to observe the sect's 'appointed times'. There is no indication, however, that the intensive study of the Torah played any part in their lives. Nor is there any mention in their regard of instruction in the doctrine of the two spirits.

How many of these people, if any, lived in Jerusalem is not known, but they must at least have visited the city from time to time, since a statute forbids them to enter the 'house of worship' in a state of ritual uncleanness, or to 'lie with a woman in the city of Sanctuary to defile the city of the Sanctuary with their uncleanness' (CD I, 22; XII, 1; TS XLV, 11–12).

Little is revealed in the Damascus Rule of how the life-span of the individual progressed in the 'towns', and for this we have to turn to the Messianic Rule in the hope that it reflects contemporary actuality as well as the ideal life of an age to come.

According to the latter Rule, members of the Covenant were permitted to marry at the age of twenty, when they were estimated to have reached adulthood and to 'know [good] and evil' (1QSa I, 9–11). For the subsequent five years they were then allowed to 'assist' (as opposed to taking an active part) at hearings and judgements. At twenty-five, they advanced one grade further and qualified to 'work in the service of the Congregation' (1QSa I, 12–13). At thirty, they were regarded as at last fully mature and could 'participate' in the affairs of the tribunals and assemblies, taking their place among the higher ranks of the sect, the 'chiefs of the thousands of Israel, the Hundreds, the chiefs of the Fifties and Tens, the judges and the officers of their tribes, in all their families [under the authority] of the sons of [Aar]on the Priests' (1QSa I, 8–16). As office-holders, they were expected to perform their duties to the best of their ability and were accorded more honour or less in conformity with their 'understanding' and the 'perfection' of their 'way'. As they grew older, so their burdens became lighter (1QSa I, 19).

As at Qumran, supreme authority rested in the hands of the priests, and every group of ten or more was to include a priest 'learned in the Book of Meditation' and to be 'ruled by him' (CD XIII). His precedence, on the other hand, is not represented as absolute in the 'towns'. It is explicitly stated that in the absence of a properly qualified priest, he was to be replaced by a Levite who would perform all the functions of a superior except those specially reserved in the Bible to the priesthood such as applying the laws of leprosy (CD XIII, 3–7).

As in the Community Rule, the head of the 'camp' is given in the Damascus Rule as the *mebaqqer*, Guardian. He appears, however, not to be supported by a council. In fact, the words 'Council of the Community' are absent from this document. There is reference to the 'company of Israel', on the advice of which it would be licit to attack Gentiles (CD XII, 8), but this type of war council, mentioned also in the Messianic Rule (1QSa I, 26), can surely have had nothing to do with the assemblies described in the Community Rule. The Guardian of the 'camps', in any case, stands on his own as teacher and helper of his people. He shall love them, writes the author,

as a father loves his children, and shall carry them in all their distress like a shepherd his sheep. He shall loosen all the fetters that bind them so that in his Congregation there may be none that are oppressed and broken (CD XIII, 9–10).

The Guardian was to examine newcomers to his congregation, though not, it should be noted, to determine their 'spirit', and was to serve as the deciding authority on the question of their admission. These offices are of course already familiar to us from the Community Rule. But an additional task of the *mebaqqer* in the towns was to ensure that no friendly contact occurred between his congregation and the 'men of the Pit', i.e. everyone outside the sect. Whatever exchanges took place had to be paid for; and even these transactions were to be subject to his consent (CD XIII, 14–16).

Instead of dealing with offenders in Community courts of inquiry, the towns had their tribunals for hearing cases, equipped moreover with 'judges'. These were to be ten in number, elected for a specific term and drawn from the tribes of Levi, Aaron and Israel; four priests and Levites, and six laymen (CD x, 4–7). They were to be not younger than twenty-five and not older than sixty – in the Messianic Rule, which also speaks of judges, the age-limits are thirty and sixty years (1QSa I, 13–15) – and were to be expert in biblical law and the 'constitutions of the Covenant'. The arrangement would seem, in fact, to be fairly straightforward. Yet it is not entirely so. For example, it is evident that the Guardian was also implicated in legal matters; he had to determine whether a proper case had been made out against a sectary and whether it should be brought before the court (CD IX, 16–20), and in certain cases he appears to have imposed penalties on his own (CD xv, 13–14). We are not told whether these ten judges sat together, whether they were all drawn from the locality in which they lived, or whether they travelled on circuit as in the present day. The code of law they were expected to administer, as laid down in the Damascus Rule, is in any case totally different in both content and tone from that of the Community Rule: the offences envisaged bear no relation to existence in a quasi-monastic community. Furthermore, although, unlike the Qumran code, a sentence is prescribed but rarely, sometimes it is the death penalty. Thus, instead of recommendations not to spit or guffaw at a meeting of the Council, we have here a sectarian reformulation of scriptural laws regulating Jewish life as such.

The first group of statutes, concerned with vows, opens with the injunction that in order to avoid being put to death for the capital sin of uttering the names of God, the sectary must swear by the Covenant alone. Such an oath would be fully obligatory and might not be cancelled (CD xvi, 7–8). If he subsequently violated his oath, he would then have only to confess to the priest and make restitution (CD xv, 1–5). The sectary is also ordered not to vow to the altar articles acquired unlawfully, or the food of his own house (CD xvi, 13–15), and not to make any vow 'in the fields' but always before the judges (CD IX, 9–10). He is threatened with death if he 'vow another to destruction by the laws of the Gentiles' (CD IX, 1). As for the right conferred by the Bible on fathers and husbands to annul vows made by their daughters or wives, the Damascus Rule limits it to the cancellation of oaths which should have never been made (CD XVI, 10–12; for a somewhat different rule, see TS LIII, 16–LIV, 5).

A few ordinances follow concerned with witnesses. No one under the age of twenty was to testify before the judges in a capital charge (CD IX, 23–X, 2). Also, whereas the normal biblical custom is that two or three witnesses are needed before any sentence can be pronounced (Deut. XIX, 15), a single witness being quite unacceptable, *unus testis nullus testis*, sectarian law allowed the indictment of a man guilty of repeating the same capital offence on the testimony of single witnesses to the separate occasions on which it was committed, providing they reported it to the Guardian at once and that the Guardian recorded it at once in writing (CD IX, 17–20). In regard to the capital cases, to which should be added apostasy in a state of demonic possession (CD XII, 2–3), the adultery of a betrothed girl (4Q Ord. 2–4: 10–11), slandering the people of Israel and treason (TS LXIV, 6–13), it is highly unlikely that either the Jewish or the Roman authorities would have granted any rights of execution to the sect. So this is probably part of the sect's vision of the future age, when it as Israel *de jure* would constitute *de facto* the government of the chosen people.

A section devoted to Sabbath laws displays a marked bias towards severity. In time, rabbinic law developed the Sabbath rules in still greater detail than appears here, but the tendency is already apparent.

The sectary was not only to abstain from labour 'on the sixth day from the moment when the sun's orb is distant by its own fullness from the gate (wherein it sinks)' (CD X, 15–16), he was not even to speak about work. Nothing associated with money or gain was to interrupt his Sabbath of rest (CD X, 18–19). No member of the Covenant of God was to go out of his house on business on the Sabbath. In fact, he was not to go out, for any reason, further than one thousand cubits (about 500 yards), though he could pasture his beast at a distance of two thousand cubits from his town (CD X, 21; XI, 5–6). He could not cook. He could not pick and eat fruit and other edible things 'lying in the fields'. He could not draw water and carry it away, but must drink where he found it (CD X, 22–23). He could not strike his beast or reprimand his servant (CD XI, 6, 12). He could not carry a child, wear perfume or sweep up the dust in his house (CD XI, 10–11). He could not assist his animals to give birth or help them if they fell into a pit; he could, however, pull a man out of water or fire with the help of a ladder or rope (CD XI, 13–14, 16–17). Interpreting the Bible restrictively (Lev. XXIII, 38), the sect's lawmaker (or makers) commanded him to offer nothing on the Sabbath save the Sabbath burnt-offering, and never to send a gift to the Temple by the hand of one 'smitten with any uncleanness permitting him thus to defile the altar' (CD XI, 19–20). And as has been said earlier (p. 9), he was also never to have intercourse while in the 'city of the Sanctuary' (CD XII, 1–2; TS XLV, 1–12).

The punishment imposed for profaning the Sabbath and the feasts in any of these ways was not death as in the Bible (Num. XV, 35), and not even expulsion as in the Community Rule. It was seven years of imprisonment.

It shall fall to men to keep him in custody. And if he is healed of his error, they shall keep him in custody for seven years and he shall afterwards approach the assembly (CD XII, 4–6).

In the last group, the ordinances appear to be only loosely connected, though some of them involve relation with the larger Jewish-Gentile world. One such forbids killing or stealing a non-Jew, 'unless so advised by the company of Israel' (CD XII, 6–8). Another proscribes the sale to Gentiles of ritually pure beasts and birds, and the produce of granary and wine-press, in case they should blaspheme by offering them in heathen sacrifice. A ban is similarly laid on selling to Gentiles foreign servants converted to the Jewish faith (CD XII, 11). But in addition to these regulations affecting contacts with non-Jews, a few are concerned with dietary restrictions. Thus:

No man shall defile himself by eating any live creature or creeping thing, from the larvae of bees to all creatures which creep in water (CD XII, 12–13).

Others deal with the laws of purity (CD XII, 16–18) and purification (CD X, 10–13).

Two types of meeting are provided for, with equal laconism; the 'assembly of the camp' presided over by a priest or a Levite (cf. above, p. 10) and the 'assembly of all the camps' (CD XIV, 3–6). Presumably the latter was the general convention of the whole sect held on the Feast of the Renewal of the Covenant, the annual great festival when both the 'men of holiness' and the 'men of the Covenant' confessed their former errors and committed themselves once more to perfect obedience to the Law and the sect's teachings. In the circumstances it would be remarkable, therefore, that so little space is given to it were we not told that a whole section dealing with the feast has disappeared from the Cairo manuscript but is attested in unpublished fragments from Cave 4. According to the available texts, the sectaries were to be mustered and inscribed in their rank by name, the priests first, the Levites second, the Israelites third. A fourth group of proselytes is unique to the 'towns', but as has been observed these were Gentile slaves converted to Judaism. A further remark that they were in this order to 'be questioned on all matters' leads one to suppose that the allusion must be to the yearly inquiry into the members' spiritual progress mentioned in the Community Rule (CD xiv, 3–6).

Apart from these familiar directions, we learn only that the priest who mustered the gathering was to be between thirty and sixty years old and, needless to say, 'learned in the Book of Meditation'. The 'Guardian of all the camps', in his turn, was to be between thirty and fifty, and to have 'mastered all the secrets of men and the language of all their clans'. He was to decide who was to be admitted, and anything connected with a 'suit or judgement' was to be brought to him (CD xiv, 7–12).

As for the initiation of new members, the Statutes appear to legislate for young men reaching their majority within the brotherhood and for recruits from outside. This is not entirely clear, but the instruction that an aspirant was not to be informed of the sect's rules until he had stood before the Guardian can hardly have applied to a person brought up within its close circle (CD xv, 5–6, 10–11).

Of the sect's own young men the Damascus Rule writes merely:

And when the children of all those who have entered the Covenant granted to all Israel for ever reach the age of enrolment, they shall swear with an oath of the Covenant (CD xv, 5–6).

The Messianic Rule is more discursive. There, enrolment into the sect is represented as the climax of a childhood and youth spent in study. Teaching in the Bible and in the 'precepts of the Covenant' began long before the age of ten, at which age a boy embarked on a further ten years of instruction in the statutes. It was not until after all this that he was finally ready.

From [his] youth they shall instruct him in the Book of Meditation and shall teach him, according to his age, the precepts of the Covenant. He [shall be edu]cated in their statutes for ten years . . . At the age of twenty [he shall be] enrolled, that he may enter upon his allotted duties in the midst of his family [and] be joined to the holy congregation (1QSa 1, 6–9).

The newcomer from outside who repented of his 'corrupted way' was to be enrolled 'with the oath of the Covenant' on the day that he spoke to the Guardian, but no sectarian statute was to be divulged to him 'lest when examining him the Guardian be deceived by him' (CD xv, 7–11). Nevertheless, if he broke that oath, 'retribution' would be exacted of him. The text subsequently becomes fragmentary and unreliable, but he is told where to find the liturgical calendar which his oath obliges him to follow.

As for the exact determination of their times to which Israel turns a blind eye, behold it is strictly defined in the Book of the Divisions of the Times into their Jubilees and Weeks (CD xvi, 2–4).

It should be added here that one big difference between the organization of the brethren in the towns and those of the monastic settlement is that new members were not required to surrender their property. There was none of the voluntary communism found at Qumran. On the other hand, where the desert sectaries practised common ownership, those of the towns contributed to the assistance of their fellows in need. Every man able to do so was ordered to hand over a minimum of two days' wages a month to a charitable fund, and from it the Guardian and the judges distributed help to the orphans, the poor, the old and sick, to unmarried women without support and to prisoners held in foreign hands and in need of redemption (CD xiv, 12–16).

When the two varieties of sectarian life are compared, the differences seem at first to outnumber the similarities. In the desert of Qumran men lived together in seclusion; in the towns they were grouped in families, surrounded by non-members with whom they were in inevitable though exiguous contact. The desert brotherhood kept apart from the Temple in Jerusalem; that of the towns participated in worship there. The 'Foundations' of the Qumran community had no counterparts in the towns; the judges of the towns had no counterparts at Qumran. The Qumran Guardian was supported by a Council; the town Guardians acted independently. Unfaithful desert sectaries were sentenced to irrevocable excommunication, or to temporary exclusion from the common life, or to suffer lighter penances; offenders from the towns were condemned to death (whether or not the verdict was carried out) or committed to corrective custody. The common table and the 'purity' associated with it played an essential role at Qumran; in connection with the towns the table goes unmentioned and 'purity' in that sense receives attention only once. Furthermore, at Qumran all the new recruits came from outside; in the towns, some were converts but others were the sons of sectaries. The desert novices underwent two years of training and were instructed in the doctrine of the 'two spirits'; the towns' converts were subjected to neither experience. In the desert, property was owned in common; in the towns, it was not. And last but not least, the desert community appears to have practised celibacy, whereas the town sectaries patently did not.

Yet despite these many dissimilarities, at the basic level of doctrine, aims and principles, a perceptible bond links the brethren of the desert with those of the towns. They both claim to represent the true Israel. They both follow the Zadokite priesthood, both form units of Thousands, Hundreds, Fifties and Tens, both insist on a whole-hearted return to the Mosaic Law in accordance with their own particular interpretation of it. They are both governed by priests (or Levites). The principal, superior, teacher and administrator of both is known by the unusual title of *mebaqqer*. In both cases, initiation into the sect is preceded by entry into the Covenant, sworn by oath. Both groups convene yearly to review the order of precedence of their members after an enquiry into the conduct of each man during the previous twelve months. Above all, both embrace the same 'unorthodox' liturgical calendar that sets them apart from the rest of Jewry.

There can be only one logical conclusion: this was a single religious movement with two branches. It does not, however, answer all our questions. It does not tell us in particular whether the sectaries of desert and towns maintained regular contact among themselves. After all, the history of religions furnishes scores of examples of sister sects which turned into mortal enemies. Did the Qumran and towns fellowships profess and practise unity? A few vital clues suggest that they did.

One indication of a living relationship between the two groups derives from the Qumran library itself. In it were discovered no less than ten copies of the Damascus Rule. It seems hardly likely that it would have been represented in such numbers if it had been the manual of some rival institution, or have figured so prominently among the Qumran literary treasures. Besides, there was no trace of any other book in the caves relating to an opposing religious faction. Another pointer towards unity appears in the passage of the Damascus Rule outlining the procedure for the 'assembly of all the camps' and prescribing that the members were to be 'inscribed by name' in hierarchical rank. This clause corresponds exactly to the statute in the Community Rule ordaining a yearly ranking of the sectaries (1QS II, 19–23), with a solemn ritual for the Renewal of the Covenant (for an analysis of the rite, see pp. 48–9). This leads us to suppose that the Feast of the Covenant, when the desert brethren held their annual spiritual survey, was also the occasion for that of the towns. Can we go further still and establish that the two ceremonies took place, not only at the same time, but at the same place? In effect, the literary and archaeological evidence tends to support the theory that the 'assembly of all the camps', identical with the yearly assembly of the Qumran branch, forgathered at Qumran.

The first clue turns on the qualifications of the *mebaqqer* of the Community Rule and the Damascus Rule respectively. As may be remembered, the superior at Qumran was required to be expert in recognizing 'the nature of all the children of men according to the kind of spirit which they possess' (1QS III, 13–14), while the *mebaqqer* of the towns was to be concerned rather more with a man's 'deeds', 'possessions', 'ability', etc., than with his inner spirit. When, however, the Damascus Rule describes the attributes needed of the 'Guardian of all the camps', what do we find but a reformulation of those accredited to the superior of the desert community, that he should know 'all the secrets of men and all the languages of their clans'? It would emerge from this, therefore, that the Guardian of all the camps and the Guardian at Qumran were one and the same person.

The next hint comes from the fact that the Damascus Rule is directed to both desert and town sectaries. As an example, the passage from the Exhortation advising men to choose whatever is pleasing to God and to reject whatever he hates, 'that you may walk perfectly in all his ways and not follow after thoughts of the guilty inclination and after eyes of lust' (CD II, 14–16), is plainly meant for celibates. Yet in this very same document we later come upon injunctions addressed explicitly to non-celibates:

And if they live in camps according to the rule of the earth, marrying and begetting children, they shall walk according to the Law and according to the statute concerning binding vows, according to the rule of the Law which says, 'Between a man and his wife and between a father and his son' (Num. xxx, 17) (CD vii, 6–9).

The Exhortation would seem in short to be a sermon intended for delivery on a certain occasion to married and unmarried members of the sect; and as its theme is perseverance in the Covenant, the appropriate setting would be the Feast of the Renewal of the Covenant, and the venue, Qumran.

These literary pointers are supported by two archaeological finds. Firstly, the twenty-six deposits of animal bones buried on the Qumran site – goats, sheep, lambs, calves, cows or oxen – have for long intrigued scholars. Can J. T. Milik be correct in identifying them as the remains of meals served to large groups of pilgrims in the Qumran mother-house of the sect (*Ten Years of Discovery in the Wilderness of Judaea*, p. 117)? Naturally, he too connects the gathering with the Covenant festival.

The second archaeological clue also is concerned with bones. The skeletons of four women and one child, and possibly of two further female bodies and those of two children, were found in the extension of the Qumran cemetery. Now, if the Renewal of the Covenant was attended by sectaries from the towns and their families, might not this account for the presence of dead women and children among the otherwise male skeletons of the grave-yard proper?

Drawing the threads of these various arguments together, there would seem to be little doubt that not only were the desert and town sectaries united in doctrine and organization, but that they remained in actual and regular touch with each other, under the ultimate administrative and spiritual authority of the shadowy figure of the Priest, of whom we hear so little, and his dominant partner, the Qumran Guardian, Guardian of all the camps. Qumran, it seems, was the seat of the sect's hierarchy and also the centre to which all those turned who professed allegiance to the sons of Zadok the Priests, the Keepers of the Covenant.

II. THE HISTORY OF THE COMMUNITY

The absence from the Dead Sea Scrolls of historical texts proper should not surprise us. Neither in the inter-Testamental period, nor in earlier biblical times, was the recording of history as we understand it a strong point among the Jews. Chroniclers are concerned not with factual information about past events, but with their religious significance. In Scripture, the 'secular' past is viewed and interpreted by the prophets as revealing God's pleasure or displeasure. Victory or defeat in war, peace or social unrest, abundance of harvest or famine, serve to demonstrate the virtue or sinfulness of the nation and to forecast its future destiny. And when prophecy declined in the fifth century B.C., it was still not succeeded by a growth of historiography: only the memoirs of Ezra and Nehemiah and the retelling of the age-old stories of the kings of Israel and Judah in the Books of Chronicles belong to the historical *genre*. It was followed instead by eschatological speculation, by apocalyptic visions of the end of time, with its awe-inspiring beasts and battles, and by announcements of the ultimate triumph of truth and justice in a future kingdom of God.

In the Scrolls, the apocalyptic compositions form part of this later tradition. On the other hand, most of the knowledge we possess of the sect's history is inserted into works of Bible interpretation. The Qumran writers, while meditating on the words of the Old Testament prophets, sought to discover in them allusions to their own past, present and future. Convinced that they were living in the last days, they read the happenings of their times as the fulfilment of biblical predictions.

Yet all that these non-historical sources provide are fragments. Even with the help of the archaeological data from Qumran they cannot be made into a consistent and continuous narrative. For an understanding of the sect's history as it occurred within the larger framework of inter-Testamental Jewish history, we have to rely principally on Flavius Josephus, the Palestinian Jew who became a Greek man of letters, and on other Jewish Hellenists, such as the authors of the Greek Books of the Maccabees, and Philo of Alexandria, all of whom inherited the Greek predilection for recording and interpreting the past and set out to depict the life of the Jews of Palestine in itself, and as part of the Graeco-Roman world, from the early second century B.C. to the first anti-Roman war in A.D. 66–70. It is only with the help of the wider canvas painted by these ancient scholars that places can be found for the often cryptic historical indications contained in the Scrolls.

1 INTER-TESTAMENTAL JEWISH HISTORY: 200 B.C.-A.D. 70

At the beginning of the second century B.C., Palestinian Jewry passed through a state of crisis. Alexander the Great had conquered the Holy Land in 332 B.C. and, after the early uncertainties which followed his death, it became part of the empire of the Greeks of Egypt, the Ptolemies. During the third century, the Ptolemies avoided, as much as possible, interfering with the internal life of the Jewish nation and, while taxes were required to be paid, it remained under the rule of the High Priest and his council. Important changes in the patterns of population nevertheless took place during this time. Hellenistic cities were built along the Mediterranean coast, such as Gaza, Ascalon (Ashkelon), Joppa (Jaffa), Dor, and Acco, re-named Ptolemais. Inland also, to the south of the Lake of Tiberias, the ancient town of Beth Shean was reborn as the Greek city of Scythopolis; Samaria, the capital city of the Samaritans, was Hellenized; and in Transjordan, Rabbath-Ammon (Amman) was re-founded as Philadelphia. In other words, Greeks, Macedonians and Hellenized Phoenicians took up permanent residence on Palestinian soil and the further spread of Greek civilization and culture was merely a matter of time.

With the conquest of the Holy Land by the Seleucids, or Syrian Greeks, in 200 B.C., the first signs appeared of Jews succumbing to a foreign cultural influence. In the apocryphal Book of Ecclesiasticus dated to the beginning of the second century B.C., its author, Jesus ben Sira, a sage from Jerusalem, rages against those 'ungodly men' who have 'forsaken the Law of the Most High God' (xli, 8). But the real trouble started when Antiochus Epiphanes (175–164 B.C.) officially promoted a Hellenizing programme in Judaea that was embraced with eagerness by the Jewish elite. The leader of the modernist faction was the brother of the High Priest Onias III. Known as Jesus among his compatriots, he adopted the Greek name of Jason, and set about to transform Jerusalem into a Hellenistic city, building a gymnasium there and persuading the Jewish youth to participate in athletic games. As 2 Maccabees describes the situation:

So Hellenism reached a high point with the introduction of foreign customs through the boundless wickedness of the impious Jason, no true High Priest. As a result, the priests no longer had any enthusiasm for their duties at the altar, but despised the temple and neglected the sacrifices; and in defiance of the law they eagerly contributed to the expenses of the wrestling-school whenever the opening gong called them. They placed no value on their hereditary dignities, but cared above everything for Hellenic honours (2 Mac. iv, 13–15).

Jason was succeeded by two other High Priests with the same Greek sympathies, Menelaus and Alcimus. In 169 B.C. Antiochus IV visited Jerusalem and looted the Temple. But when in 167 B.C. he actually prohibited the practice of Judaism under pain of death and re-dedicated the Jerusalem Sanctuary to Olympian Zeus, the 'abomination of desolation', the opponents of the Hellenizers finally rose up in violent resistance. An armed revolt was instigated by the priest Mattathias and his sons the Maccabee brothers, supported by all the traditionalist Jews, and in particular by the company of the Pious, the Asidaeans or Hasidim, 'stalwarts of Israel, every one of them a volunteer in the cause of the Law' (1 Mac. ii, 42–3). Led by Judas Maccabaeus and, after his death on the battlefield, by his brothers Jonathan and Simon, the fierce defenders of Judaism were able not only to restore Jewish worship in Jerusalem, but against all expectations even managed to eject the ruling Seleucids and to liberate Judaea.

The Maccabaean triumph was however not simply a straightforward victory of godliness and justice over idolatry and tyranny; it was accompanied by serious social and religious upheavals. There was firstly a change in the pontifical succession. With the murder of Onias III and the deposition of the usurper, his brother Jason, the Zadokite family, from which the incumbents of the High Priest's office traditionally came, lost the monopoly which it had held for centuries. Furthermore, when Onias IV, the son of Onias III, was prevented from taking over the High Priesthood from Menelaus, he emigrated to Egypt and in direct breach of biblical law erected a Jewish temple in Leontopolis with blessing of King Ptolemy Philometor (182–146 B.C.). His inauguration of Israelite worship outside the Jerusalem sanctuary, with the connivance of some priests and Levites, must have scandalized every Palestinian conservative, even those priests who belonged, or were allied, to the Zadokite dynasty.

There was trouble also within the ranks of the Maccabees themselves. The Hasidim – or part of their group – defected when Alcimus was appointed High Priest in 162 B.C. This move on their part turned out to be naïve; Alcimus's Syrian allies massacred sixty of them in one day (1 Mac. vii, 12–20).

Lastly, a major political change came about when Jonathan Maccabaeus, himself a priest but not a Zadokite, accepted in 153–2 B.C. pontifical office from Alexander Balas, a usurper of the Seleucid throne. Alexander was anxious for Jewish support and was not mistaken in thinking that an offer of the High Priesthood would be irresistible. For the conservatives this was an illegal seizure of power. But they were even more scandalized by the appointment in 140 B.C., following Jonathan's execution in 143–2 B.C. by the Syrian general Tryphon, of Simon Maccabee as High Priest and leader of the people by means of a decree passed by a Jewish national assembly.

From then on, until Pompey's transformation of the independent Jewish state into a Roman province in 63 B.C., Judaea was ruled by a new dynasty of High Priests, later Priest-Kings, known as the Hasmonaeans after the grandfather of the Maccabees, Hasmon, or Asamonaeus according to Josephus, *War* I, 36. During the intervening years, all Simon's successors, but especially John Hyrcanus I (134–104 B.C.) and Alexander Jannaeus (103–76 B.C.), for whom their political role took precedence over their office of High Priest, occupied one by one the Hellenistic cities of Palestine and conquered the neighbouring territories of Idumaea, Samaria and Ituraea.

Throughout this period of territorial expansion, the Hasmonaean rulers enjoyed the support of the Sadducees, one of the three religious parties first mentioned under Jonathan Maccabaeus (cf. Josephus, *Antiquities* XIII, 171) and regular allies of the government. They were opposed by the Pharisees, an essentially lay group formed from one of the branches of the Hasidim of the Maccabaean age. Already in the days of John Hyrcanus I there was Pharisaic objection to his usurpation of the High Priesthood, though they were willing to recognize him as national leader (*Antiquities* XIII, 288–98), but on one other occasion, at least, their opposition was overcome by force. Accused of plotting against Alexander Jannaeus in 88 B.C. in collusion with the Syrian

Seleucid king Demetrius Eucaerus, eight hundred Pharisees were condemned by Jannaeus to die on the cross (*Antiquities* XIII, 380–3; *War* I, 96–8).

After Pompey's seizure of Jerusalem, the Hasmonaean High Priesthood continued for another three decades, but the political power formerly belonging to them passed to the Judaized Idumaean, Herod the Great, when he was promoted to the throne of Jerusalem by Rome in 37 B.C. It is to the last year or two of his reign – he died in 4 B.C. – that the Gospels of Matthew and Luke date the birth of Jesus of Nazareth (Matth. ii:1; Lk. i, 15).

After the ephemeral rule of the successor to Herod the Great, Herod Archelaus (4 B.C.-A.D. 6), who was deposed by Augustus for his misgovernment of Jews and Samaritans alike, Galilee continued in semi-autonomy under the Herodian princes Antipas (4 B.C.-A.D. 39) and Agrippa (A.D. 39–41), but Judaea was placed under the direct administration of Roman authority. In A.D. 6, Coponius, the first Roman prefect of Judaea, arrived to take up his duties there. This prefectorial regime, whose most notorious representative was Pontius Pilate (A.D. 26–36), lasted for thirty-five years until A.D. 41, when the emperor Claudius appointed Agrippa I as king. He died, however, three years later, and in A.D. 44 the government of the province once more reverted to Roman officials, this time with the title of procurator. Their corrupt and unwise handling of Jewish affairs was one of the chief causes of the war of A.D. 66 which led to the destruction of Jerusalem in A.D. 70, and to the subsequent decline of the Sadducees, the extinction of the Zealots in Masada in A.D. 74, the disappearance of the Essenes, and the survival and uncontested domination of the Pharisees and their rabbinic successors.

It is into this general course of events that the history of Qumran has to be inserted. Document by document the Scrolls will be scrutinized and the literary information combined, both with the findings of Qumran archaeology and with the incidental reports provided by Josephus. In the end it is hoped that the history of the Essene sect will begin to fall reliably into place.

2 THE HISTORY OF THE ESSENES

(a) Concealed References in the Scrolls

The search for clues to the origins and story of the movement begins with the Damascus Rule because it is a document particularly rich in such hints. Here, the birth of the Community is said to have occurred in the 'age of wrath', 390 years after the destruction of Jerusalem by Nebuchadnezzar, king of Babylon. At that time, a 'root' sprung 'from Israel and Aaron', i.e. a group of pious Jews, laymen and priests, came into being in a situation of general ungodliness. These people 'groped for the way' for twenty years, and then God sent them a 'Teacher of Righteousness' to guide them 'in the way of His heart'. The Teacher did not meet with unanimous approval within the congregation, and a faction described as 'seekers of smooth things', 'removers of the bounds' and 'builders of the wall', all metaphors seeming to point to religious laxity and infidelity, turned against him and his followers. The leader of the breakaway party is accorded the unflattering sobriquets of 'Scoffer', 'Liar' or 'Spouter of Lies'. His associates erred in matters of ritual cleanness, justice, chastity, the dates of festivals and Temple worship; they were lovers of money and enemies of peace. In the ensuing fratricidal struggle, the Teacher and those who remained faithful to him went into exile in the 'land of Damascus' where they entered into a 'new Covenant'. There, the Teacher of Righteousness was 'gathered in', meaning that he died. In the meantime, the wicked dominated over Jerusalem and the Temple, though not without experiencing God's vengeance at the hands of the 'Chief of the Kings of Greece'.

A similar picture emerges from the Habakkuk Commentary with its explicit reference to desertion by disciples of the Teacher of Righteousness to the Liar, but also by members unfaithful to the 'new Covenant'. The allusions to the protagonists of the conflict are sharper in this document than in the Damascus Rule. We learn that the villain, known in this Scroll as the 'Wicked Priest' as well as the 'Liar' and 'Spouter of Lies', was 'called by the name of truth' before he became Israel's ruler and was corrupted by wealth and power – the implication being that for a time he had met with the sect's approval. Subsequently, however, he defiled Jerusalem and the Temple. He also sinned against the Teacher of Righteousness and his disciples, chastising him while the 'House of Absalom' looked silently on, and confronting him in his place of exile on the sect's Day of Atonement. He 'vilified and outraged the elect of God', 'plotted to destroy the Poor', i.e. the Community, and stole their riches. As a punishment, God delivered him 'into the hand of his enemies', who 'took vengeance on his body of flesh'. At the last judgement, predicts the Commentary, the Wicked Priest will empty 'the cup of wrath of God'. His successors, the 'last Priests of Jerusalem', are also charged with amassing 'money and wealth by plundering the peoples', i.e. foreigners. But, so the commentator asserts, all their riches and booty will be snatched from them by the Kittim, the conquerors of the world commissioned by God to pay them their just deserts.

Because of lacunae, one cannot be quite sure from the Habakkuk Commentary that the Teacher was a priest. The Commentary on Psalm xxxvii, by contrast, makes this plain. Interpreting verses 23–4, it reads: 'this concerns the Priest, the Teacher of [Righteousness]'. It further supplies a significant detail by assigning to 'the violent of the nations', that is to say to the Gentiles as opposed to the Jews, the execution of judgement on the Wicked Priest. Another point of interest is that the enemies of the sect are alluded to as 'the wicked of Ephraim and Manasseh', i.e. as of two distinct factions.

In the Messianic Anthology or Testimonia, references appear in the final section to two 'instruments of violence' who ruled Jerusalem. They are cursed for making the city a 'stronghold of ungodliness' and for committing 'an abomination' in the land. They are also said to have shed blood 'like water on the ramparts of the daughter of Zion'. The relationship of the two tyrants to one another cannot be established with certainty because of the fragmentary nature of the manuscript. They could be father and son. On the other hand, the expression, 'instruments of violence', depends on Genesis xlix, where it describes the brother murderers, Simeon and Levi, the destroyers of Shechem.

The Nahum Commentary moves on to an age following that of the Teacher of Righteousness and the Wicked Priest. The principal character here is the 'furious young lion', a Jewish ruler of Jerusalem. He is said to have taken revenge on the 'seekers of smooth things', whom he reproached for having invited 'Demetrius' the king of Greece to Jerusalem. The attempt failed; no foreigner entered the city 'from the time of Antiochus until the coming of the rulers of the Kittim'. The enemies of the 'furious young lion' were 'hanged alive on the tree', a Hebrew circumlocution for crucifixion. As in the Commentary on Psalm xxxvii, the sobriquets 'Ephraim' and 'Manasseh' are attached to the Community's opponents. 'Ephraim' is said to 'walk in lies and falsehood', but because of gaps in the manuscript, the description of 'Manasseh' is less clear. It seems nevertheless that this party included 'great men', 'mighty men', 'men of dignity'.

The Nahum Commentary was the first of the Qumran Scrolls to disclose historical names: those of two Seleucid kings, Antiochus and Demetrius. But their identity has still to be determined because nine monarchs in all bore the first name, and three the second. Apparently, three additional names figure in an unpublished liturgical calendar: 'Shelamzion', the Hebrew name of Queen Alexandra-Salome, widow of Alexander Jannaeus, who reigned from 76 to 67 B.C.; 'Hyrcanus', probably John Hyrcanus II, son of Alexandra and High Priest from 76 to 67 and again from 63 to 40 B.C.; and 'Emilius', no doubt M. Aemilius Scaurus, the first Roman governor of Syria from 65 to 62 B.C.

In the Commentaries on Habakkuk and Nahum, the Kittim are represented as instruments appointed by God to punish the ungodly priests of Jerusalem. The War Rule, however, testifies to a changed attitude towards them on the part of the sect by making the Kittim appear as the chief allies of Satan and the final foe to be subjugated by the hosts of the sons of Light.

Several Qumran Hymns reflect the career and sentiments of a teacher, possibly of the Teacher of Righteousness himself. According to them, he was opposed by 'interpreters of error', 'traitors', 'deceivers', by 'those who seek smooth things', all of whom were formerly his 'friends' and 'members of (his) Covenant', bearers of the 'yoke of (his) testimony'. In one of them, the reference to a 'devilish scheme' is reminiscent of the allusion in the Habakkuk Commentary to the visit of the Wicked Priest to the Community's place of exile in order to cause them 'to stumble':

> Teachers of lies [have smoothed] Thy people with words
>   and false prophets have led them astray . . .
> They have banished me from my land
>   like a bird from its nest . . .
> And they, teachers of lies and seers of falsehood,
>   have schemed against me a devilish scheme,
> to exchange the Law engraved on my heart by Thee
>   for the smooth things [which they speak] to Thy people.
> And they withhold from the thirsty the drink of knowledge,
>   and assuage their thirst with vinegar,
> that they may gaze on their straying,
>   on their folly concerning their feast-days,
>   on their fall into the snares;

> (1QH IV, 7–12)

Another Hymn appears to hint at the Teacher's withdrawal

from society and to announce with confidence his eventual glorious justification:

> For Thou, O God, hast sheltered me
>   from the children of men,
> and hast hidden Thy Law within me
>   against the time when Thou shouldst reveal
>   Thy salvation to me.

(1QH v, 11–12)

It would be unrealistic, taking into account the vagueness of all these statements, the cryptic nature of the symbolism and the entire lack of any systematic exposition of the sect's history, to expect every detail to be identified. We can however attempt to define the chronological framework of the historical references and thus be in a position to place at least some of the key events and principal personalities within the context of Jewish history as we know it.

(b) The Chronological Framework

The chronological setting of Qumran history may be reconstructed from archaeological and literary evidence. The excavations of 1951–6 date the beginning, the *terminus a quo*, of the sectarian establishment to 150–140 B.C. and its end, the *terminus ad quem*, to the middle of the first war against Rome, A.D. 68. The literary allusions, particularly the identifiable historical names, confirm this general finding. It goes without saying, however, that the initial phases of the Community's existence must have preceded by some years or decades the actual establishment of the sect at Qumran. The first task therefore is to examine the Scrolls for indications of its origins. The Nahum Commentary implies that a king by the name of Antiochus was alive at the beginning of the period with which the documents are concerned. This Antiochus, although one among several so called, can only have been Antiochus IV Epiphanes, notorious for his looting of Jerusalem and the profanation of the Temple in 169–168 B.C.

More significant as a chronological pointer is the dating, in the Damascus Rule, of the sect's beginnings to the 'age of wrath', 390 years after the conquest of Jerusalem by Nebuchadnezzar in 586 B.C. This should bring us to 196 B.C. but, as is well known, Jewish historians are not very reliable in their time-reckoning for the post-exilic era. They do not seem to have had a clear idea of the length of the Persian domination, and they were in addition not free of the theological influence of the Book of Daniel, where a period of seventy weeks of years, i.e. 490 years, is given as separating the epoch of Nebuchadnezzar from that of the Messiah. As it happens, if to this figure of 390 years is added, firstly twenty (during which the Community 'groped' for its way until the entry on the scene of the Teacher of Righteousness), then another forty (the timespan between the death of the Teacher and the dawn of the messianic epoch), the total stretch of years arrived at is 450. And if to this total is added the duration of the Teacher's ministry of, say, forty years – a customary round figure – the final result is the classic seventy times seven years.

Yet even if the literal figure of 390 is rejected, there are still compelling reasons for placing the 'age of wrath' in the opening decades of the second century B.C. Only the Hellenistic crisis which occurred at that time, and which is recalled in various Jewish literary sources from the last two centuries of the pre-Christian era, provides a fitting context for the historical allusions made in the sectarian writings (cf. Daniel ix–xi; Enoch xc, 6–7; Jubilees xxiii, 14–19; Testament of Levi xvii; Assumption of Moses iv–v). Also, it is the Hasidim of the pre-Maccabaean and early Maccabaean era who best correspond to the earlier but unorganized group as it is described there (cf. pp. 21–2).

As for the *terminus ad quem* of Qumran history, as this is linked to the appearance of the Kittim, we have to determine who these people were. In its primitive sense, the word 'Kittim' described the inhabitants of Kition, a Phoenician colony in Cyprus. Later, the name tended to be applied indiscriminately to those living in 'all islands and most maritime countries' (Josephus, *Antiquities* I, 128). But from the second century B.C., Jewish writers also used 'Kittim' more precisely to denote the greatest world power of the day. In 1 Maccabees (i, 1; viii, 5) they are Greeks; Alexander the Great and Perseus are called kings of the 'Kittim'. In Daniel xi, 30 on the other hand, the 'Kittim' are Romans; it was the ambassador of the Roman senate, Poppilius Laenas, brought to Alexandria by 'ships of Kittim', who instructed the 'king of the North', the Seleucid monarch Antiochus Epiphanes, to withdraw at once from Egypt. The term 'Romans' is substituted for 'Kittim' already in the old Greek or Septuagint version of Daniel xi, 30. None of these texts is critical of the 'Kittim'. They are seen as the ruling force of the time, but not as hostile to Israel. In fact, in Daniel they humiliate the enemy of the Jews. It is not till a later stage, especially after A.D. 70, that they come to symbolize oppression and tyranny.

In the Habakkuk Commentary, the portrait of the Kittim is neutral, as in Maccabees and Daniel. (In the Damascus Rule they play no part; the alien adversary there is the 'Chief of the Kings of Greece'.) Feared and admired by all, they are seen to be on the point of defeating the 'last Priests of Jerusalem' and confiscating their wealth, as they have done to many others before. Such a representation of a victorious and advancing might would hardly apply to the Greek Seleucids of Syria, who by the second half of the second century B.C. were in grave decline. But it does correspond to the Romans, whose thrust to the east in the first century B.C. resulted in their triumphs over Pontus, Armenia and Seleucid Syria, and finally, with the arrival of Pompey in Jerusalem in 63 B.C., in the transformation of the Hasmonaean state into a province of the Roman republic.

Since the identification of the 'Kittim' as Romans is nowadays generally accepted, it will suffice to cite a single, but very striking, feature in the Habakkuk Commentary to support it. Interpreting Hab. i, 14–16 as referring to the 'Kittim', the commentator writes: 'This means that they sacrifice to their standards and worship their weapons of war' (1QpHab. VI, 3–5). Now this custom of worshipping the *signa* was a characteristic of the religion of the Roman armies, as Josephus testifies in his report of the capture of the Temple of Jerusalem by the legionaries of Titus in A.D. 70.

The Romans, now that the rebels had fled to the city, and the Sanctuary itself and all around it were in flames, carried their standards into the Temple court, and setting them up opposite the eastern gate, there sacrificed to them (*War* VI, 316).

It is also worth noting that the 'Kittim', the final opponents of the eschatological Israel, are subject to a king or emperor (*melekh*).

In brief, the time-limits of the sect's history appear to be at one extreme, the beginning of the second century B.C., and at the other, some moment during the Roman imperial epoch, i.e. after 27 B.C. And this latter date is determined by Qumran archaeology as coinciding with the first Jewish war, and even more precisely, with the arrival of the armies of Vespasian and Titus in the neighbourhood of the Dead Sea in June A.D. 68.

(c) Decipherment of Particular Allusions

The 'age of wrath' having been identified as that of the Hellenistic crisis of the beginning of the second century B.C., the 'root' as the Hasidim of the pre-Maccabaean age, and the 'Kittim' as the Romans, the next major problem is to discover who was, or were, the principal Jewish enemy or enemies of the sect at the time of the ministry of the Teacher of Righteousness variously known as 'the Scoffer', 'the Liar', 'the Spouter of Lies' and 'the Wicked Priest'.

It is not unreasonable to conclude that all these insults are directed at the same individual. It would appear from the Damascus Rule that the 'Scoffer' and the 'Liar' were one and the same ('when the Scoffer arose who shed over Israel the waters of lies', CD I, 14). And we read of the 'Wicked Priest' that he was called 'by the name of truth' (1QpHab VIII, 8–9) at the outset of his career, the inference being that later he changed into a 'Liar'.

Another basic premise must be that the person intended by the fragments of information contained in the Scrolls became the head, the national leader, of the Jewish people. For although biblical names are often used symbolically, including that of 'Israel', the actions attributed to the 'Wicked Priest' make little sense if the person in question did not exercise pontifical and secular power. He 'ruled over Israel'. He 'robbed . . . the riches of the men of violence who rebelled against God', probably Jewish apostates, as well as 'the wealth of the peoples', i.e. the Gentiles. He built 'his city of vanity with blood', committed 'abominable deeds in Jerusalem and defiled the Temple of God'. Taken separately, these observations might be understood allegorically, but considered together, they constitute a strong argument for recognizing the 'Wicked Priest' as a ruling High Priest in Jerusalem.

The 'Wicked Priest', then, was a Pontiff who enjoyed good repute before he assumed office. He was victorious over his adversaries at home and abroad. He re-built Jerusalem. And he was eventually captured and put to death by a foreign rival.

The chronological guide-lines established in the preceding section locate the period in which this individual flourished between the reign of Antiochus Epiphanes (175–164 B.C.) and the probable date of the foundation at Qumran (150–140 B.C.). During that time, five men held the office of High Priest. Three of them were pro-Greek: Jason, Menelaus and Alcimus. The remaining two were the Maccabee brothers, Jonathan and Simon. All the

Hellenizers can be eliminated as candidates for the role of 'Wicked Priest' since none can be said to have enjoyed anything like good repute at the beginning of their ministry. Jason and Alcimus fail also because neither was killed by an enemy: Jason died in exile (2 Mac. v, 7–9) and Alcimus in office (1 Mac. ix, 54–56). The Maccabee brothers, by contrast, meet all the conditions. The careers of both men fall easily into two stages marked, in the case of Jonathan, by his acceptance of the High Priesthood from Alexander Balas, and in the case of Simon, by his willingness to become a hereditary High Priest. Both were also 'instruments of violence' and both died by violence. Jonathan is nevertheless to be chosen rather than Simon because he alone suffered the vengeance of the 'Chief of the Kings of Greece' and died at the hands of the 'violent of the nations', whereas Simon was murdered by his son-in-law (1 Mac. xvi, 14–16). A gallant defender of Jewish religion and independence, Jonathan succeeded the heroic Judas in 161 B.C. when the latter fell in battle. But he qualified for the epithet 'Wicked Priest' when he accepted in 153–2 B.C., from Alexander Balas, a heathen usurper of the Seleucid throne who had no right to grant them, the pontifical vestments which Jonathan was not entitled to wear. Captured later by Tryphon, a former general of Alexander and protector of his son, he was killed by the Syrian at Bascama in Transjordan (1 Mac. xiii, 23).

Concerning the identity of the 'last Priests of Jerusalem', the passion for conquest, wealth and plunder for which they are reproached points to the Hasmonaean priestly rulers, from Simon's son, John Hyrcanus I (134–104 B.C.), to Judas Aristobulus II (67–63 B.C.). There can in particular be little doubt that the 'furious young lion', designated also 'the last Priest' in a badly damaged Commentary on Hosea (4QpHos II, 2–3), was one of them, namely Alexander Jannaeus. The application to him of the words of Nahum, 'who chokes prey for its lionesses', and the report that the 'young lion' executed the 'seekers of smooth things' by 'hanging men alive', accord perfectly with the known story that Jannaeus crucified eight hundred Pharisees whilst feasting with his concubines (cf. above, p. 22–3).

From this it follows that 'Ephraim', equated in the Commentary on Nahum with the 'seekers of smooth things', symbolizes the Pharisees, and that if so, 'Manasseh' and his dignitaries must refer to the Sadducees. In other words, the political and doctrinal opponents of the Essene community were the Pharisees and the Sadducees.

This division of Jewish society into three opposing groups corresponds to the conformation described by Josephus as existing from the time of Jonathan Maccabaeus, but the new insight provided by the Scrolls suggests that the united resistance to Hellenism first fell apart when the Maccabees, and more precisely Jonathan, refused to acknowledge the spiritual leadership of the Teacher of Righteousness, the priestly head of the Hasidim. From then on, the sect saw its defectors as 'Ephraim' and 'Manasseh', these being the names of the sons of Joseph, associated in biblical history with the apostate North of the kingdom, and referred to itself as the 'House of Judah', the faithful South.

Unfortunately, on the most vital topic of all, the question of the identity of the Teacher of Righteousness, we can be nothing like as clear. If the 'Wicked Priest' was Jonathan Maccabaeus, the Teacher would, of course, have been one of his contemporaries. Yet all we know of him is that he was a priest, no doubt of Zadokite affiliation, though obviously opposed to Onias IV since he did not follow him to Egypt and to his unlawful Temple in Leontopolis. He founded or re-founded the Community. He transmitted to them his own distinctive interpretation of the Prophets and, if we can rely on the Hymns, of the laws relating to the celebration of festivals. The 'Liar' and his sympathizers in the congregation of the Hasidim disagreed with him, and after a violent confrontation between the two factions in which the 'Liar' gained the upper hand, the Teacher and his remaining followers fled to a place of refuge called 'the land of Damascus': it has been suggested that this is a cryptic designation of Babylonia, the original birthplace of the group, or that 'Damascus' is a symbolical name for Qumran. The 'House of Absalom' gave the Teacher of Righteousness no help against the 'Liar', writes the Habakkuk commentator (1QpHab v, 9–12), the implication being that this was support on which he might have relied. If 'Absalom' is also a symbol, it doubtless recalls the rebellion of Absalom against his father David, and thus points to the perfidy of a close relation or intimate friend of the Teacher. On the other hand, since the 'House of Absalom' is accused not of an actual attack but simply of remaining silent during the Teacher's 'chastisement', this allegorical solution may not be convincing. The allusion may then be a straightforward one. A certain Absalom was an ambassador of Judas Maccabaeus (2 Mac. xi, 17), and his son Mattathias was one of Jonathan's gallant officers (1 Mac. xi, 70). Another of his sons, Jonathan, commanded Simon's army which captured Joppa (1 Mac xiii, 11).

Meanwhile, even in his 'place of exile' the Teacher continued to be harassed and persecuted by the Wicked Priest. In this connection, the most important and painful episode appears to have been the Priest's pursuit of the Teacher to his settlement with the purpose of confusing him 'with his venomous fury'. Appearing before the sectaries on 'their sabbath of repose', at the 'time appointed for rest, for the Day of Atonement', his intention was to cause them 'to stumble on the Day of Fasting'. It is impossible to say, from the evidence so far available, precisely what happened on this portentous occasion, or whether it was then or later that the Wicked Priest 'laid hands' on the Teacher 'that he might put him to death'. The wording is equivocal. For example, the verb in 1QpHab xi, 5, 7, translated 'to confuse' can also mean 'to swallow up', and some scholars have chosen to understand that the Teacher was killed by the Wicked Priest at the time of the visit. On the other hand, we find recounted in the imperfect tense (which can be rendered in English into either the future or the present tense): 'The wicked of Ephraim and Manasseh . . seek/ will seek to lay hands on the Priest and the men of his Council . . But God redeems/will redeem them from out of their hand' (4QpPs.xxxvii II, 17–19). In other words, we neither know who the founder of the Essenes was, nor how, nor where, nor when he died.

It has been argued that this inability to identify the Teacher of Righteousness in the context of the Maccabaean period undermines the credibility of the reconstruction as a whole. Is it conceivable, it is asked, that a figure of the stature of the Teacher should have left no trace in the literature relating to that time? The answer to this objection is that such writings are to all intents and purposes restricted to the Books of the Maccabees, sources politically biased in favour of their heroes and virtually oblivious of the very existence of opposition movements. Josephus himself relies largely on 1 Maccabees and cannot therefore be regarded as an independent witness. But even were this not so, and he had additional material at his disposition, his silence *vis-à-vis* the Teacher of Righteousness would still not call for particular comment since he also makes no mention of the founders of the Pharisees and Sadducees. And incidentally, not a few historians hold that he has nothing to say either of Jesus of Nazareth. The so-called Testimonium Flavianum (*Antiquities* XVIII, 63–64), they maintain, is a Christian interpolation into the genuine text of Antiquities, (though others, myself included, think that part of the text is authentic). Be this as it may, not a word is breathed by him about Hillel, the greatest of the Pharisee masters, or about Yohanan ben Zakkai, who re-organized Judaism after the destruction of the Temple, although both of these men lived in Josephus's own century.

Admittedly, the various fragments of information gleaned from the Dead Sea Scrolls result in an unavoidably patchy story, but it is fundamentally sound, and the continuing anonymity of the Teacher does nothing to impair it. For the present synthesis to be complete it remains now to turn to Josephus for his occasional historical references to individual Essenes and to Essenism.

To begin with it should be pointed out that four members of the Community are actually mentioned by the Jewish historian, three of them associated with prophecy, one of the distinctive interests of the Teacher of Righteousness himself. The first, called Judas, is encountered in Jerusalem surrounded by a group of pupils taking instruction in 'foretelling the future', which probably means, in how to identify prophetic pointers to future events. Josephus writes of him that he had 'never been known to speak falsely in his prophecies', and that he predicted the death of Antigonus, the brother of Aristobulus I (104–103 B.C.) (*Antiquities* XIII, 311–13). A second Essene prophet, Menahem, apparently foretold that Herod would rule over the Jews (XV, 373–8). Herod showed his gratitude to him by dispensing the Essenes, who were opposed to all oaths except their own oath of the Covenant, from taking the vow of loyalty imposed on all his Jewish subjects. A third Essene named Simon interpreted a dream of Archelaus, ethnarch of Judaea (4 B.C.-A.D. 6), in 4 B.C. to mean that his rule would last for ten years (XVII, 345–8). John the Essene, the last sectary to be referred to by Josephus, was not a prophet, but the commander or *strategos* of the district of Thamna in north-western Judaea, and of the cities of Lydda (Lod), Joppa (Jaffa) and Emmaus at the beginning of the first revolution (*War* II, 567). Said to have been a man of 'first-rate prowess and ability', he fell in battle at Ascalon (iii, 11, 19).

Finally, Josephus depicts in vivid language the bravery of the Essenes subjected to torture by the Romans.

The war with the Romans tried their souls through and through by every variety of test. Racked and twisted, burned and broken, and made to pass through every instrument of torture in order to induce them to blaspheme their lawgiver or to eat some forbidden thing, they refused to yield to either demand, nor ever once did they cringe to their persecutors or shed a tear. Smiling in their agonies and mildly deriding their tormentors, they cheerfully resigned their souls, confident that they would receive them back again (*War* II, 152–3).

Since it would appear from this passage that the Romans were persecuting not individuals, but a group, it is tempting, bearing in mind the archaeologists' claim that the Qumran settlement was destroyed by the Romans, to associate it with the story of Essenes captured by the Dead Sea. If such a surmise is correct, the sect's disappearance from history may well have been brought about in the lethal blow suffered by its central establishment during the fateful summer of A.D. 68.

III. THE RELIGIOUS IDEAS OF THE COMMUNITY

⌾⌾⌾

The first essays in the 1950s on the religious outlook of the Qumran sect all suffered from a serious defect in that scholars in those days tended to envisage the Scrolls as self-contained and entitled to independent treatment. Today, with the hindsight of four decades of research and a considerably increased, though still incomplete, documentation, it is easier to conceive of the theology of the Community as part of the general doctrinal evolution of ancient Judaism.

On the other hand, it is no simple task to follow that evolution itself, the reason being that the systematic exposition of beliefs and customs is not a traditional Jewish discipline. The theology of Judaism, biblical, inter-Testamental, medieval or modern, even when written by Jews, is often modelled consciously or unconsciously on Christian dogmatic structures: God, creation, human destiny, messianic redemption, judgement, resurrection, heaven and hell. Such structures may and sometimes do distort the religious concepts of Judaism. For example, the interest of the Church in the messianic role of Jesus is apt to assign a greater importance to Messianism in Jewish religion than the historical evidence justifies, and Paul's hostility to the 'legalism' of Israel obscures the Jewish recognition of the humble realities of everyday life prescribed by the law as no mere 'works' but as a path to holiness walked in obedience to God's commandments.

1 THE COVENANT

Since the key to any understanding of Judaism must be the notion of the Covenant, it may safely be taken as an introduction to Essene religious thought. The history of mankind and of the Jewish people has seen a series of such covenants. God undertook never to destroy mankind again by a flood; in exchange, Noah and his descendants were required to abstain from shedding human blood and, on the ritual level, from eating animal 'flesh with the life, which is the blood, still in it' (Gen. ix, 1–17). To Abraham, who was childless and landless, God offered posterity and country provided he led a perfect life and marked his body and that of all his male progeny with a visible reminder of the Covenant between himself and heaven, circumcision (Gen. xvii, 1–14). Again, in the days of Moses the Israelites were declared 'a kingdom of priests, and a holy nation' (Exod. xix, 5), God's special possession, on condition that they obeyed the Torah, the divine Teaching of the religious, moral, social and ritual precepts recorded in the Pentateuch from Exodus chapter xx and repeated in the farewell discourse addressed by Moses to his people in the Book of Deuteronomy.

After the conquest of Canaan and the distribution of the land to the tribes, the fulfilment of God's promise to Abraham, the Covenant was renewed by Joshua and the Israelites reasserted their commitment to their heavenly Helper (Jos. xxiv). From then on, the biblical story is one of continuous unfaithfulness to the Covenant. But God was not to be thwarted by human unworthiness and ingratitude, and for the sake of the handful of just men appearing in every generation he allowed the validity of the Covenant to endure. Though he punished the sinful and the rebellious, he spared the 'remnant' because of their fidelity to it.

From time to time, saintly leaders of the Jewish people, King David and King Josiah before the Babylonian exile (2 Sam. vii; 2 Kings xxiii, 1–3) and Ezra the Priest after the return from Mesopotamia (Neh. viii–x), persuaded them to remember their Covenant with God with solemn vows of repentance and national re-dedication; but the promises were usually short-lived. This would no doubt account for the development of an idea in the sixth century B.C. of a 'new Covenant' founded not so much on undertakings entered into by the community as on the inner transformation of every individual Jew for whom the will of God was to become, as it were, second nature.

The time is coming . . . when I will make a new Covenant with Israel . . . This is the new Covenant which I will make with Israel in those days . . . I will set my law within them and write it on their hearts . . . (Jer. xxxi, 31–33; Isa. liv, 13).

It was this same Covenant theology that served as the foundation of the Qumran Community's basic beliefs. The Essenes not only considered themselves to be the 'remnant' of their time, but the 'remnant' of all time, the final 'remnant'. In the 'age of wrath', while God was making ready to annihilate the wicked, their founders had repented. They had become the 'Converts of Israel' (cf. CD IV, 2). As a reward for their conversion, the Teacher of Righteousness had been sent to establish for them a 'new Covenant', which was to be the sole valid form of the eternal alliance between God and Israel. Consequently, their paramount aim was to pledge themselves to observe its precepts with absolute faithfulness. Convinced that they belonged to a Community which alone interpreted the Holy Scriptures correctly, they devoted their exile in the wilderness to the study of the Bible. Their intention was to do according to all that had been 'revealed from age to age, and as the Prophets had revealed by His Holy Spirit' (1QS VIII, 14–16).

Without an authentic interpretation it was not possible properly to understand the Torah. All the Jews of the inter-Testamental era, the Essenes as well as their rivals, agreed that true piety entails obedience to the Law, but although its guidance reaches into so many corners of life – into business and prayer, law court and kitchen, marriage-bed and Temple – the 613 positive and negative commandments of which it consists still do not provide for all the problems encountered, especially those which arose in the centuries following the enactment of biblical legislation. To give but one example, the diaspora situation was not envisaged by the jurists of an autonomous Jewish society.

Torah interpretation was entrusted to the priests and Levites during the first two or three centuries following the Babylonian exile. Ezra and his colleagues, the ancient scribes of Israel, 'read from the book of the Law . . . made its sense plain and gave instruction in what was read'. In this passage from the Book of Nehemiah viii, 8, Jewish tradition acknowledges the institution of a regular paraphrase of Scripture known as Targum, or translation into the vernacular of the members of the congregation. When the parties of the Pharisees, Sadducees, Essenes, etc., came into being with their different convictions, they justified them by interpretations suited to their needs.

A classic example in the Scrolls of idiosyncratic Bible interpretation concerns a law on marriage. Since no directly relevant ruling is given in the Pentateuch on whether a niece may marry her uncle, Pharisaic and rabbinic Judaism understands this scriptural silence to mean that such a union is licit. When the Bible wishes to declare a degree of kinship unlawful, it does so: thus we read apropos of marriage between nephew and aunt, 'You shall not approach your mother's sister' (Lev. xviii, 13). So a tradition surviving in the Babylonian Talmud is able to go so far as even to praise marriage with a 'sister's daughter' and to proclaim it as a particularly saintly and generous act comparable to the loving kindness shown to the poor and needy (Yebamoth 62b). The Qumran Essenes did not adopt this attitude at all. On the contrary, they regarded an uncle/niece union as straightforward 'fornication'. Interpreted correctly, they maintained, the Leviticus precept signifies the very opposite of the meaning accepted by their opponents; the truth is that whatever applies to men in this respect applies also to women.

Moses said, 'You shall not approach your mother's sister (i.e. your aunt); she is your mother's near kin' (Lev. xviii, 13). But although the laws against incest are written for men, they also apply to women. When therefore a brother's daughter uncovers the nakedness of her father's brother, she is (also his) near kin' (CD v, 7–9; cf. TS LXVI, 16–17).

Again, according to the strict views of the sectaries, fidelity to the Covenant demanded not only obedience to the Law, to all that God has 'commanded by the hand of Moses', but also adherence to the teaching of 'all his servants, the Prophets' (1QS 1, 2–3). Although not expressly stated, this special attention to the Prophets implies, firstly, that the Essenes subscribed to the principle incorporated into the opening paragraph of the Sayings of the Fathers in the Mishnah that the Prophets served as an essential link in the transmission of the Law from Moses to the rabbis.

Moses received the Torah from (God on) Sinai and passed it on to Joshua; Joshua to the Elders (= Judges); the Elders to the Prophets; and the Prophets passed it on to the members of the Great Assembly (= the leaders of Israel in the post-exilic age) (Aboth i, 1).

The second inference to be drawn is that the sect believed the Prophets to be not only teachers of morality, but also guides in the domain of the final eschatological realities. But as in the case of the Law, their writings were considered to contain pitfalls for the ignorant and the misinformed, and only the Community's sages knew how to expound them correctly. Properly understood, the books of Isaiah, Hosea and the rest indicate the right path to be followed in the terrible cataclysms of the last days. A simple reading can convey only their superficial meaning, but not their profounder significance. The Book of Daniel sets the biblical example here when it announces that Jeremiah's prediction that the Babylonian domination would last for seventy years is not to be taken literally; the real and final message is that seventy times seven years would separate Nebuchadnezzar from the coming of the Messiah (Dan. ix, 21–24). But the Qumran sectaries went even further than Daniel. They argued that it is quite impossible to discover the meaning without an inspired interpreter because the Prophets themselves were ignorant of the full import of what they wrote. Habakkuk, for instance, was commanded to recount the history of the 'final generation', but he did so without having any clear idea of how far ahead the eschatological age lay. God 'did not make known to him when time would come to an end'. Knowledge of the authentic teaching of the Prophets was the supreme talent of the Teacher of Righteousness. The surviving Bible commentaries, whether or not the Teacher was directly responsible for them, are almost all concerned with predictions concerning the ultimate destiny of the righteous and the wicked, the tribulations and final triumph of the 'House of Judah' and the concomitant annihilation of those who had rebelled against God. But in addition to this general evidence of the subject-matter, the Scrolls directly impute to the Teacher a particular God-given insight into the hidden significance of prophecy. He was 'the Teacher of Righteousness to whom God made known all the mysteries of His servants the Prophets' (1QpHab. vii, 1–5). He was 'the Priest (in whose heart) God set (understanding) that he might interpret all the words of his servants the Prophets, through whom he foretold all that would happen to His people' (1QpHab. ii, 8–10). He was the Teacher who 'made known to the latter generations that which God would do to the last generation, the congregation of traitors, those who depart from the way' (CD i, 12–13). The Teacher's interpretation alone, propagated by his disciples, offered true enlightenment and guidance.

Supported in this way by the infallible teaching of the Community, the sectary believed himself to be living in the true city of God, the city of the Covenant built on the Law and the Prophets (cf. CD vii, 13–18).

Again and again, the architectural metaphors used in the Scrolls suggest security and protection. The sect is a 'House of Holiness', a 'House of Perfection and Truth', (1QS viii, 5, 9), a 'House of the Law' (CD xix, (B2): 10, 13); it is a 'sure House' (CD

III, 19) constructed on solid foundations. Indeed the language used is reminiscent of Isaiah xxviii, 16, and of Jesus' simile about the Church built not on sand but on rock (Matth. vii, 24–27; xvi, 18):

> But I shall be as one who enters a *fortified city*,
>   as one who seeks refuge behind a *high wall* . . .
> I will [lean on] Thy truth, O my God.
> For Thou wilt set the *foundation* on *rock*
>   and the *framework* by the *measuring cord* of justice;
> and the tried *stones* [Thou wilt lay]
>   by the *plumb-line* [of the truth],
> to [build] a mighty [wall] which shall not sway;
>   and no man entering there shall stagger.
>
> (1QS VI, 24–27)

Fortified by his membership of the brotherhood, the sectary could even carry his notions of solidity and firmness over into his own self so that he too became a 'strong tower':

> Thou hast strengthened me
>   before the battles of wickedness . . .
> Thou hast made me like a *strong tower*, a *high wall*,
>   and hast established my *edifice* upon the rock;
> *eternal foundations* serve for my ground,
>   and all my *ramparts* are a *tried wall* which shall not sway.
>
> (1QH VII, 7–9)

2 ELECTION AND HOLY LIFE IN THE COMMUNITY OF THE COVENANT

In the ideology of the Old Testament, to be a member of the chosen people is synonymous with being party to the Covenant. Israel willingly accepts the yoke of the Law given on Sinai, and God in his turn acknowledges her as his 'special possession' (Exod. xix, 5):

For you are a people holy to the Lord your God; the Lord your God has chosen you to be a people for his own possession, out of all the peoples that are on the face of the earth . . . You shall therefore be careful to do the commandment, and the statutes, and the ordinances which I command you this day (Deut. vii, 6, 11).

Theoretically, there is no distinction between election *de jure* and election *de facto*: every Jew is chosen. But already in biblical times a deep gulf is in fact seen to divide righteous observers of the Covenant from the wicked of Israel. Though not deprived of their birthright, the unfaithful are viewed as burdened with guilt and as such excluded, provisionally at least, from the congregation of the sons of God. The fully developed concept of election is summarized in the Palestinian Talmud by the third century A.D. Galilean Rabbi Lazar. Expounding the words of Deuteronomy quoted above, he comments:

When the Israelites do the will of the Holy One, blessed by He, they are called sons; but when they do not do His will, they are not called sons (Kiddushin 61c).

Inevitably, for the Qumran Essenes such a notion of Covenant membership was far too elastic. Consistent with their approach to legal matters, their attitude in regard to the Covenant was that only the initiates of their own 'new Covenant' were to be reckoned among God's elect and, as such, united already on earth with the angels of heaven.

> [God] has caused [His chosen ones] to inherit
>   the lot of the Holy Ones.
> He has joined their assembly
>   to the Sons of Heaven,
> to be a Council of the Community,
>   a foundation of the Building of Holiness,
>   an eternal Plantation throughout all ages to come.

(1QS xi, 7–9)

They insisted moreover, on the individual election of each sectary. The ordinary Jew envisaged entry into the congregation of the chosen primarily through birth, and secondly through the symbolical initiation of an eight-day-old infant submitted to circumcision. An Essene became a member of his sect by virtue of the deliberate and personal adult commitment of himself. For this reason, as will be remembered, even children born to married members and brought up in their schools had to wait until their twentieth birthday before they were allowed to make their solemn vows of entry into the Covenant. Also, believing in divine foreknowledge, they considered their adherence to the 'lot of God' as the effect of grace, as having been planned for each of them in heaven from all eternity. They, the elect, were guided by the spirit of truth in the ways of light, while the unprivileged, Jew and Gentile alike, were doomed to wander along paths of darkness. The Community Rule gives a fascinating description of these two human groups, the chosen and the unchosen.

The Master shall instruct all the sons of light and shall teach them the nature of all the children of men according to the kind of spirit which they possess . . .

From the God of Knowledge comes all that is and shall be. Before ever they existed He established their whole design, and when, as ordained for them, they come into being, it is in accord with His glorious design that they accomplish their task without change . . .

He has created man to govern the world, and has appointed for him two spirits in which to walk until the time of His visitation: the spirits of truth and falsehood.

Those born of truth spring from a fountain of light, but those born of falsehood spring from a source of darkness. All the children of righteousness are ruled by the Prince of Light and walk in the ways of light, but all the children of falsehood are ruled by the Angel of Darkness and walk in the ways of darkness.

The Angel of Darkness leads all the children of righteousness astray, and until his end, all their sins, iniquities, wickednesses, and all their unlawful deeds are caused by his dominion in accordance with the mysteries of God . . .

But the God of Israel and His Angel of Truth will succour all the sons of light. For it is He who created the spirits of Light and Darkness and founded every action upon them and established every deed (upon) their (ways).

And He loves the one everlastingly and delights in its works for ever; but the counsel of the other He loathes and for ever hates its ways (1QS III, 13–14:1).

Convictions of this kind, with their theories of individual election and predestination, coupled with a precise knowledge of the boundary dividing right from wrong, can lead to self-righteousness and arrogant intolerance of the masses thought to be rejected by God. The Essenes, however, appear to have concentrated more on the blessedness of the chosen than on the damnation of the unjust. Besides, they could always argue that Jews who refused to repent and remained outside the new Covenant were responsible for their own doom.

But the spiritual masters of the Community were doubtless aware of the danger of the sin of pride to which their less enlightened brothers were exposed and attacked it on three fronts. The Qumran Hymns, unlike certain biblical Psalms (e.g. Psalm xxvi) which testify to an acute form of sanctimoniousness, never cease to emphasize the sectary's frailty, unworthiness and total dependence on God.

> Clay and dust that I am,
>   what can I devise unless Thou will it,
>   and what contrive unless Thou desire it?
> What strength shall I have
>   unless Thou keep me upright
> and how shall I understand
>   unless by (the spirit) which Thou hast shaped for me?
>
> (1QH x, 5–7)

Not only is election itself owed to God's grace, but perseverance in the way of holiness cannot be counted on unless he offers his continuous help and support.

> When the wicked rose against Thy Covenant
>   and the damned against Thy word,
> I said in my sinfulness,
>   'I have been forsaken by Thy Covenant'.
> But calling to mind the might of Thy hand
>   and the greatness of Thy compassion,
> I rose and stood . . .
>   I lean on Thy grace and on the multitude of Thy mercies.
>
> (1QH iv, 34–37)

Another theme constantly stressed in Essene teaching is that not only is God's assistance necessary in order to remain faithful to his Law; the very knowledge of that Law is a gift from heaven. All their special understanding and wisdom comes from God.

> From the source of His righteousness
>   is my justification,
> and from His marvellous mysteries
>   is the light in my heart.
> My eyes have gazed
>   on that which is eternal,
> on wisdom concealed from men,
>   on knowledge and wise design
>   (hidden) from the sons of men;
> on a fountain of righteousness
>   and on a storehouse of power,
> on a spring of glory
>   (hidden) from the assembly of flesh.
> God has given them to His chosen ones
>   as an everlasting possession,
> and has caused them to inherit

the lot of the Holy Ones.

(1QS XI, 5–8)

The sentiments expressed in the Hymns, of love and gratitude and awareness of God's presence, represent a true religiousness and must have helped the sectary not to allow his life – governed as it was by laws and precepts – to slide into one of mere religious formalism.

> Thou hast upheld me with certain truth;
>> Thou hast delighted me with Thy Holy Spirit
>> and [hast opened my heart] till this day . . .
> The abundance of Thy forgiveness is with my steps
>> and infinite mercy accompanies Thy judgement of me.
> Until I am old Thou wilt care for me;
>> for my father knew me not
>> and my mother abandoned me to Thee.
> For Thou art a father
>> to all [the sons] of Thy truth,
> and as a woman who tenderly loves her babe,
>> so dost Thou rejoice in them;
> and as a nurse bearing a child in her lap,
>> so carest Thou for all Thy creatures.

(1QH IX, 32–36)

Whether the average Essene actually succeeded in fulfilling his high ideals, we cannot of course know: experience past and present has shown that paths to sanctity devised by organized religion are beset with snares. But there can be no doubt of their intention. The aim of a holy life lived within the Covenant was to penetrate the secrets of heaven in this world and to stand before God forever in the next. Like Isaiah, who beheld the Seraphim proclaiming 'Holy, holy, holy', and like Ezekiel, who in a trance watched the winged Cherubim drawing the divine Throne-Chariot, and like the ancient Jewish mystics who consecrated themselves, despite official disapproval by the rabbis, to the contemplation of the same Throne-Chariot and the heavenly Palaces, the Essenes, too, strove for a similar mystical knowledge, as one of their number testifies in a description of his own vision of the ministers of the 'Glorious Face'.

The [cheru]bim prostrate themselves before him and bless. As they rise, a whispered divine voice [is heard], and there is a roar of praise. When they drop their wings, there is a [whispere]d divine voice. The cherubim bless the image of the throne-chariot above the firmament, [and] they praise [the majes]ty of the luminous firmament beneath his seat of glory. When the wheels advance, angels of holiness come and go. From between his glorious wheels there is as it were a fiery vision of most holy spirits. About them, the appearance of rivulets of fire in the likeness of gleaming brass, and a work of . . . radiance in many-coloured glory, marvellous pigments, clearly mingled. The spirits of the living 'gods' move perpetually with the glory of the marvellous chariot(s). The whispered voice of blessing accompanies the roar of their advance, and they praise the Holy One on their way of return. When they ascend, they ascend marvellously, and when they settle, they stand still. The sound of joyful praise is silenced and there is a whispered blessing of the 'gods' in all the camps of God (4Q **405** 20ii–22).

3 Worship in the Community of the Covenant

In addition to the worship of God offered through a life of holiness, the Qumran sectary had more particularly to perform the ritual acts prescribed by Moses in the correct manner and at the right times. The earthly liturgy was intended to be a replica of that sung by the choirs of angels in the celestial Temple.

To judge from the many references to it, the time element both calendric and horary was crucial. The Community Rule lays down that the Community was not to 'depart from any command of God concerning their appointed times; they shall be neither early nor late for any of their appointed times, they shall stray neither to the right nor to the left of any of His true precepts' (1QS I, 13–15). This injunction asks for exact punctuality in regard to the two daily moments of prayer meant to coincide with and replace the perpetual burnt-offering sacrificed in the Temple at sunrise and sunset (Exod. xxix, 30; Num. xxviii, 4), but it demands in addition a strict observance of the sect's own liturgical calendar.

To understand the peculiarity of Essenism in this respect, a few words need to be said about the calendar followed by non-sectarian Judaism. Essentially, this was regulated by the movements of the moon; months varied in duration from between twenty-nine and thirty days and the year consisted of twelve months of 354 days. Needless to say, such a lunar year does not correspond to the four seasons determined by the movements of the sun, by solstices and equinoxes. The shortfall of about ten days between the lunar and the solar year was therefore compensated for by means of 'intercalation', i.e. by inserting after Adar

(February/March), the twelfth month of the year, a supplementary 'Second Adar' at the end of every thirty-six lunar months.

The Qumran sect rejected this seemingly artificial system and adopted instead a chronological reckoning, probably of priestly origin, based on the sun, a practice attested also in the Book of Jubilees and 1 Enoch. The outstanding feature of this solar calendar was its absolute regularity in that, instead of 354 days, not divisible by seven, it consisted of 364 days, i.e. fifty-two weeks precisely. Each of its four seasons was thirteen weeks long divided into three months of thirty days each, plus an additional 'remembrance' day (1QS x, 5) linking one season to another $(13 \times 7 = 91 = 3 \times 30 + 1)$. In tune in this way with the 'laws of the Great Light of heaven' (1QH XII, 5) and not with the 'festivals of the nations' (4QpHos II, 16), Qumran saw its calendar as corresponding to 'the certain law from the mouth of God' (1QH XII, 9). Its unbroken rhythm meant furthermore that the first day of the year and of each subsequent season always fell on the same day of the week. For the Essenes this was Wednesday, since according to Genesis i, 14–19, it was on the fourth day that the sun and the moon were created. Needless to add, the same monotonous sequence also implied that all the feasts of the year always fell on the same day of the week: Passover, the fifteenth day of the first month, was always celebrated on a Wednesday; the Feast of Weeks, the fifteenth day of the third month, always on a Sunday; the Day of Atonement, the tenth day of the seventh month, on a Friday; the Feast of Tabernacles, the fifteenth day of the seventh month, on a Wednesday, etc. This solar calendar with its eternal regularity cannot of course stand up to the astronomical calculation of 365 days 5 hours 48 minutes and 48 seconds to the year, but the Scrolls so far published give no indication of how the Essenes proposed to cope with this inconvenience, or whether indeed they were even aware of it.

One practical consequence of the sect's adherence to a calendar at variance with that of the rest of Judaism was that its feast-days were working days for other Jews and vice versa. The Wicked Priest was thus able to travel (journeys of any distance being forbidden on holy days of rest) to the place of exile of the Teacher of Righteousness while he and his followers were celebrating the Day of Atonement (cf. above, p. 24). In fact, it is likely that the persecutors of the sect deliberately chose that date to oblige the sectaries to attend to them on what they considered to be their 'Day of Fasting' and 'Sabbath of repose', and thus 'confuse them and cause them to stumble'. The same sort of story is told in the Mishnah of the Patriarch Gamaliel II, who endeavoured to humiliate Rabbi Joshua ben Hananiah by requiring him to visit him, carrying his stick and purse (also forbidden in the circumstances), on what Joshua reckoned to be the Day of Atonement (Rosh Ha-shanah ii, 9).

Another peculiarity of the liturgical calendar of the Community, attested in the Temple Scroll, was the division of the year into seven fifty-day periods – hence the name pentecontad calendar – each marked by an agricultural festival, e.g. the Feast of New Wine, the Feast of Oil, etc. A similar system is mentioned by Philo in connection with the Therapeutae in his book, *On the Contemplative Life*. One of these festivals, the Feast of the New Wheat, coincided with the Feast of Weeks and was for the Essenes/Therapeutae also the principal holy day of the year, that of the Renewal of the Covenant, the importance of which is discussed in Chapter I. From the Book of Jubilees, where, as has been said, the same calendar is followed, it is clear that Pentecost (the Feast of Weeks), together with the Feast of the Renewal of the Covenant, were celebrated on the fifteenth day of the third month (Jub. vi, 17–19). An outline of the ceremony performed on this holy day, with its acknowledgements of sin and its blessings and curses, is preserved in the Community Rule (1QS i, 16–ii, 25). The sectaries assemble in the service in strict hierarchical order: the priests first, ranked in order of status, after them the Levites, and lastly 'all the people one after another in their Thousands, Hundreds, Fifties and Tens, that every Israelite may know his place in the Community of God according to the everlasting design' (1QS ii, 22–23). Blessing God, the priests then recite his acts of loving-kindness to Israel and the Levites, Israel's rebellions against him. This recognition of guilt is followed by an act of public repentance appropriate to a community of converts.

We have strayed! We have [disobeyed]! We and our fathers before us have sinned and acted wickedly in walking [counter to the precepts] of truth and righteousness. [And God has] judged us and our fathers also; but He has bestowed His bountiful mercy on us from everlasting to everlasting (1QS i, 24–ii, 1).

After the confession, the priests solemnly bless the converts of Israel, calling down on them in particular the gifts of wisdom and knowledge:

May he bless you with all good and preserve you from all evil! May He lighten your heart with life-giving wisdom and grant you eternal knowledge! May He raise his merciful face towards you for everlasting bliss! (1QS II, 2–4).

This paraphrase of the blessing of Israel which God commanded Moses to transmit to Aaron and his sons in Numbers vi, 24–26, and which recalls the fourth of the daily Eighteen Benedictions of traditional Judaism, is accompanied by a Levitical curse of the party of Satan and a special malediction directed by both priests and Levites at any sectary whose conversion may be insincere:

Cursed be the man who enters this Covenant while walking among the idols of his heart, who sets up before himself his stumbling-block of sin so that he may backslide! Hearing the words of this Covenant, he blesses himself in his heart and says, 'Peace be with me, even though I walk in the stubbornness of my heart' (1QS II, 11–12).

Each benediction and curse is approved by the whole congregation with a twice repeated 'Amen'.

The ceremony of the Renewal of the Covenant is the only rite described in any detail among the Scrolls so far published, but as the Essenes laid so much emphasis on the full and punctilious observance of the Law of Moses it may be taken for granted that they did not omit the many other basic acts of Jewish religion and worship. Circumcision, for example, was certainly practised, though it is referred to only figuratively in the context of severing the 'foreskin of the evil inclination' (1QS v, 5), or possibly as the 'Covenant of Abraham' (CD XII, 11; XVI, 6). The laws of purity were also assuredly essential to the sect, despite the absence of any practical guidance on them. The same applies to the dietary laws, though a glimpse of information on these comes from the Damascus Rule declaring the eating of 'live creatures' prohibited (e.g. larvae of bees, fish and locusts – CD XII, 11–15), and from Josephus's remark that an Essene was forbidden to eat food prepared by people not belonging to the brotherhood (*War* II, 143).

On three other topics, the Qumran sources are less taciturn: ritual ablutions, Temple worship and the sacred meal. Discussed in Chapter I as part of the life of the sect, it remains now to consider the doctrinal significance of these rites.

Josephus, as will be recalled, observes that the Essenes took a ritual bath twice daily before meals (cf. *War* II, 129, 132). To this the Scrolls add that the minimum quantity of clean water required for a valid act of purification was to be the amount necessary to cover a man (CD x, 12–13). This is not of course an Essene invention, but typically, where the Mishnah prescribes a minimum of forty seahs (about 120 gallons), the sect's teaching concentrates on the practical purpose of the Mishnaic rule, namely that 'in them men may immerse themselves' (Mikwaoth vii, 1) and eliminates the obligation of having carefully to measure out what that quantity should be. Of greater interest, however, is the theological aspect, with its insistence on a correlation between the inner condition of a man and the outer rite. The wicked, according to the Community Rule, 'shall not enter the water . . . for they shall not be cleansed unless they turn from their wickedness' (1QS v, 13–14). True purification comes from the 'spirit of holiness' and true cleansing from the 'humble submission' of the soul to all God's precepts.

For it is through the spirit of true counsel concerning the ways of man that all his sins shall be expiated . . . He shall be cleansed from all his sins by the spirit of holiness . . . and his iniquity shall be expiated by the spirit of uprightness and humility. And when his flesh is sprinkled with purifying water and sanctified by cleansing water, it shall be made clean by the humble submission of his soul to all the precepts of God (1QS III, 6–9).

The second issue has to do with the sect's attitude towards the Temple and Temple sacrifice. While some Essenes, notwithstanding their vow of total fidelity to the Law of Moses, rejected the validity of the sanctuary and refused to participate (temporarily) in its rites (cf. Philo, *Omnis probus* 75; Josephus, *Antiquities* XVIII, 19), they evaded the theological dilemma in which this stand might have placed them by contending that until the re-dedication of the Temple, the only true worship of God was to be offered in their establishment. The Council of the Community was to be the 'Most Holy Dwelling for Aaron' where, 'without the flesh of holocausts and the fat of sacrifice', a 'sweet fragrance' was to be sent up to God, and where prayer was to serve 'as an acceptable fragrance of righteousness' (1QS VIII, 8–9; IX, 4–5). The Community itself was to be the sacrifice offered to God in atonement for Israel's sins (1QS VIII, 4–5).

Besides this evidence in the Community Rule, the same equation of Council of the Community = the Temple appears in the Habakkuk Commentary (XII, 3–4) in a most interesting interpretation of the word 'Lebanon'. Traditionally, 'Lebanon' is understood by ancient Jewish interpreters to symbolize 'the Temple'. For example, Deuteronomy iii, 25, 'Let me go over . . . and see . . . that goodly mountain and Lebanon', is rendered in Targum Onkelos as, 'Let me go over . . . and see . . . that goodly mountain and the Temple'. The Qumran commentator, explaining the Habakkuk text, 'For the violence done to Lebanon shall overwhelm you' (Hab. ii, 17), proceeds from the belief that the Council of the Community is the one valid Temple. He then sets out to prove it by directly associating Lebanon with the Council in the conviction that the traditional exegesis will be familiar to all his readers: Lebanon = Temple. Temple = Council of the Community, *ergo* Lebanon = Council of the Community.

The symbolical approach of the sect to sacrificial worship may account for Essene celibacy (where it was practised). Sexual abstinence was imposed on those participating in the Temple services, both priests and laymen; no person who had sexual intercourse (or an involuntary emission, or even any contact with a menstruating woman) could lawfully take part. More importantly still, bearing in mind the central place occupied by prophecy in Essene doctrine, clear indications exist in inter-Testamental and rabbinic literature that a similar renunciation was associated with the prophetic state. Thus Moses, in order always to be ready to hear the voice of God, is said by Philo to have cleansed himself of 'all calls of mortal nature, food, drink, and intercourse with women' (*Life of Moses* ii, 68–9). Consequently, despite the attempt made by this writer and by Josephus to attribute the sect's celibacy to misogyny, a more reasonable explanation would be that it was thought that lives intended to be wholly consecrated to worship and wholly preoccupied with meditation on prophecy should be kept wholly, and not intermittently, pure.

The common table of the Essenes, the third special cultic subject to be examined, has already been discussed in Chapter I (pp. 6–7), but one remaining point needs to be mentioned, namely that since the rules relating to the daily meal and the messianic meal are the same, it is not unreasonable to infer from the New Testament parallel that the former was thought to prefigure the latter. As is well known, the evangelist Matthew portrays the Last Supper as the prototype of the great eschatological feast, quoting Jesus as saying:

I tell you, I shall not drink again of this fruit of the vine until that day when I drink it new with you in my Father's Kingdom (Matth. xxvi, 29).

4 Future Expectations in the Community of the Covenant

The Essene sect was born into a world of eschatological ferment, of intense expectation of the end foretold by the prophets. Using biblical models as vehicles for their own convictions, the Teacher of Righteousness and the Community's sages projected an image of the future which is detailed and colourful, but which cannot always be fully comprehended by us, partly because some of the associations escape us, and partly because of gaps in the extant texts and the incompleteness of the documentation in general. They foresaw their Community as fulfilling the prophetic expectations of the salvation of the righteous. It was from their ranks, swollen by the re-conversion of some of the 'Simple of Ephraim' (4QpNah III, 4–5) who had caused such distress by their previous apostasy, and by other Jewish recruits (1QSa I, 1–), that the sons of Light would go to battle against the sons of Darkness. The Community, the 'exiles of the desert', would after a preliminary attack on the 'army of Satan' symbolized by the 'ungodly of the Covenant' and their foreign allies from the environs of Judaea, followed by an assault on the Kittim occupying the Holy Land, move to Jerusalem. These events were expected to cover a period of six years. The seventh, the first sabbatical year of the War, would see the restoration of the Temple worship.

Of the remaining thirty-three years of its duration, four would be sabbatical years, so the War would be waged during twenty-nine: against the 'sons of Shem' for nine years, against the 'sons of Ham' for ten years, and against the 'sons of Japheth' for another ten years (1QM I-II). The final conflict would end with the total defeat of the 'King of the Kittim' and of Satan's hosts, and the joyful celebrations of the Hero, God, by the victorious sons of Light.

> Rise up, O Hero!
> Lead off Thy captives, O Glorious One!
> Gather up Thy spoils, O Author of mighty deeds!
> Lay Thy hand on the neck of Thine enemies
>   and Thy feet on the pile of the slain!
> Smite the nations, Thine adversaries,
>   and devour flesh with Thy sword!
> Fill Thy land with glory
>   and Thine inheritance with blessing!
> Let there be a multitude of cattle in Thy fields,
>   and in Thy palaces silver and gold and precious stones!

O Zion, rejoice greatly!
  Rejoice all you cities of Judah!
Keep your gates ever open
  that the host of the nations may be brought in!
Their kings shall serve you
  and all your oppressors shall bow down before you;
  they shall lick the dust of your feet.
Shout for joy, O daughters of my people!
Deck yourselves with glorious jewels
  and rule over the kingdom of the nations!
Sovereignty shall be to the Lord
  and everlasting dominion to Israel.

(1QM xix, 2–8)

Such was to be the course of the War in its earthly dimensions. But it would possess in addition a cosmic quality. The hosts of the sons of Light, commanded by the 'Prince of the Congregation', were to be supported by the angelic armies led by the 'Prince of Light', also known in the Scrolls as the archangel Michael or Melchizedek. Similarly, the 'ungodly of the Covenant' and their Gentile associates were to be aided by the demonic forces of Satan, or Belial, or Melkiresha. These two opposing camps were to be evenly matched, and God's intervention alone would bring about the destruction of evil (1QM xviii, 1–3). Elsewhere the grand finale is represented as a judgement scene in which the heavenly prince Melchizedek recompenses 'the holy ones of God' and executes 'the vengeance of the judgements of God' over Satan and his lot (11QMelch ii, 9, 13).

The role of the priests and Levites in this imaginary ultimate grappling of good with evil emerges as that of non-combatants, but it is difficult to determine the function of the commander-in-chief, the so-called 'Prince of the Congregation'. We learn that on his shield will be inscribed his name, the names of Israel, Levi and Aaron, and those of the twelve tribes and their chiefs (1QM v, 1–2); but little room appears to be left in the War Rule for him to act as the royal Messiah. God himself is the supreme agent of salvation and after him in importance is Michael.

In the other Scrolls, by contrast, the theme of Messianism is prominent. Complex and *sui generis*, it envisages everywhere except in the Damascus Rule not one, but two, and possibly even three, messianic figures. The lay King-Messiah, otherwise known as the 'Branch of David', the 'Messiah of Israel', the 'Prince of [all] the Congregation' and the 'Sceptre', was to usher in, according to the sect's book of Blessings, 'the Kingdom of his people' and 'bring death to the ungodly' and defeat '[the kings of the] nations' (1QSb v, 21, 25, 28). As befits a priestly sect, however, the Priest-Messiah comes first in the order of precedence, the 'Messiah of Aaron', the 'Priest', the 'Interpreter of the Law' (cf. 1QSa II, 20). The King-Messiah was to defer to him and to the priestly authority in general in all legal matters: 'As they teach him, so shall he judge' (4QpIsa VIII–XI, 23). The 'Messiah of Aaron' was to be the final Teacher, 'he who shall teach righteousness at the end of days' (CD VI, 11). But he was also to preside over the battle liturgy (1QM xv, 4; xvi, 13; xviii, 5) and the eschatological banquet (1QSa II, 12–21).

The third figure, 'the Prophet', is mentioned directly though briefly only once: we are told that his arrival was expected together with that of the Messiahs of Aaron and Israel (1QS IX, 11). Viewed in the context of inter-Testamental Jewish ideas, the Prophet was to be either an Elijah returned as a precursor of the Messiah (Mal. iv, 5; 1 Enoch xc, 31, 37; Matth. xi, 13; xvii, 12), or as a divine guide sent to Israel in the final days (1 Mac. iv, 46; xiv, 41; Jn. i, 21) no doubt identical with 'the Prophet' promised by God to Moses ('I will raise up for them a prophet like you . . . He shall convey all my commands to them', Deut. xviii, 15–18; cf. Acts iii, 22–23; 7:37). An identification of 'the Prophet' with a 'new Moses' is supported by the inclusion of the Deuteronomy passage in the Messianic Anthology or *Testimonia* from cave 4 as the first of three messianic proof texts, the second being Balaam's prophecy concerning the Star to rise out of Jacob (Num. xxiv, 15–17), and the third, the blessing of Levi by Moses (Deut. xxxiii, 11), prefiguring respectively the royal Messiah and the Priest-Messiah.

If it is proper to deduce from these not too explicit data that the messianic Prophet (or prophetic Messiah) was to teach the truth revealed on the eve of the establishment of the Kingdom, it would follow that his part was to all intents and purposes to be the same as that attributed by the Essenes to the Teacher of Righteousness. In consequence, it would not be unreasonable to suggest that at some point of the sect's history the coming of the Prophet was no longer expected; he was believed to have already appeared in the person of the Teacher of Righteousness.

The evidence so far published does not permit categorical statements on the sectaries' views of what was to follow the days of the Messiahs. Some kind of metamorphosis was awaited by them, as is clear from the Community Rule – 'until the determined end, and until the Renewal' (1QS iv, 25). But one cannot be sure that it was understood as synonymous with the new creation of the Apocalypses of Ezra (vii, 75) and Baruch (xxxii, 6). Similarly, the 'new Jerusalem' described in various manuscripts does not match by definition the Holy City descending from above of 1 Enoch (xc, 28–29) or Revelation xxi, but could be an earthly city rebuilt according to the plans of angelic architects.

As for the after-life proper, and the place it occupied in Essene thought, for many centuries in the biblical age Jews paid little attention to this question. They believed with most peoples in antiquity that after death the just and wicked alike would share a miserable, shadowy existence in Sheol, the underworld, where even God is forgotten: 'Turn, O Lord, save my life,' cries the psalmist, 'for in death there is no remembrance of thee; in Sheol who can give thee praise?' (Ps. vi, 5; cf. Isa. xxxviii, 18; Ps. lxxxviii, 10–12, etc.) The general hope was for a long and prosperous life, many children, a peaceful death in the midst of one's family, and burial in the tomb of one's fathers. Needless to say, with this simple outlook went a most sensitive appreciation of the present time as being the only moment in which man can be with God.

Eventually, the innate fear of death, and the dissatisfaction of later biblical thinkers with a divine justice that allowed the wicked to flourish on earth and the just to suffer, led to attempts in the post-exilic era to solve this fundamental dilemma. The idea of resurrection, or rather of the reunification of body and soul after death, first appears as a metaphor in Ezekiel's vision of the rebirth of the Jewish nation after the Babylonian captivity as the re-animation of dry bones (Ezek. xxxvii). Later, after the historical experience of martyrdom under the persecution of Antiochus Epiphanes, resurrection was expected to be the true reward of individuals who freely gave their lives for God – i.e., for their religion (Dan. xii, 2; 2 Mac. vii, 9; xii, 44; xiv, 46, etc.). At the same time, the notion of immortality also emerged, the idea that the righteous are to be vindicated and live for ever in God's presence. This view is developed fully in the Greek apocryphal Book of Wisdom (iii, 1–v, 16).

Josephus tells us that the Essenes subscribed to this second school of thought. According to him, they adopted a distinctly Hellenistic concept of immortality, holding the flesh to be a prison out of which the indestructible soul of the just escapes into limitless bliss 'in an abode beyond the ocean' after its final deliverance (*War* II, 154–8). Resurrection, implying a return of the spirit to a material body, can thus play no part in this scheme.

The Scrolls themselves, however, are not particularly helpful because they never confront the issue as such. We encounter statements such as, 'Hoist a banner, O you who lie in the dust! O bodies gnawed by worms, raise up an ensign . . .!' (1QH VI, 34-35; cf. XI, 10–14), which may connote bodily resurrection. On the other hand, the poet's language may just be allegorical. Immortality, as distinct from resurrection, is better attested. The substance of Josephus's account is confirmed, though not surprisingly without any typically Hellenistic colouring (no doubt introduced by him to please his Greek readers). The Community Rule, discussing the reward of the righteous and the wicked, assures the just of 'eternal joy in life without end, a crown of glory and a garment of majesty in unending light' (1QS IV, 7–8), and sinners of 'eternal torment and endless disgrace together with shameful extinction in the fire of the dark regions' (1QS IV, 12–13).

It is interesting to observe that immortality was not conceived of as an entirely new state, but rather as a direct continuation of the position attained on entry into the Community. From that moment, the sectary was raised to an 'everlasting height' and joined to the 'everlasting Council', the 'Congregation of the Sons of Heaven' (1QH III, 20–22).

In sum, the portrait of the sectary as it is reflected in his religious ideas and ideals bears the marks of a fanatical observance of the Mosaic Law, an overwhelming assurance of the correctness of his beliefs, and certainty of his own eventual salvation. But whereas these characteristics may make little appeal to modern man, we would do well not to overlook other traits conspicuous in particular, in his prayers and hymns, which testify to his absolute dependence on God and his total devotion to what he believed to be God's cause.

> For without Thee no way is perfect,
>   and without Thy will nothing is done.
> It is Thou who hast taught all knowledge
>   and all things come to pass by Thy will.
> There is none beside Thee to dispute Thy counsel
>   or to understand all Thy holy design
> or to contemplate the depth of Thy mysteries
>   and the power of Thy might.

Who can endure Thy glory,
  and what is the son of man
  in the midst of Thy wonderful deeds?
What shall one born of woman
  be accounted before Thee?
Kneaded from the dust,
  his abode is the nourishment of worms.
He is but a shape, but moulded clay,
  and inclines towards the dust.

(1QS XI, 17–22)

NOTE ON THE TEXTS

✦

TRANSLATORS of the Scrolls are tempted to render them either with extreme freedom at the expense of fidelity, or else literally, word for word and line for line. I have tried to avoid both these pitfalls by providing an interpretation in simple English which is at the same time faithful and intelligible.

Lacunae impossible to complete with any measure of confidence are indicated by dots.

Hypothetical but likely reconstructions are placed between [ ] and glosses necessary for fluency between ( ).

Biblical quotations appearing in the text are printed in italics, as well as the titles and headings which figure in the manuscripts.

Each scroll is divided into columns. The beginning of each of these columns is indicated in the translation by bold Roman numerals: **I, II, III**, etc.

I have included only those fragments which are large enough to convey some meaning and have similarly omitted from the Scrolls any passage too mutilated to reconstruct.

A. THE RULES

1. THE COMMUNITY RULE (1QS)

Discovered in cave 1, the eleven relatively well preserved columns of this manuscript were first published in 1951 by M. Burrows under the title, *The Manual of Discipline* (*The Dead Sea Scrolls of St Mark's Monastery* II, New Haven). Important fragments of eleven other manuscripts of the Rule containing a certain number of variant readings were also found in caves IV and V. A list of these has been drawn up by J. T. Milik (*Revue Biblique*, 1960, pp. 412–15) and some of them have been adopted in the present translation.

The principal manuscript bears the stamp of editorial modification. For instance, in column X the original 'I will *conceal* knowledge with discretion' is corrected to 'I will *impart* knowledge with discretion'. The section covered by columns VIII-IX was particularly subject to alteration and is considerably abridged in one of the fragmentary manuscripts.

The Community Rule is probably one of the oldest documents of the sect; its original composition may date to around 100 B.C. It seems to have been intended for the Community's teachers, for its Masters or Guardians, and contains extracts from liturgical ceremonies, an outline of a model sermon on the spirits of truth and falsehood, statutes concerned with initiation into the sect and with its common life, organization and discipline, a penal code, and finally a poetic dissertation on the fundamental religious duties of the Master and his disciples, and on the sacred seasons proper to the Community.

There are, to my knowledge, no writings in ancient Jewish sources parallel to the Community Rule, but a similar type of literature flourished among Christians between the second and fourth centuries, the so-called 'Church Orders' represented by the Didache, the Didascalia, the Apostolic Constitution, etc.

The contents may be divided into three main sections, but further sub-headings appear in the text itself:

1. Entry into the Covenant, followed by an instruction on the two spirits (I-IV).
2. Statutes relating to the Council of the Community (V-IX).
3. Directives addressed to the Master, and the Master's Hymn (IX-XI).

I [The Master shall teach the sai]nts to live [according to] the

Book of the Community Rule, that they may seek God with a whole heart and soul, and do what is good and right before Him as He commanded by the hand of Moses and all His servants the Prophets; that they may love all that He has chosen and hate all that he has rejected; that they may abstain from all evil and hold fast to all good; that they may practise truth, righteousness, and justice upon earth and no longer stubbornly follow a sinful heart and lustful eyes committing all manner of evil. He shall admit into the Covenant of Grace all those who have freely devoted themselves to the observance of God's precepts, that they may be joined to the counsel of God and may live perfectly before Him in accordance with all that has been revealed concerning their appointed times, and that they may love all the sons of light, each according to his lot in God's design, and hate all the sons of darkness, each according to his guilt in God's vengeance.

All those who freely devote themselves to His truth shall bring all their knowledge, powers, and possessions into the Community of God, that they may purify their knowledge in the truth of God's precepts and order their powers according to His ways of perfection and all their possessions according to His righteous counsel. They shall not depart from any command of God concerning their times; they shall be neither early nor late for any of their appointed times, they shall stray neither to right nor to left of any of His true precepts. All those who embrace the Community Rule shall enter into the Covenant before God to obey all His commandments so that they may not abandon Him during the dominion of Satan because of fear or terror or affliction.

On entering the Covenant, the Priests and Levites shall bless the God of salvation and all His faithfulness, and all those entering the Covenant shall say after them, 'Amen, Amen!'

Then the Priests shall recite the favours of God manifested in His mighty deeds and shall declare all His merciful grace to Israel, and the Levites shall recite the iniquities of the children of Israel, all their guilty rebellions and sins during the dominion of Satan. And after them, all those entering the Covenant shall confess and say: 'We have strayed! We have [disobeyed!] We and our fathers before us have sinned and done wickedly in walking [counter to the precepts] of truth and righteousness. [And God has] judged us and our fathers also; **II** but He has bestowed His bountiful mercy on us from everlasting to everlasting.' And the Priests shall bless all the men of the lot of God who walk perfectly in all His ways, saying: 'May He bless you with all good and preserve you from all evil! May He lighten your heart with life-giving wisdom and grant you eternal knowledge! May he raise His merciful face towards you for everlasting bliss!'

And the Levites shall curse all the men of the lot of Satan, saying: 'Be cursed because of all your guilty wickedness! May He deliver you up for torture at the hands of the vengeful Avengers! May He visit you with destruction by the hand of all the Wreakers of Revenge! Be cursed without mercy because of the darkness of your deeds! Be damned in the shadowy place of everlasting fire! May God not heed when you call on Him, nor pardon you by blotting out your sin! May He raise His angry face towards you for vengeance! May there be no "Peace" for you in the mouth of those who hold fast to the Fathers!' And after the blessing and the cursing, all those entering the Covenant shall say, 'Amen, Amen!'

And the Priests and Levites shall continue, saying: 'Cursed be the man who enters this Covenant while walking among the idols of his heart, who sets up before himself his stumbling-block of sin so that he may backslide! Hearing the words of this Covenant, he blesses himself in his heart and says, "Peace be with me, even though I walk in the stubbornness of my heart" (Deut. xxix, 18–19), whereas his spirit, parched (for lack of truth) and watered (with lies), shall be destroyed without pardon. God's wrath and His zeal for His precepts shall consume him in everlasting destruction. All the curses of the Covenant shall cling to him and God will set him apart for evil. He shall be cut off from the midst of all the sons of light, and because he has turned aside from God on account of his idols and his stumbling-block of sin, his lot shall be among those who are cursed for ever.' And after them, all those entering the Covenant shall answer and say, 'Amen, Amen!'

Thus shall they do, year by year, for as long as the dominion of Satan endures. The Priests shall enter first, ranked one after another according to the perfection of their spirit; then the Levites; and thirdly, all the people one after another in their Thousands, Hundreds, Fifties, and Tens, that every Israelite may know his place in the Community of God according to the ever-lasting design. No man shall move down from his place nor move up from his allotted position. For according to the holy design, they shall all of them be in a Community of truth and virtuous humility, of loving kindness and good intent one towards the other, and (they shall all of them be) sons of the everlasting Company.

No man [shall be in the] Community of His truth who refuses to enter [the Covenant of] God so that he may walk in the stubbornness of his heart, for **III** his soul detests the wise teaching of just laws. He shall not be counted among the upright for he has not persisted in the conversion of his life. His knowledge, powers, and possessions shall not enter the Council of the Community, for whoever ploughs the mud of wickedness returns defiled (?). He shall not be justified by that which his stubborn heart declares lawful, for seeking the ways of light he looks towards darkness. He shall not be reckoned among the perfect; he shall neither be purified by atonement, nor cleansed by purifying waters, nor sanctified by seas and rivers, nor washed clean with any ablution. Unclean, unclean shall he be. For as long as he despises the precepts of God he shall receive no instruction in the Community of His counsel.

For it is through the spirit of true counsel concerning the ways of man that all his sins shall be expiated that he may contemplate the light of life. He shall be cleansed from all his sins by the spirit of holiness uniting him to His truth, and his iniquity shall be expiated by the spirit of uprightness and humility. And when his flesh is sprinkled with purifying water and sanctified by cleansing water, it shall be made clean by the humble submission of his soul to all the precepts of God. Let him then order his steps to walk perfectly in all the ways commanded by God concerning the times appointed for him, straying neither to right nor to left and transgressing none of His words, and he shall be accepted by virtue of pleasing atonement before God and it shall be to him a Covenant of the everlasting Community.

The Master shall instruct all the sons of light and shall teach them the nature of all the children of men according to the kind of spirit which they possess, the signs identifying their works during their lifetime, their visitation for chastisement, and the time of their reward.

From the God of Knowledge comes all that is and shall be. Before ever they existed He established their whole design, and when, as ordained for them, they come into being, it is in accord with His glorious design that they accomplish their task without change. The laws of all things are in His hand and He provides them with all their needs.

He has created man to govern the world, and has appointed

for him two spirits in which to walk until the time of His visitation: the spirits of truth and falsehood. Those born of truth spring from a fountain of light, but those born of falsehood spring from a source of darkness. All the children of righteousness are ruled by the Prince of Light and walk in the ways of light, but all the children of falsehood are ruled by the Angel of Darkness and walk in the ways of darkness.

The Angel of Darkness leads all the children of righteousness astray, and until his end, all their sin, iniquities, wickedness, and all their unlawful deeds are caused by his dominion in accordance with the mysteries of God. Every one of their chastisements, and every one of the seasons of their distress, shall be brought about by the rule of his persecution; for all his allotted spirits seek the overthrow of the sons of light.

But the God of Israel and His Angel of Truth will succour all the sons of light. For it is He who created the spirits of Light and Darkness and founded every action upon them and established every deed [upon] their [ways]. And He loves the one **IV** everlastingly and delights in its works for ever; but the counsel of the other He loathes and for ever hates its ways.

These are their ways in the world for the enlightenment of the heart of man, and that all the paths of true righteousness may be made straight before him, and that the fear of the laws of God may be instilled in his heart: a spirit of humility, patience, abundant charity, unending goodness, understanding, and intelligence; (a spirit of) mighty wisdom which trusts in all the deeds of God and leans on His great lovingkindness; a spirit of discernment in every purpose, of zeal for just laws, of holy intent with steadfastness of heart, of great charity towards all the sons of truth, of admirable purity which detests all unclean idols, of humble conduct sprung from an understanding of all things, and of faithful concealment of the mysteries of truth. These are the counsels of the spirit to the sons of truth in this world.

And as for the visitation of all who walk in this spirit, it shall be healing, great peace in a long life, and fruitfulness, together with every everlasting blessing and eternal joy in life without end, a crown of glory and a garment of majesty in unending light.

But the ways of the spirit of falsehood are these: greed, and slackness in the search for righteousness, wickedness and lies, haughtiness and pride, falseness and deceit, cruelty and abundant evil, ill-temper and much folly and brazen insolence, abominable deeds (committed) in a spirit of lust, and ways of lewdness in the service of uncleanness, a blaspheming tongue, blindness of eye and dullness of ear, stiffness of neck and heaviness of heart, so that man walks in all the ways of darkness and guile.

And the visitation of all who walk in this spirit shall be a multitude of plagues by the hand of all the destroying angels, everlasting damnation by the avenging wrath of the fury of God, eternal torment and endless disgrace together with shameful extinction in the fire of the dark regions. The times of all their generations shall be spent in sorrowful mourning and in bitter misery and in calamities of darkness until they are destroyed without remnant or survivor.

The nature of all the children of the men is ruled by these (two spirits), and during their life all the hosts of men have a portion of their divisions and walk in (both) their ways. And the whole reward for their deeds shall be, for everlasting ages, according to whether each man's portion in their two divisions is great or small. For God has established the spirits in equal measure until the final age, and has set everlasting hatred between their divisions. Truth abhors the works of falsehood, and falsehood hates all the ways of truth. And their struggle is fierce in all their arguments for they do not walk together.

But in the mysteries of His understanding, and in His glorious wisdom, God has ordained an end for falsehood, and at the time of the visitation He will destroy it for ever. Then truth, which has wallowed in the ways of wickedness during the dominion of falsehood until the appointed time of judgement, shall arise in the world for ever. God will then purify every deed of man with his truth; He will refine for Himself the human frame by rooting out all spirit of falsehood from the bounds of his flesh. He will cleanse him of all wicked deeds with the spirit of holiness; like purifying waters He will shed upon him the spirit of truth (to cleanse him) of all abomination and falsehood. And he shall be plunged into the spirit of purification that he may instruct the upright in the knowledge of the Most High and teach the wisdom of the sons of heaven to the perfect of way. For God has chosen them for an everlasting Covenant and all the glory of Adam shall be theirs. There shall be no more lies and all the works of falsehood shall be put to shame.

Until now the spirits of truth and falsehood struggle in the hearts of men and they walk in both wisdom and folly. According to his portion of truth so does a man hate falsehood, and according to his inheritance in the realm of falsehood so is he wicked and so hates truth. For God has established the two spirits in equal measure until the determined end, and until the Renewal, and He knows the reward of their deeds from all eternity. He has allotted them to the children of men that they may know good [and evil, and] that the destiny of all the living may be according to the spirit within [them at the time] of the visitation.

V *And this is the Rule for the men of the Community who have freely pledged themselves to be converted from all evil and to cling to all His commandments according to His will.*

They shall separate from the congregation of the men of falsehood and shall unite, with respect to the Law and possessions, under the authority of the sons of Zadok, the Priests who keep the Covenant, and of the multitude of the men of the Community who hold fast to the Covenant. Every decision concerning doctrine, property, and justice shall be determined by them.

They shall practise truth and humility in common, and justice and uprightness and charity and modesty in all their ways. No man shall walk in the stubbornness of his heart so that he strays after his heart and eyes and evil inclination, but he shall circumcise in the Community the foreskin of evil inclination and of stiffness of neck that they may lay a foundation of truth for Israel, for the Community of the everlasting Covenant. They shall atone for all those in Aaron who have freely pledged themselves to holiness, and for those in Israel who have freely pledged themselves to the House of Truth, and for those who join them to live in community and to take part in the trial and judgement and condemnation of all those who transgress the precepts.

On joining the Community, this shall be their code of behaviour with respect to all these precepts.

Whoever approaches the Council of the Community shall enter the Covenant of God in the presence of all who have freely pledged themselves. He shall undertake by a binding oath to return with all his heart and soul to every commandment of the Law of Moses in accordance with all that has been revealed of it to the sons of Zadok, the Keepers of the Covenant and Seekers of His will, and to the multitude of the men of their Covenant who together have freely pledged themselves to His truth and to walking in the way of His delight. And he shall undertake by the Covenant to separate from all the men of falsehood who walk in the way of wickedness.

For they are not reckoned in His Covenant. They have neither inquired nor sought after Him concerning His laws that they might know the hidden things in which they have sinfully erred; and matters revealed they have treated with insolence. Therefore Wrath shall rise up to condemn, and Vengeance shall be executed by the curses of the Covenant, and great chastisements of eternal destruction shall be visited on them, leaving no remnant. They shall not enter the water to partake of the pure Meal of the saints, for they shall not be cleansed unless they turn from their wickedness: for all who transgress His word are unclean. Likewise, no man shall consort with him with regard to his work or property lest he be burdened with the guilt of his sin. He shall indeed keep away from him in all things: as it is written, *Keep away from all that is false* (Exod. xxiii, 7). No member of the Community shall follow them in matters of doctrine and justice, or eat or drink anything of theirs, or take anything from them except for a price; as it is written, *Keep away from the man in whose nostrils is breath, for wherein is he counted?* (Isa. ii, 22). For all those not reckoned in His Covenant are to be set apart, together with all that is theirs. None of the saints shall lean upon works of vanity: for they are all vanity who know not His Covenant, and He will blot from the earth all them that despise His word. All their deeds are defilement before Him, and all their possessions unclean.

But when a man enters the Covenant to walk according to all these precepts that he may join the holy Congregation, they shall examine his spirit in community with respect to his understanding and practice of the Law, under the authority of the sons of Aaron who have freely pledged themselves in the Community to restore His Covenant and to heed all the precepts commanded by Him, and of the multitude of Israel who have freely pledged themselves in the Community to return to His Covenant. They shall inscribe them in the order, one after another, according to their understanding and their deeds, that every one may obey his companion, the man of lesser rank obeying his superior. And they shall examine their spirit and deeds yearly, so that each man may be advanced in accordance with his understanding and perfection of way, or moved down in accordance with the offences committed by him.

They shall rebuke one another in truth, humility, and charity. Let no man address his companion with anger, or ill-temper, or obduracy, or with envy prompted by the spirit of wickedness. Let him not hate him [because of his uncircumcised] heart, but let him rebuke him on the very same day lest **VI** he incur guilt because of him. And furthermore, let no man accuse his companion before the Congregation without having first admonished him in the presence of witnesses.

These are the ways in which all of them shall walk, each man with his companion, wherever they dwell. The man of lesser rank shall obey the greater in matters of work and money. They shall eat in common and pray in common and deliberate in common.

Wherever there are ten men of the Council of the Community there shall not lack a Priest among them. And they shall all sit before him according to their rank and shall be asked their counsel in all things in that order. And when the table has been prepared for eating, and the new wine for drinking, the Priest shall be the first to stretch out his hand to bless the first-fruits of the bread and new wine.

And where the ten are, there shall never lack a man among them who shall study the Law continually, day and night, concerning the right conduct of a man with his companion. And the Congregation shall watch in community for a third of every night of the year, to read the Book and to study Law and to pray together.

This is the Rule for an Assembly of the Congregation

Each man shall sit in his place: the Priests shall sit first, and the elders second, and all the rest of the people according to their rank. And thus shall they be questioned concerning the Law, and concerning any counsel or matter coming before the Congregation, each man bringing his knowledge to the Council of the Community.

No man shall interrupt a companion before his speech has ended, nor speak before a man of higher rank; each man shall speak in his turn. And in an Assembly of the Congregation no man shall speak without the consent of the Congregation, nor indeed of the Guardian of the Congregation. Should any man wish to speak to the Congregation, yet not be in a position to question the Council of the Community, let him rise to his feet and say: 'I have something to say to the Congregation.' If they command him to speak, he shall speak.

Every man, born of Israel, who freely pledges himself to join the Council of the Community shall be examined by the Guardian at the head of the Congregation concerning his understanding

and his deeds. If he is fitted to the discipline, he shall admit him
into the Covenant that he may be converted to the truth and
depart from all falsehood; and he shall instruct him in all the rules
of the Community. And later, when he comes to stand before the
Congregation, they shall all deliberate his case, and according to
the decision of the Council of the Congregation he shall either
enter or depart. After he has entered the Council of the Community he shall not touch the pure Meal of the Congregation
until one full year is completed, and until he has been examined
concerning his spirit and deeds; nor shall he have any share of
the property of the Congregation. Then when he has completed
one year within the Community, the Congregation shall deliberate his case with regard to his understanding and observance of
the Law. And if it be his destiny, according to the judgement of
the Priests and the multitude of the men of their Covenant, to
enter the company of the Community, his property and earnings
shall be handed over to the Bursar of the Congregation who shall
register it to his account and shall not spend it for the Congregation. He shall not touch the Drink of the Congregation until
he has completed a second year among the men of the Community. But when the second year has passed, he shall be examined, and if it be his destiny, according to the judgement of the
Congregation, to enter the Community, then he shall be inscribed
among his brethren in the order of his rank for the Law, and for
justice, and for the pure Meal; his property shall be merged and
he shall offer his counsel and judgement to the Community.

These are the Rules by which they shall judge at a Community (Court of)
Inquiry according to the cases

If one of them has lied deliberately in matters of property, he
shall be excluded from the pure Meal of the Congregation for
one year and shall do penance with respect to one quarter of his
food.

Whoever has answered his companion with obstinacy, or has
addressed him impatiently, going so far as to take no account of
the dignity of his fellow by disobeying the order of a brother
inscribed before him, he has taken the law into his own hand;
therefore he shall do penance for one year [and shall be
excluded].

If any man has uttered the [Most] Venerable Name
VII even though frivolously, or as a result of shock or for any

other reason whatever, while reading the Book or praying, he shall be dismissed and shall return to the Council of the Community no more.

If he has spoken in anger against one of the Priests inscribed in the Book, he shall do penance for one year and shall be excluded for his soul's sake from the pure Meal of the Congregation. But if he has spoken unwittingly, he shall do penance for six months.

Whoever has deliberately lied shall do penance for six months.

Whoever has deliberately insulted his companion unjustly shall do penance for one year and shall be excluded.

Whoever has deliberately deceived his companion by word or by deed shall do penance for six months.

If he has failed to care for his companion, he shall do penance for three months. But if he has failed to care for the property of the Community, thereby causing its loss, he shall restore it in full. And if he be unable to restore it, he shall do penance for sixty days.

Whoever has borne malice against his companion unjustly shall do penance for six months/one year; and likewise, whoever has taken revenge in any matter whatever.

Whoever has spoken foolishly: three months.

Whoever has interrupted his companion whilst speaking: ten days.

Whoever has lain down to sleep during an Assembly of the Congregation: thirty days. And likewise, whoever has left, without reason, an Assembly of the Congregation as many as three times during one Assembly, shall do penance for ten days. But if he has departed whilst they were standing he shall do penance for thirty days.

Whoever has gone naked before his companion, without having been obliged to do so, he shall do penance for six months.

Whoever has spat in an Assembly of the Congregation shall do penance for thirty days.

Whoever has been so poorly dressed that when drawing his hand from beneath his garment his nakedness has been seen, he shall do penance for thirty days.

Whoever has guffawed foolishly shall do penance for thirty days.

Whoever has drawn out his left hand to gesticulate with it shall do penance for ten days.

Whoever has gone about slandering his companion shall be

excluded from the pure Meal of the Congregation for one year and shall do penance. But whoever has slandered the Congregation shall be expelled from among them and shall return no more.

Whoever has murmured against the authority of the Community shall be expelled and shall not return. But if he has murmured against his companion unjustly, he shall do penance for six months.

Should a man return whose spirit has so trembled before the authority of the Community that he has betrayed the truth and walked in the stubbornness of his heart, he shall do penance for two years. During the first year he shall not touch the pure Meal of the Congregation, and during the second year he shall not touch the Drink of the Congregation and shall sit below all the men of the Community. Then when his two years are completed, the Congregation shall consider his case, and if he is admitted he shall be inscribed in his rank and may then question concerning the Law.

If, after being in the Council of the Community for ten full years, the spirit of any man has failed so that he has betrayed the Community and departed from the Congregation to walk in the stubbornness of his heart, he shall return no more to the Council of the Community. Moreover, if any member of the Community has shared with him his food or property which . . . of the Congregation, his sentence shall be the same; he shall be ex[pelled].

VIII   In the Council of the Community there shall be twelve men and three Priests, perfectly versed in all that is revealed of the Law, whose works shall be truth, righteousness, justice, loving kindness and humility. They shall preserve the faith in the Land with steadfastness and meekness and shall atone for sin by the practice of justice and by suffering the sorrows of affliction. They shall walk with all men according to the standard of truth and the rule of the time.

When these are in Israel, the Council of the Community shall be established in truth. It shall be an Everlasting Plantation, a House of Holiness for Israel, an Assembly of Supreme Holiness for Aaron. They shall be witnesses to the truth at the Judgement, and shall be the elect of Goodwill who shall atone for the Land and pay to the wicked their reward. It shall be that tried wall, that *precious corner-stone*, whose foundations shall neither rock nor sway in their place (Isa. xxviii, 16). It shall be a Most Holy Dwelling for Aaron, with everlasting knowledge of the Covenant of justice, and shall offer up sweet fragrance. It shall be a House of Perfection and Truth in Israel that they may establish a Covenant according to the everlasting precepts. And they shall be an agreeable offering, atoning for the Land and determining the judgement of wickedness, and there shall be no more iniquity. When they have been confirmed for two years in perfection of way by the authority of the Community, they shall be set apart as holy within the Council of the men of the Community. And the Interpreter shall not conceal from them, out of fear of the spirit of apostasy, any of those things hidden from Israel which have been discovered by him.

And when these become members of the Community in Israel according to all these rules, they shall separate from the habitation of ungodly men and shall go into the wilderness to prepare the way of Him; as it is written, *Prepare in the wilderness the way of . . ., make straight in the desert a path for our God* (Isa. xl, 3). This (path) is the study of the Law which He commanded by the hand of Moses, that they may do according to all that has been revealed from age to age, and as the Prophets have revealed by His Holy Spirit.

And no man among the members of the Covenant of the Community who deliberately, on any point whatever, turns aside from all that is commanded, shall touch the pure Meal of the men of holiness or know anything of their counsel until his deeds are purified from all falsehood and he walks in perfection of way. And then, according to the judgement of the Congregation, he shall be admitted to the Council and shall be inscribed in his rank. This rule shall apply to whoever enters the Community.

And these are the rules which the men of perfect holiness shall follow in their commerce with one another

Every man who enters the Council of Holiness, (the Council of those) who walk in the way of perfection as commanded by God, and who deliberately or through negligence transgresses one word of the Law of Moses, on any point whatever, shall be expelled from the Council of the Community and shall return no more; no man of holiness shall be associated in his property or counsel in any matter at all. But if he has acted inadvertently, he shall be excluded from the pure Meal and the Council and they shall interpret the rule (as follows). For two years he shall take no part in judgement or ask for counsel; but if, during that time, his way becomes perfect, then he shall return to the (Court of) Inquiry and the Council, in accordance with the judgement of the Congregation, provided that he commit no further inadvertent sin during two full years. **IX** For one sin of inadvertence (alone) he shall do penance for two years. But as for him who has sinned deliberately, he shall never return; only the man who has sinned inadvertently shall be tried for two years that his way and counsel may be made perfect according to the judgement of the Congregation. And afterwards, he shall be inscribed in his rank in the Community of Holiness.

When these become members of the Community in Israel according to all these rules, they shall establish the spirit of holiness according to everlasting truth. They shall atone for guilty rebellion and for sins of unfaithfulness that they may obtain lovingkindness for the Land without the flesh of holocausts and the fat of sacrifice. And prayer rightly offered shall be as an acceptable fragrance of righteousness, and perfection of way as a delectable free-will offering. At that time, the men of the Community shall set apart a House of Holiness in order that it may be united to the most holy things and a House of Community for Israel, for those who walk in perfection. The sons of Aaron alone shall command in matters of justice and property, and every rule concerning the men of the Community shall be determined according to their word.

As for the property of the men of holiness who walk in perfection, it shall not be merged with that of the men of falsehood who have not purified their life by separating themselves from iniquity and walking in the way of perfection. They shall depart from none of the counsels of the Law to walk in the stubbornness of their hearts, but shall be ruled by the primitive precepts in which the men of the Community were first instructed until there shall come the Prophet and the Messiahs of Aaron and Israel.

These are the precepts in which the Master shall walk in his commerce with all the living, according to the rule proper to every season and according to the worth of every man

He shall do the will of God according to all that has been revealed from age to age.

He shall measure out all knowledge discovered throughout the ages, together with the Precept of the age.

He shall separate and weigh the sons of righteousness according to their spirit.

He shall hold firmly to the elect of the time according to His will, as He has commanded.

He shall judge every man according to his spirit. He shall admit him in accordance with the cleanness of his hands and advance him in accordance with his understanding. And he shall love and hate likewise.

He shall not rebuke the men of the Pit nor dispute with them.

He shall conceal the teaching of the Law from men of falsehood, but shall impart true knowledge and righteous judgement to those who have chosen the Way. He shall guide them all in knowledge according to the spirit of each and according to the rule of the age, and shall thus instruct them in the mysteries of marvellous truth that in the midst of the men of the Community they may walk perfectly together in all that has been revealed to them. This is the time for the preparation of the way into the wilderness, and he shall teach them to do all that is required at that time and to separate from all those who have not turned aside from all ungodliness.

These are the rules of conduct for the Master in those times with respect to his loving and hating

Everlasting hatred in a spirit of secrecy for the men of perdition! He shall leave to them wealth and earnings like a slave to his lord and like a poor man to his master.

He shall be a man zealous for the Precept whose time is for the Day of Revenge. He shall perform the will of God in all his deeds, and in all his dominion as He has commanded. He shall freely delight in all that befalls him and nothing shall please him save God's will. He shall delight in all the words of His mouth and shall desire nothing except His command. He shall watch always [for] the judgement of God, and shall bless his Maker [for all His goodness] and declare [His mercies] in all that befalls.

He shall bless Him [with the offering] of the lips **X** at the times ordained by Him: at the beginning of the dominion of light, and at its end when it retires to its appointed place; at the beginning of the watches of darkness when He unlocks their storehouse and spreads them out, and also at their end when they retire before the light; when the heavenly lights shine out from the dwelling-place of Holiness, and also when they retire to the place of Glory; at the entry of the (monthly) seasons on the days of the new moon, and also at their end when they succeed to one another. Their renewal is a great day for the Holy of Holies, and a sign for the unlocking of everlasting mercies at the beginning of seasons in all times to come.

> At the beginning of the months of the (yearly) seasons
>   and on the holy days appointed for remembrance,
> in their seasons I will bless Him
>   with the offering of the lips
>   according to the Precept engraved for ever:
> at the beginning of the years
>   and at the end of their seasons
>   when their appointed law is fulfilled,
> on the day decreed by Him
>   that they should pass from one to the other –
> the season of early harvest to the summer time,
> the season of sowing to the season of grass,
> the seasons of years to their weeks (of years) –
> and at the beginning of their weeks
>   for the season of Jubilee.
> All my life the engraved Precept shall be on my tongue
>   as the fruit of praise
>   and the portion of my lips.
>
> I will sing with knowledge and all my music
>   shall be for the glory of God.
> (My) lyre (and) my harp shall sound
>   for His holy order
> and I will tune the pipe of my lips
>   to His right measure.
> With the coming of day and night
>   I will enter the Covenant of God,
> and when evening and morning depart
>   I will recite His decrees.
> I will place in them my bounds without return.
>
> I will declare His judgement concerning my sins,
>   and my transgressions shall be before my eyes
>   as an engraved Precept.
> I will say to God, 'My Righteousness'
>   and 'Author of my Goodness' to the Most High,
> 'Fountain of Knowledge' and 'Source of Holiness',
>   'Summit of Glory' and 'Almighty Eternal Majesty'.
> I will choose that which He teaches me
>   and will delight in His judgement of me.
>
> Before I move my hands and feet

I will bless His Name.
I will praise Him before I go out or enter,
   or sit or rise,
    and whilst I lie on the couch of my bed.
I will bless Him with the offering
   of that which proceeds from my lips
    from the midst of the ranks of men,
and before I lift my hands to eat
   of the pleasant fruits of the earth.
I will bless Him for His exceeding wonderful deeds
   at the beginning of fear and dread
    and in the abode of distress and desolation.
I will meditate on His power
   and will lean on His mercies all day long.
I know that judgement of all the living
   is in His hand,
    and that all His deeds are truth.
I will praise Him when distress is unleashed
   and will magnify Him also because of His salvation.

I will pay to no man the reward of evil;
   I will pursue him with goodness.
For judgement of all the living is with God
   and it is He who will render to man his reward.
I will not envy in a spirit of wickedness,
   my soul shall not desire the riches of violence.
I will not grapple with the men of perdition
   until the Day of Revenge,
but my wrath shall not turn from the men of falsehood
   and I will not rejoice until judgement is made.
I will bear no rancour
   against them that turn from transgression,
but will have no pity
   on all who depart from the way.
I will offer no comfort to the smitten
   until their way becomes perfect.

I will not keep Satan within my heart,
and in my mouth shall be heard
   no folly or sinful deceit,
    no cunning or lies shall be found on my lips.
The fruit of holiness shall be on my tongue
   and no abominations shall be found upon it.
I will open my mouth
   in songs of thanksgiving,
and my tongue shall always proclaim
   the goodness of God and the sin of men

until their transgression ends.
I will cause vanities
    to cease from my lips,
uncleanness and crookedness
    from the knowledge of my heart.

I will impart/conceal knowledge with discretion
    and will prudently hedge it within a firm bound
to preserve faith and strong judgement
    in accordance with the justice of God.
I will distribute the Precept
    by the measuring-cord of the times,
and . . . righteousness
    and lovingkindness towards the oppressed,
encouragement to the troubled heart
    XI   and discernment to the erring spirit,
teaching understanding to them that murmur
    that they may answer meekly
    before the haughty of spirit
and humbly before men of injustice
    who point the finger and speak of iniquity
    and who are zealous for wealth.

As for me,
    my justification is with God.
In His hand are the perfection of my way
    and the uprightness of my heart.
He will wipe out my transgression
    through His righteousness.

For my light has sprung
    from the source of His knowledge;
my eyes have beheld His marvellous deeds,
    and the light of my heart, the mystery to come.
He that is everlasting
    is the support of my right hand;
the way of my steps is over stout rock
    which nothing shall shake;
for the rock of my steps is the truth of God
    and His might is the support of my right hand.

From the source of His righteousness
    is my justification,
and from His marvellous mysteries
    is the light in my heart.
My eyes have gazed
    on that which is eternal,
on wisdom concealed from men,

on knowledge and wise design
 (hidden) from the sons of men;
on a fountain of righteousness
 and on a storehouse of power,
on a spring of glory
 (hidden) from the assembly of flesh.
God has given them to His chosen ones
 as an everlasting possession,
and has caused them to inherit
 the lot of the Holy Ones.
He has joined their assembly
 to the Sons of Heaven
to be a Council of the Community,
a foundation of the Building of Holiness,
and eternal Plantation throughout all ages to come.

As for me,
 I belong to wicked mankind,
 to the company of ungodly flesh.
My iniquities, rebellions, and sins,
 together with the perversity of my heart,
belong to the company of worms
 and to those who walk in darkness.
For mankind has no way,
 and man is unable to establish his steps
since justification is with God
 and perfection of way is out of His hand.
All things come to pass by His knowledge;
He establishes all things by His design
 and without Him nothing is done.

As for me,
 if I stumble, the mercies of God
 shall be my eternal salvation.
If I stagger because of the sin of flesh,
 my justification shall be
by the righteousness of God which endures for ever.
When my distress is unleashed
 He will deliver my soul from the Pit
 and will direct my steps to the way.
He will draw me near by His grace,
 and by His mercy will He bring my justification.
He will judge me in the righteousness of His truth
 and in the greatness of His goodness
 He will pardon all my sins.
Through His righteousness he will cleanse me
 of the uncleanness of man

and of the sins of the children of men,
that I may confess to God His righteousness,
  and His majesty to the Most High.

Blessed art Thou, my God,
  who openest the heart of Thy servant to knowledge!
Establish all his deeds in righteousness,
and as it pleases Thee to do for the elect of mankind,
  grant that the son of Thy handmaid
  may stand before Thee for ever.

For without Thee no way is perfect,
  and without Thy will nothing is done.
It is Thou who hast taught all knowledge
  and all things come to pass by Thy will.
There is none beside Thee to dispute Thy counsel
  or to understand all Thy holy design,
or to contemplate the depth of Thy mysteries
  and the power of Thy might.

Who can endure Thy glory,
  and what is the son of man
  in the midst of Thy wonderful deeds?
What shall one born of woman
  be accounted before Thee?
Kneaded from the dust,
  his abode is the nourishment of worms.
He is but a shape, but moulded clay,
  and inclines towards dust.
What shall hand-moulded clay reply?
  What counsel shall it understand?

2. THE DAMASCUS RULE (CD)

⟨∾⟩⟨∾⟩

Extensive fragments of the Damascus Rule have been recovered from three of the Qumran caves, but two incomplete medieval copies of this document had been found already many years earlier, in 1896–7, amongst a mass of discarded manuscripts in a store-room (*geniza*) of an old Cairo synagogue. Published in 1910 by S. Schechter (*Fragments of a Zadokite Work*, Cambridge), they were reprinted with a new Prolegomenon by J. A. Fitzmyer in 1970, and re-edited by Chaim Rabin under the title, *The Zadokite Documents* (Oxford, 1954).

Dating from the tenth and twelfth centuries respectively, the manuscripts found in Cairo – Manuscript A and Manuscript B – raise a certain number of textual problems in that they present two different versions of the original composition. I have settled the difficulty as satisfactorily as I can by following Manuscript A, to which the unpublished Qumran fragments correspond, and by inserting the Manuscript B variants in brackets or footnotes. At a certain point, as the reader will see, Manuscript A comes to an end and we then have to rely entirely on Manuscript B. Furthermore, following the suggestion made by J. T. Milik in *Ten Years of Discovery in the Wilderness of Judaea* (London, 1959, pp. 151–2), I have rearranged the order of the pages and placed pages xv and xvi before page ix.

The title 'Damascus Rule' derives from the references in the Exhortation to the 'New Covenant' made 'in the land of Damascus'. The significance of this phrase is discussed in Chapter II (p. 32) together with the chronological data included in the manuscript. They suggest that the document was written in about 100 B.C. and this hypothesis is indirectly supported by the absence of any mention in the historical passages of the Kittim (Romans) whose invasion of the Orient did not take place until after 70 B.C.

The work is divided into an Exhortation and a list of Statutes. In the Exhortation, the preacher – probably a Guardian of the Community – addresses his 'sons' on the themes of the sect's teaching, many of which appear also in the Community Rule. His aim is to encourage the sectaries to remain faithful, and with this end in view he sets out to demonstrate from the history of Israel and the Community that fidelity is always rewarded and apostasy chastised.

During the course of his argument, the author of the Damascus Rule frequently interprets biblical passages in a most unexpected way. I have mentioned one of these commentaries on the marriage laws in Chapter III (p. 38–9), but there is another involved exposition of Amos v, 26–7 on page 88–9 which may not be easy to understand.

In the Bible these verses convey a divine threat: the Israelites were to take themselves and their idols into exile. 'You shall take up Sakkuth your king and Kaiwan your star-god, your images which you made for yourselves, for I will take you into exile beyond Damascus.' But the Damascus Rule transforms this threat into a promise of salvation; by changing certain words in the biblical text and omitting others its version reads: 'I will exile the tabernacle of your king and the bases of your statues from my tent to Damascus.'

In this new text, the three key phrases are interpreted symbolically as follows: 'tabernacle' = 'Books of the Law'; 'king' = 'congregation'; 'bases of statues' = 'Books of the Prophets'. Thus: 'The Books of the Law are the *tabernacle* of the king; as God said, *I will raise up the tabernacle of David which is fallen* (Amos ix, 11). The *king* is the congregation; and the *bases of the statues* are the Books of the Prophets whose sayings Israel despised.'

The omission of any reference to the 'star-god' is made good by introducing a very different 'Star', the Messianic 'Interpreter of the Law' with his companion the 'Prince of the congregation'. 'The star is the Interpreter of the Law who shall come to Damascus; as it is written, *A star shall come forth out of Jacob and a sceptre shall rise out of Israel* (Num. xxiv, 17). The sceptre is the Prince of the whole congregation . . .'

The second part of the Damascus Rule, the Statutes, consists of a collection of laws which mostly reflect a sectarian reinterpretation of the biblical commandments relative to vows and oaths, tribunals, purification, the Sabbath, and the distinction between ritual purity and impurity. They are followed by rules concerned with the institutions and organization of the Community. Some of the particular laws of the Damascus Rule appear also in the Temple Scroll. (cf. p.129).

Whereas the Exhortation represents a literary *genre* adopted by both Jewish and Christian religious teachers (e.g. the Letter to the Hebrews), the methodical grouping of the Statutes prefigures that of the Mishnah, the oldest Jewish code extant.

The Statutes as they appear in the Qumran fragments include the form of the ritual for the Feast of the Renewal of the Covenant, so it may be assumed that the entire Damascus Rule was originally connected with that festival.

The Exhortation

I   Hear now, all you who know righteousness, and consider the works of God; for He has a dispute with all flesh and will condemn all those who despise Him.

For when they were unfaithful and forsook Him, He hid His face from Israel and His Sanctuary and delivered them up to the sword. But remembering the Covenant of the forefathers, He left a remnant to Israel and did not deliver it up to be destroyed. And in the age of wrath, three hundred and ninety years after He had given them into the hand of king Nebuchadnezzar of Babylon, He visited them, and He caused a plant root to spring from Israel and Aaron to inherit His Land and to prosper on the good things of His earth. And they perceived their iniquity and recognized that they were guilty men, yet for twenty years they were like blind men groping for the way.

And God observed their deeds, that they sought Him with a whole heart, and He raised for them a Teacher of Righteousness to guide them in the way of His heart. And he made known to the latter generations that which God had done to the latter generation, the congregation of traitors, to those who departed from the way. This was the time of which it is written, *Like a stubborn heifer thus was Israel stubborn* (Hos. iv, 16), when the Scoffer arose who shed over Israel the waters of lies. He caused them to wander in a pathless wilderness, laying low the everlasting heights, abolishing the ways of righteousness and removing the boundary with which the forefathers had marked out their inheritance, that he might call down on them the curses of His Covenant and deliver them up to the avenging sword of the Covenant. For they sought smooth things and preferred illusions (Isa. xxx, 10) and they watched for breaks (Isa. xxx, 13) and chose the fair neck; and they justified the wicked and condemned the just, and they transgressed the Covenant and violated the Precept. They banded together against the life of the righteous (Ps. xciv, 21) and loathed all who walked in perfection; they pursued them with the sword and exulted in the strife of the people. And the anger of God was kindled against **II** their congregation so that He ravaged all their multitude; and their deeds were defilement before Him.

Hear now, all you who enter the Covenant, and I will unstop your ears concerning the ways of the wicked.

God loves knowledge. Wisdom and understanding He has set before Him, and prudence and knowledge serve Him. Patience and much forgiveness are with Him towards those who turn from transgression; but power, might, and great flaming wrath by the hand of all the Angels of Destruction towards those who depart from the way and abhor the Precept. They shall have no remnant or survivor. For from the beginning God chose them not; He knew their deeds before ever they were created and He hated their generations, and He hid His face from the Land until they were consumed. For He knew the years of their coming and the length and exact duration of their times for all ages to come and throughout eternity. He knew the happenings of their times throughout all the everlasting years. And in all of them He raised for Himself men called by name, that a remnant might be left to the Land, and that the face of the earth might be filled with their seed. And He made known His Holy Spirit to them by the hand of His anointed ones, and He proclaimed the truth (to them). But those whom He hated He led astray.

Hear now, my sons, and I will uncover your eyes that you may see and understand the works of God, that you choose that which pleases Him and reject that which He hates, that you may walk perfectly in all His ways and not follow after thoughts of the guilty inclination and after eyes of lust. For through them, great men have gone astray and mighty heroes have stumbled from former times till now. Because they walked in the stubbornness of their heart the Heavenly Watchers fell; they were caught because they did not keep the commandments of God. And their sons also fell who were tall as cedar trees and whose bodies were like mountains. All flesh on dry land perished; they were as though they had never been because they did their own will and did not keep the commandment of their Maker so that His wrath was kindled against them.   **III**   Through it, the children of Noah went astray, together with their kin, and were cut off. Abraham did not walk in it, and he was accounted a friend of God because he kept the commandments of God and did not choose his own will. And he handed them down to Isaac and Jacob, who kept them, and were recorded as friends of God and party to the Covenant for ever.

The children of Jacob strayed through them and were punished in accordance with their error. And their sons in Egypt walked in the stubbornness of their hearts, conspiring against the commandments of God and each of them doing that which seemed right in his own eyes. They ate blood, and He cut off their males in the wilderness.

And at Kadesh He said to them, *Go up and possess the land* (Deut. ix, 23). But they chose their own will and did not heed the voice of their Maker, the commands of their Teacher, but murmured in their tents; and the anger of God was kindled against their congregation. Through it their sons perished, and through it their kings were cut off; through it their mighty heroes perished and through it their land was ravaged. Through it the first members of the Covenant sinned and were delivered up to the sword, because they forsook the Covenant of God and chose their own will and walked in the stubbornness of their hearts each of them doing his own will.

But with the remnant which held fast to the commandments of God He made His Covenant with Israel for ever, revealing to them the hidden things in which all Israel had gone astray. He unfolded before them His holy Sabbaths and his glorious feasts, the testimonies of His righteousness and the ways of His truth, and the desires of His will which a man must do in order to live. And they dug a well rich in water; and he who despises it shall not live. Yet they wallowed in the sin of man and in ways of uncleanness, and they said, 'This is our (way).' But God, in His wonderful mysteries, forgave them their sin and pardoned their wickedness; and He built them a sure house in Israel whose like has never existed from former times till now. Those who hold fast to it are destined to live for ever and all the glory of Adam shall be theirs. As God ordained for them by the hand of the Prophet Ezekiel, saying, *The Priests, the Levites, and the sons* **IV** *of Zadok who kept the charge of my sanctuary when the children of Israel strayed from me, they shall offer me fat and blood* (Ezek. xliv, 15).

The *Priests* are the converts of Israel who departed from the land of Judah, and (the *Levites* are) those who joined them. The *sons of Zadok* are the elect of Israel, the men called by name who shall stand at the end of days. Behold the exact list of their names according to their generations, and the time when they lived, and the number of their trials, and the years of their sojourn, and the exact list of their deeds . . .

(They were the first men) of holiness whom God forgave, and who justified the righteous and condemned the wicked. And until the age is completed, according to the number of those years, all who enter after them shall do according to that interpretation of the Law in which the first were instructed. According to the Covenant which God made with the forefathers, forgiving their sins, so shall He forgive their sins also. But when the age is completed, according to the number of those years, there shall be no more joining the house of Judah, but each man shall stand on his watchtower: *The wall is built, the boundary far removed* (Mic. vii, 11).

During all those years Satan shall be unleashed against Israel, as He spoke by the hand of Isaiah, son of Amoz, saying, *Terror and the pit and the snare are upon you, O inhabitant of the land* (Isa. xxiv, 17). Interpreted, these are the three nets of Satan with which Levi son of Jacob said that he catches Israel by setting them up as three kinds of righteousness. The first is fornication, the second is riches, and the third is profanation of the Temple. Whoever escapes the first is caught in the second, and whoever saves himself from the second is caught in the third (Isa. xxiv, 18).

The 'builders of the wall' (Ezek. xiii, 10) who have followed after 'Precept' – 'Precept' was a spouter of whom it is written, *They shall surely spout* (Mic. ii, 6) – shall be caught in fornication twice by taking a second wife while the first is alive, whereas the principle of creation is, *Male and female created He them* (Gen. i, 27). V Also, those who entered the Ark went in two by two. And concerning the prince it is written, *He shall not multiply wives to himself* (Deut. xvii, 17); but David had not read the sealed book of the Law which was in the ark (of the Covenant), for it was not opened in Israel from the death of Eleazar and Joshua, and the elders who worshipped Ashtoreth. It was hidden and (was not) revealed until the coming of Zadok. And the deeds of David rose up, except for the murder of Uriah, and God left them to him.

Moreover, they profane the Temple because they do not observe the distinction (between clean and unclean) in accordance with the Law, but lie with a woman who sees her bloody discharge.

And each man marries the daughter of his brother or sister, whereas Moses said, *You shall not approach your mother's sister; she is your mother's near kin* (Lev. xviii, 13). But although the laws against incest are written for men, they also apply to women. When, therefore, a brother's daughter uncovers the nakedness of her father's brother, she is (also his) near kin.

Furthermore, they defile their holy spirit and open their mouth with a blaspheming tongue against the laws of the Covenant of God saying, 'They are not sure.' They speak abominations concerning them; *they are all kindlers of fire and lighters of brands* (Isa. l, 11), *their webs are spiders' webs and their eggs are vipers' eggs* (Isa. lix, 5). No man that approaches them shall be free from guilt; the more he does so, the guiltier shall he be, unless he is pressed. For (already) in ancient times God visited their deeds and His anger was kindled against their works; *for it is a people of no discernment* (Isa. xxvii, 11), *it is a nation void of counsel inasmuch as there is no discernment in them* (Deut. xxxii, 28). For in ancient times, Moses and Aaron arose by the hand of the Prince of Lights and Satan in his cunning raised up Jannes and his brother when Israel was first delivered.

And at the time of the desolation of the Land there arose removers of the bound who led Israel astray. And the land was ravaged because they preached rebellion against the command-ments of God given by the hand of Moses and **VI** of His holy anointed ones, and because they prophesied lies to turn Israel away from following God. But God remembered the Covenant with the forefathers, and he raised from Aaron men of discern-ment and from Israel men of wisdom, and He caused them to hear. And they dug the Well: *the well which the princes dug, which the nobles of the people delved with the stave* (Num. xxi, 18).

The *Well* is the Law, and those who dug it were the converts of Israel who went out of the land of Judah to sojourn in the land of Damascus. God called them all *princes* because they sought Him, and their renown was disputed by no man. The *Stave* is the Interpreter of the Law of whom Isaiah said, *He makes a tool for His work* (Isa. liv, 16); and the *nobles of the people* are those who come to dig the *Well* with the staves with which the *Stave* ordained that they should walk in all the age of wickedness – and without them they shall find nothing – until he comes who shall teach righteousness at the end of days.

None of those brought into the Covenant shall enter the Temple to light His altar in vain. They shall bar the door, foras-much as God said, *Who among you will bar its door?* And, *You shall not light my altar in vain* (Mal. i, 10). They shall take care to act according to the exact interpretation of the Law during the age of wickedness. They shall separate from the sons of the Pit, and shall keep away from the unclean riches of wickedness acquired by vow or anathema or from the Temple treasure; they shall not rob the poor of His people, to make of widows their prey and of the fatherless their victim (Isa. x, 2). They shall distinguish between clean and unclean, and shall proclaim the difference between holy and profane. They shall keep the Sabbath day according to its exact interpretation, and the feasts and the Day of Fasting according to the finding of the members of the New Covenant in the land of Damascus. They shall set aside the holy things according to the exact teaching concerning them. They shall love each man his brother as himself; they shall succour the poor, the needy, and the stranger.

A man shall seek his brother's well-being **VII** and shall not sin against his near kin. They shall keep from fornication according to the statute. They shall rebuke each man his brother according to the commandment and shall bear no rancour from one day to the next. They shall keep apart from every uncleanness according to the statutes relating to each one, and no man shall defile his holy spirit since God has set them apart. For all who walk in these (precepts) in perfect holiness, according to all the teaching of God, the Covenant of God shall be an assurance that they shall live for thousands of generations (Ms. B: as it is written, *Keeping the Covenant and grace with those who love me and keep my commandments, to a thousand generations*, Deut. vii, 9).

And if they live in camps according to the rule of the Land (Ms. B: as it was from ancient times), marrying (Ms. B according to the custom of the Law) and begetting children, they shall walk according to the Law and according to the statute concerning binding vows, according to the rule of the Law which says, *Between a man and his wife and between a father and his son* (Num. xxx, 17). And all those who despise (Ms. B the commandments and the statutes) shall be rewarded with the retribution of the wicked when God shall visit the Land, when the saying shall come to pass which is written* among the words of the Prophet Isaiah son of Amoz: *He will bring upon you, and upon your people, and upon your father's house, days such as have not come since the day that Ephraim departed from Judah* (Isa. vii, 17). When the two houses of Israel were divided, Ephraim departed from Judah. And all the apostates were given up to the sword, but those who held fast escaped to the land of the north; as God said, *I will exile the tabernacle of your king and the bases of your statues from my tent to Damascus* (Amos v, 26–7).

---

*Ms. B continues: by the hand of the prophet Zechariah: *Awake, O Sword, against my shepherd, against my companion, says God. Strike the shepherd that the flock may be scattered and I will stretch my hand over the little ones* (Zech. xiii, 7). The humble of the flock are those who watch for Him. They shall be saved at the time of the Visitation whereas the others shall be delivered up to the sword when the Anointed of Aaron and Israel shall come, as it came to pass at the time of the former Visitation concerning which God said by the hand of Ezekiel: *They shall put a mark on the foreheads of those who sigh and groan* (Ezek. ix, 4). But the others were delivered up to the avenging sword of the Covenant.

The Books of the Law are the *tabernacle* of the king; as God said, *I will raise up the tabernacle of David which is fallen* (Amos ix, 11). The *king* is the congregation; and the *bases of the statues* are the Books of the Prophets whose sayings Israel despised. The *star* is the Interpreter of the Law who shall come to Damascus; as it is written, *A star shall come forth out of Jacob and a sceptre shall rise out of Israel* (Num. xxiv, 17). The *sceptre* is the Prince of the whole congregation, and when he comes *he shall smite all the children of Seth* (Num. xxiv, 17).

At the time of the former Visitation they were saved, whereas the apostates **VIII** were given up to the sword; and so shall it be for all the members of His Covenant who do not hold steadfastly to these (Ms. B: to the curse of the precepts). They shall be visited for destruction by the hand of Satan. That shall be the day when God will visit. (Ms. B: As He said,) *The princes of Judah have become* (Ms. B: *like those who remove the bound*); *wrath shall be poured upon them* (Hos. v, 10). For they shall hope for healing but He will crush them. They are all of them rebels, for they* have not turned from the way of traitors but have wallowed in the ways of whoredom and wicked wealth. They have taken revenge and borne malice, every man against his brother, and every man has hated his fellow, and every man has sinned against his near kin, and has approached for unchastity, and has acted arrogantly for the sake of riches and gain. And every man has done that which seemed right in his eyes and has chosen the stubbornness of his heart. They have not kept apart from the people (Ms. B: and their sin) and have wilfully rebelled by walking in the ways of the wicked of whom God said, *Their wine is the venom of serpents, the cruel poison* (or *head*) *of asps* (Deut. xxxii, 33).

The *serpents* are the kings of the peoples and their *wine* is their ways. And the *head of asps* is the chief of the kings of Greece who came to wreak vengeance upon them. But all these things the *builders of the wall and those who daub it with plaster* (Ezek. xiii, 10) have not understood because a follower of the wind, one who raised storms and rained down lies, had preached to them (Mic. ii, 11), against all of whose assembly the anger of God was kindled.

And as for that which Moses said, *You enter to possess these nations not because of your righteousness or the uprightness of your hearts* (Deut. ix, 5) *but because God loved your fathers and kept the oath* (Deut. vii,

---

*Ms. B inserts: they have entered the Covenant of repentance but they have not turned, etc.

8), thus shall it be with the converts of Israel who depart from the way of the people. Because God loved the first who* testified in His favour, so will He love those who come after them, for the Covenant of the fathers is theirs. But He hated the *builders of the wall* and His anger was kindled (Ms. B against them and against all those who followed them); and so shall it be for all who reject the commandments of God and abandon them for the stubbornness of their hearts. This is the word which Jeremiah spoke to Baruch son of Neriah, and which Elisha spoke to his servant Gehazi.

None of the men who enter the New Covenant in the land of Damascus, (B I) and who again betray it and depart from the fountain of living waters, shall be reckoned with the Council of the people or inscribed in its Book from the day of the gathering in (B II) of the Teacher of the Community until the coming of the Messiah out of Aaron and Israel.

And thus shall it be for every man who enters the congregation of men of perfect holiness but faints in performing the duties of the upright. He is a man who has melted in the furnace (Ezek. xxii, 22); when his deeds are revealed he shall be expelled from the congregation as though his lot had never fallen among the disciples of God. The men of knowledge shall rebuke him in accordance with his sin against the time when he shall stand again before the Assembly of the men of perfect holiness. But when his deeds are revealed, according to the interpretation of the Law in which the men of perfect holiness walk, let no man defer to him with regard to money or work, for all the Holy Ones of the Most High have cursed him.

And thus shall it be for all among the first and the last who reject (the precepts), who set idols upon their hearts and walk in the stubbornness of their hearts; they shall have no share in the house of the Law. They shall be judged in the same manner as their companions were judged who deserted to the Scoffer. For they have spoken wrongly against the precepts of righteousness, and have despised the Covenant and the Pact – the New Covenant – which they made in the land of Damascus. Neither they nor their kin shall have any part in the house of the Law.

From the day of the gathering in of the Teacher of the Community until the end of all the men of war who deserted to the Liar there shall pass about forty years (Deut. ii, 14). And during

---

*Ms. B adds: bore witness against the people, so will He love, etc.

that age the wrath of God shall be kindled against Israel; as He said, *There shall be no king, no prince, no judge, no man to rebuke with justice* (Hos. iii, 4). But those who turn from the sin of Jacob, who keep the Covenant of God, shall then speak each man to his fellow, to justify each man his brother, that their step may take the way of God. And God will heed their words and will hear, and a Book of Reminder shall be written before Him of them that fear God and worship His Name, against the time when salvation and righteousness shall be revealed to them that fear God. *And then shall you distinguish once more between the just and the wicked, between one that serves God and one that serves Him not* (Mal. iii, 18); *and He will show lovingkindness to thousands, to them that love Him and watch for Him, for a thousand generations* (Exod. xx, 6).

And every member of the House of Separation who went out of the Holy City and leaned on God at the time when Israel sinned and defiled the Temple, but returned again to the way of the people in small matters, shall be judged according to his spirit in the Council of Holiness. But when the glory of God is made manifest to Israel, all those members of the Covenant who have breached the bound of the Law shall be cut off from the midst of the camp, and with them all those who condemned Judah in the days of its trials.

But all those who hold fast to these precepts, going and coming in accordance with the Law, who heed the voice of the Teacher and confess before God, (saying), 'Truly we have sinned, we and our fathers, by walking counter to the precepts of the Covenant, Thy judgements upon us are justice and truth'; who do not lift their hand against His holy precepts or His righteous statutes or His true testimonies; who have learned from the former judgements by which the members of the Community were judged; who have listened to the voice of the Teacher of Righteousness and have not despised the precepts of righteousness when they heard them; they shall rejoice and their hearts shall be strong, and they shall prevail over all the sons of the earth. God will forgive them and they shall see His salvation because they took refuge in His holy Name.

The Statutes

. . . (He shall not) **XV** swear by (the Name), nor by *Aleph* and *Lamed* (Elohim), nor by *Aleph* and *Daleth* (Adonai), but a binding oath by the curses of the Covenant.

He shall not mention the Law of Moses for . . . were he to swear and then break (his oath) he would profane the Name.

But if he has sworn an oath by the curses of the Covenant before the judges and has transgressed it, then he is guilty and shall confess and make restitution; but he shall not be burdened with a capital sin.

And when the children of all those who have entered the Covenant, granted to all Israel for ever, reach the age of enrolment, they shall swear with the oath of the Covenant. And thus shall it be during all the age of wickedness for every man who repents of his corrupted way. On the day that he speaks to the Guardian of the congregation, they shall enrol him with the oath of the Covenant which Moses made with Israel, the Covenant to return to the Law of Moses with a whole heart and soul, to whatever is found should be done at that time. No man shall make known the statutes to him until he has stood before the Guardian, lest when examining him the Guardian be deceived by him. But if he transgresses after swearing to return to the Law of Moses with a whole heart and soul, then retribution shall be exacted from him . . . And all that is revealed of the Law . . . the Guardian shall examine him and shall issue directions concerning him . . . for a full year according to . . .

No madman, or lunatic, or simpleton, or fool, no blind man, or maimed, or lame, or deaf man, and no minor, shall enter into the Community, for the Angels of Holiness are with them . . .

(For God made) **XVI** a Covenant with you and all Israel; therefore a man shall bind himself by oath to return to the Law of Moses, for in it all things are strictly defined.

As for the exact determination of their times to which Israel turns a blind eye, behold it is strictly defined in the *Book of the Divisions of the Times into their Jubilees and Weeks.* And on the day that a man swears to return to the Law of Moses, the Angel of Persecution shall cease to follow him provided that he fulfils his word: for this reason Abraham circumcised himself on the day that he knew.

And concerning the saying, *You shall keep your vow by fulfilling it* (Deut. xxiii, 24), let no man, even at the price of death, annul any binding oath by which he has sworn to keep a commandment of the Law.

But even at the price of death, a man shall fulfil no vow by which he has sworn to depart from the Law.

Concerning the oath of a woman

Inasmuch as He said, *It is for her husband to cancel her oath* (Num. xxx, 9), no husband shall cancel an oath without knowing whether it should be kept or not. Should it be such as to lead to transgression of the Covenant, he shall cancel it and shall not let it be kept. The rule for her father is likewise.

Concerning the statute for free-will offerings

No man shall vow to the altar anything unlawfully acquired. Also, no Priest shall take from Israel anything unlawfully acquired.

And no man shall consecrate the food of his house to God, for it is as He said, *Each hunts his brother with a net* (or *votive-offering*: Mic. vii, 2).

IX Every man who vows another to destruction by the laws of the Gentiles shall himself be put to death.

And concerning the saying, *You shall not take vengeance on the children of your people, nor bear any rancour against them* (Lev. xix, 18), if any member of the Covenant accuses his companion without first rebuking him before witnesses; if he denounces him in the heat of his anger or reports him to his elders to make him look contemptible, he is one that takes vengeance and bears rancour, although it is expressly written, *He takes vengeance upon His adversaries and bears rancour against His enemies* (Nah. i, 2). If he holds his peace towards him from one day to another, and thereafter speaks of him in the heat of his anger, he testifies against himself concerning a capital matter because he has not fulfilled the commandment of God which tells him: *You shall rebuke your companion and not be burdened with sin because of him* (Lev. xix, 17).

Concerning the oath with reference to that which He said, You shall not take the law into your own hands (1 Sam. xxv, 26)

Whoever causes another to swear in the field instead of before the Judges, or at their decree, takes the law into his own hands. When anything is lost, and it is not known who has stolen it from the property of the camp in which it was stolen, its owner shall pronounce a curse, and any man who, on hearing (it), knows but does not tell, shall himself be guilty.

When anything is returned which is without an owner, whoever returns it shall confess to the Priest, and apart from the ram of the sin-offering, it shall be his.

And likewise, everything which is found but has no owner shall go to the Priests, for the finder is ignorant of the rule concerning it. If no owners are discovered they shall keep it.

Every sin which a man commits against the Law, and which his companion witnesses, he being alone, if it is a capital matter he shall report it to the Guardian, rebuking him in his presence, and the Guardian shall record it against him in case he should commit it again before one man and he should report it to the Guardian once more. Should he repeat it and be taken in the act before one man, his case shall be complete.

And if there are two (witnesses), each testifying to a different matter, the man shall be excluded from the pure Meal provided that they are trustworthy and that each informs the Guardian on the day that they witnessed (the offence). In matters of property, they shall accept two trustworthy witnesses and shall exclude (the culprit) from the pure Meal on the word of one witness alone.

No **X** Judge shall pass sentence of death on the testimony of a witness who has not yet attained the age of enrolment and who is not God-fearing.

No man who has wilfully transgressed any commandment shall be declared a trustworthy witness against his companion until he is purified and able to return.

And this is the Rule for the Judges of the Congregation

Ten shall be elected from the congregation for a definite time, four from the tribe of Levi and Aaron, and six from Israel. (They shall be) learned in the Book of Meditation and in the constitutions of the Covenant, and aged between twenty-five and sixty years. No man over the age of sixty shall hold office as Judge of the Congregation, for 'because man sinned his days have been shortened, and in the heat of His anger against the inhabitants of the earth God ordained that their understanding should depart even before their days are completed' (Jubilees, xxiii, 11).

Concerning purification by water

No man shall bathe in dirty water or in an amount too shallow to cover a man. He shall not purify himself with water contained in a vessel. And as for the water of every rock-pool too shallow to cover a man, if an unclean man touches it he renders its water as unclean as water contained in a vessel.

Concerning the Sabbath to observe it according to its law

No man shall work on the sixth day from the moment when the sun's orb is distant by its own fulness from the gate (wherein it sinks); for this is what He said, *Observe the Sabbath day to keep it holy* (Deut. v, 12). No man shall speak any vain or idle word on the Sabbath day. He shall make no loan to his companion. He shall make no decision in matters of money and gain. He shall say nothing about work or labour to be done on the morrow.

No man shall walk abroad to do business on the Sabbath. He shall not walk more than one thousand cubits beyond his town.

No man shall eat on the Sabbath day except that which is already prepared. He shall eat nothing lying in the fields. He shall not drink except in the camp. **XI** If he is on a journey and goes down to bathe, he shall drink where he stands, but he shall not draw water into a vessel. He shall send out no stranger on his business on the Sabbath day.

No man shall wear soiled garments, or garments brought to the store, unless they have been washed with water or rubbed with incense.

No man shall willingly mingle (with others) on the Sabbath.

No man shall walk more than two thousand cubits after a beast to pasture it outside his town. He shall not raise his hand to strike it with his fist. If it is stubborn he shall not take it out of his house.

No man shall take anything out of the house or bring anything in. And if he is in a booth, let him neither take anything out nor bring anything in. He shall not open a sealed vessel on the Sabbath.

No man shall carry perfumes on himself whilst going and coming on the Sabbath. He shall lift neither sand nor dust in his dwelling. No man minding a child shall carry it whilst going and coming on the Sabbath.

No man shall chide his manservant or maidservant or labourer on the Sabbath.

No man shall assist a beast to give birth on the Sabbath day. And if it should fall into a cistern or pit, he shall not lift it out on the Sabbath.

No man shall spend the Sabbath in a place near to Gentiles on the Sabbath.

No man shall profane the Sabbath for the sake of riches or gain on the Sabbath day. But should any man fall into water or fire, let him be pulled out with the aid of a ladder or rope or (some such) utensil.

No man on the Sabbath shall offer anything on the altar except the Sabbath burnt-offering; for it is written thus: *Except your Sabbath offerings* (Lev. xxiii, 38).

No man shall send to the altar any burnt-offering, or cereal offering, or incense, or wood, by the hand of one smitten with any uncleanness, permitting him thus to defile the altar. For it is written, *The sacrifice of the wicked is an abomination, but the prayer of the just is as an agreeable offering* (Prov. xv, 8).

No man entering the house of worship shall come unclean and in need of washing. And at the sounding of the trumpets for assembly, he shall go there before or after (the meeting), and shall not cause the whole service to stop,   **XII**   for it is a holy service.

No man shall lie with a woman in the city of the Sanctuary, to defile the city of the Sanctuary with their uncleanness.

Every man who preaches apostasy under the dominion of the spirits of Satan shall be judged according to the law relating to those possessed by a ghost or familiar spirit (Lev. xx, 27). But no man who strays so as to profane the Sabbath and the feasts shall be put to death; it shall fall to men to keep him in custody. And if he is healed of his error, they shall keep him in custody for seven years and he shall afterwards approach the Assembly.

No man shall stretch out his hand to shed the blood of a Gentile for the sake of riches and gain. Nor shall he carry off anything of theirs, lest they blaspheme, unless so advised by the company of Israel.

No man shall sell clean beasts or birds to the Gentiles lest they offer them in sacrifice. He shall refuse, with all his power, to sell them anything from his granary or wine-press, and he shall not sell them his manservant or maidservant inasmuch as they have been brought by him into the Covenant of Abraham.

No man shall defile himself by eating any live creature or creeping thing, from the larvae of bees to all creatures which creep in water. They shall eat no fish unless split alive and their blood poured out. And as for locusts, according to their various kinds they shall plunge them alive into fire or water, for this is what their nature requires.

All wood and stones and dust defiled by the impurity of a man shall be reckoned like men with regard to conveying defilement; whoever touches them shall be defiled by their defilement. And every nail or peg in the wall of a house in which a dead man lies shall become unclean as any working tool becomes unclean (Lev. xi, 32).

The Rule for the assembly of the towns of Israel shall be according to these precepts that they may distinguish between unclean and clean, and discriminate between the holy and the profane.

And these are the precepts in which the Master shall walk in his commerce with all the living in accordance with the statute proper to every age. And in accordance with this statute shall the seed of Israel walk and they shall not be cursed.

This is the Rule for the assembly of the camps

Those who follow these statutes in the age of wickedness until the coming of the Messiah of Aaron **XIII** and Israel shall form groups of at least ten men, by *Thousands, Hundreds, Fifties, and Tens* (Exod. xviii, 25). And where the ten are, there shall never be lacking a Priest learned in the Book of Meditation; they shall all be ruled by him.

But should he not be experienced in these matters, whereas one of the Levites is experienced in them, then it shall be determined that all the members of the camp shall go and come according to the latter's word.

But should there be a case of applying the law of leprosy to a man, then the Priest shall come and shall stand in the camp and the Guardian shall instruct him in the exact interpretation of the Law.

Even if the Priest is a simpleton, it is he who shall lock up (the leper); for theirs is the judgement.

This is the Rule for the Guardian of the Camp

He shall instruct the Congregation in the works of God. He shall cause them to consider His mighty deeds and shall recount all the happenings of eternity to them. . . He shall love them as a father loves his children, and shall carry them in all their distress like a shepherd his sheep. He shall loosen all the fetters which bind them that in his Congregation there may be none that are oppressed or broken. He shall examine every man entering his Congregation with regard to his deeds, understanding, strength, ability and possessions, and shall inscribe him in his place according to his rank in the lot of L[ight].

No member of the camp shall have authority to admit a man to the Congregation against the decision of the Guardian of the camp.

No member of the Covenant of God shall give or receive anything from the sons of the Pit except for payment.

No man shall form any association for buying and selling without informing the Guardian of the camp . . .

This is the Rule for the assembly of the camps during all [the age of wickedness, and whoever does not hold fast to] these (statutes) shall not be fit to dwell in the Land [when the Messiah of Aaron and Israel shall come at the end of days].

[And] these are the [precepts] in which the Master [shall walk in his commerce with all the living until God shall visit the earth. As He said, *There shall come upon you, and upon your people, and upon your father's house, days*] **XIV** *such as have not come since Ephraim departed from Judah* (Isa. vii, 17); but for whoever shall walk in these (precepts), the Covenant of God shall stand firm to save him from all the snares of the Pit, whereas the foolish shall be punished.

The Rule for the assembly of all the camps

They shall all be enrolled by name: first the Priests, second the Levites, third the Israelites, and fourth the proselytes. And they shall be inscribed by name, one after the other: the Priests first, the Levites second, the Israelites third, and the proselytes fourth. And thus shall they sit and thus be questioned on all matters. And the Priest who enrols the Congregation shall be from thirty to sixty years old, learned in the Book of Meditation and in all the judgements of the Law so as to pronounce them correctly.

The Guardian of all the camps shall be from thirty to fifty years old, one who has mastered all the secrets of men and the languages of all their clans. Whoever enters the Congregation shall do so according to his word, each in his rank. And whoever has anything to say with regard to any suit or judgement, let him say it to the Guardian.

This is the Rule for the Congregation by which it shall provide for all its needs

They shall place the earnings of at least two days out of every month into the hands of the Guardian and the Judges, and from it they shall give to the fatherless, and from it they shall succour the poor and the needy, the aged sick and the homeless, the captive taken by a foreign people, the virgin with no near kin, and the ma[id for] whom no man cares . . .

And this is the exact statement of the assembly . . .

This is the exact statement of the statutes in which [they shall walk until the coming of the Messia]h of Aaron and Israel who will pardon their iniquity

[Whoever] deliberately lies in a matter of property . . . and shall do penance for six days . . .

[Whoever slanders his companion or bears rancour] unjustly [shall do penance for one] year . . .

3. THE MESSIANIC RULE (1QSa)

❦

The Messianic Rule was published in 1955 by D. Barthélemy in *DJD* I (Oxford, 1955, pp. 107–18). Originally included in the same Scroll as the Community Rule, this short but complete work presents the translator with great difficulties owing to its bad state of preservation and to the carelessness of the scribe.

Barthélemy named the work 'The Rule of the Congregation', but I have given it a new title for the following reasons: (1) it was intended for 'all the congregation in the *last days*'; (2) it is a Rule for a Community adapted to the requirements of the Messianic war against the nations; (3) it refers to the presence of the Priest and the Messiah of Israel at the Council, and at the Meal described in column II.

In the main, the precepts and the doctrinal concepts of the Messianic Rule foreshadow those of the War Rule. A mid first century B.C. date may safely be proposed.

I *This is the Rule for all the congregation of Israel in the last days, when they shall join [the Community to wa]lk according to the law of the sons of Zadok the Priests and of the men of their Covenant who have turned aside [from the] way of the people, the men of His Council who keep His Covenant in the midst of iniquity, offering expiation [for the Land].*

When they come, they shall summon them all, the little children and the women also, and they shall read into their [ears] the precepts of the Covenant and shall expound to them all their statutes that they may no longer stray in their [errors].

And this is the Rule for all the hosts of the congregation, for every man born in Israel.

From [his] youth they shall instruct him in the Book of Meditation and shall teach him, according to his age, the precepts of the Covenant. He [shall be edu]cated in their statutes for ten years . . .

At the age of twenty years [he shall be] enrolled, that he may enter upon his allotted duties in the midst of his family (and) be joined to the holy congregation. He shall not [approach] a woman to know her by lying with her before he is fully twenty years old, when he shall know [good] and evil. And thereafter, he shall be accepted when he calls to witness the judgements of the Law, and shall be (allowed) to assist at the hearing of judgements.

At the age of twenty-five years he may take his place among the foundations (i.e. the officials) of the holy congregation to work in the service of the congregation.

At the age of thirty years he may approach to participate in lawsuits and judgements, and may take his place among the chiefs of the Thousands of Israel, the chiefs of the Hundreds, Fifties, and Tens, the Judges and the officers of their tribes, in all their families, [under the authority] of the sons of [Aar]on the Priests. And every head of family in the congregation who is chosen to hold office, [to go] and come before the congregation, shall strengthen his loins that he may perform his tasks among his brethren in accordance with his understanding and the perfection of his way. According to whether this is great or little, so shall one man be honoured more than another.

When a man is advanced in years, he shall be given a duty in the [ser]vice of the congregation in proportion to his strength.

No simpleton shall be chosen to hold office in the congregation of Israel with regard to lawsuits or judgement, nor carry any responsibility in the congregation. Nor shall he hold any office in the war destined to vanquish the nations; his family shall merely inscribe him in the army register and he shall do his service in task-work in proportion to his capacity.

The sons of Levi shall hold office, each in his place, under the authority of the sons of Aaron. They shall cause all the congregation to go and come, each man in his rank, under the direction of the heads of family of the congregation – the leaders, Judges, and officers, according to the number of all their hosts – under the authority of the sons of Zadok the Priests, [and] (under the direction) [of all the] heads of family of the congregation. And when the whole assembly is summoned for judgement, or for a Council of the Community, or for war, they shall sanctify them for three days that every one of its members may be prepared.

These are the men who shall be called to the Council of the Community . . .

All the wi[se men] of the congregation, the learned and the intelligent, men whose way is perfect and men of ability, together with the tribal chiefs and all the Judges and officers, and the chiefs of the Thousands, [Hundreds,] **II** Fifties, and Tens, and the Levites, each man in the [cla]ss of his duty; these are the men of renown, the members of the assembly summoned to the Council of the Community in Israel before the sons of Zadok the Priests.

And no man smitten with any human uncleanness shall enter the assembly of God; no man smitten with any of them shall be confirmed in his office in the congregation. No man smitten in his flesh, or paralysed in his feet or hands, or lame, or blind, or deaf, or dumb, or smitten in his flesh with a visible blemish; no old and tottery man unable to stay still in the midst of the congregation; none of these shall come to hold office among the congregation of the men of renown, for the Angels of Holiness are [with] their [congregation]. Should [one] of them have something to say to the Council of Holiness, let [him] be questioned privately; but let him not enter among [the congregation] for he is smitten.

[This shall be the ass]embly of the men of renown [called] to the meeting of the Council of the Community when [the Priest-]Messiah shall summon them

He shall come [at] the head of the whole congregation of Israel with all [his brethren, the sons] of Aaron the Priests, [those called] to the assembly, the men of renown; and they shall sit [before him, each man] in the order of his dignity. And then [the Mess]iah of Israel shall [come], and the chiefs of the [clans of Israel] shall sit before him, [each] in the order of his dignity, according to [his place] in their camps and marches. And before them shall sit all the heads of [family of the congreg]ation, and the wise men of [the holy congregation,] each in the order of his dignity.

And [when] they shall gather for the common [tab]le, to eat and [to drink] new wine, when the common table shall be set for eating and the new wine [poured] for drinking, let no man extend his hand over the first-fruits of bread and wine before the Priest; for [it is he] who shall bless the first-fruits of bread and wine, and shall be the first [to extend] his hand over the bread. Thereafter, the Messiah of Israel shall extend his hand over the bread, [and] all the congregation of the Community [shall utter a] blessing, [each man in the order] of his dignity.

It is according to this statute that they shall proceed at every me[al at which] at least ten men are gathered together.

4. THE WAR RULE (1QM, 4QM)

∽∘∾

The nineteen badly mutilated columns of this manuscript from cave 1 first appeared in 1954 in a posthumous work by E. L. Sukenik, and were re-edited in 1955, with an English introduction, under the title *The Dead Sea Scrolls of the Hebrew University* (Jerusalem). Copious fragments of six further manuscripts were discovered in cave 4, and published in 1982 by M. Baillet in *DJD* VII (4Q491–496 or 4QM^{a-f}). Some of these basically reflect the cave 1 text and help to complete its gaps: M^a, M^b, M^d and M^e have been used for this purpose, especially in columns I, XIV and XIX. On the other hand, M^a and M^c attest different recensions of the War Rule. Representative sections from these manuscripts will be translated separately.

The contents of the War Rule are as follows:
    Proclamation of war against the Kittim (col. I)
    Reorganization of Temple worship (col. II)
    Programme of the forty years' war (col. II)
    The trumpets (col. III)
    The standards (cols. III-IV)
    Disposition and weapons of the front formations (col. V)
    Movements of the attacking infantry (col. VI)
    Disposition and movements of the cavalry (col. VI)
    Age of the soldiers (cols. VI-VII)
    The camp (col. VII)
    Duties of the Priests and Levites
      (exhortation, trumpet signals) (cols. VII-IX)
    Addresses and prayers of the battle liturgy (cols. X-XII)
    Prayer recited at the moment of victory (col. XIII)
    Thanksgiving ceremony (col. XIV)
    Battle against the Kittim (cols. XV-XIX)

Since the five last columns are more or less repetitious, there has been some doubt concerning the unity of the composition. Those who consider all nineteen columns to be the work of one writer find in column I an introduction, in columns II-XIV general rules, and in columns XV-XIX a 'prophetic' description of the final battle fought according to those rules. Other experts explain that columns XV-XIX are a Rule annexe dependent on the principal Rule (cols. II-XIV).

I am myself inclined to follow the theory first advanced by J. van der

Ploeg (*Le Rouleau de la guerre*, Leiden, 1959, pp. 11–22). The primitive work, represented in the present composition by columns I and xv-xix, draws its inspiration from Daniel xi, 40–xii, 3, and describes the final battle against the Kittim. This account was later combined with the concept of a holy forty years' war against the entire Gentile world, and was extended by the addition of a long series of Rules concerned with the military and religious preparation and with the conduct of the fighting (cols. II-xIV). This appears to me to offer a more satisfactory explanation of the literary complexities of the manuscript than do the previous hypotheses. The text of the manuscripts from cave 4, especially 4QM^a and M^c, indicate that diverse redactions of the War Rule co-existed in the Qumran library.

The only certain pointer to the date of the compilation of the War Rule is that, since the author made use of the book of Daniel written in about 160 B.C., his own work must have been started after that time. But a more accurate dating may be attempted by studying the military strategy and tactics described in the Scroll. Scholars are divided in their opinion as to whether the sons of light modelled them on Greek or Roman custom, or whether they merely drew their ideas from the Bible. Scripture doubtless exercised a definite influence on the author of this Rule, but there is nevertheless a great deal of material completely foreign to it, and he must have possessed, in addition, at least some acquaintance with contemporary warfare.

With Y. Yadin and other archaeologists and historians, I believe that both the weapons and the tactics of the War Rule correspond to the art of war practised by the Roman legion rather than by the Greek phalanx. In particular, the square shield (*scutum*) of the foot-soldier, and the buckler of the horseman (*parma* or *clipeus*), the battle array of three lines (*acies triplex*), the openings between the units, viz. the 'gates of war' (*intervalla*), seem to be characteristically Roman. In addition, only the cavalry were to wear greaves – a custom introduced into the Roman army during the time of Julius Caesar in the middle of the first century B.C. This and similar details, as well as the general representation of the Kittim as masters of the world, lead one to conclude that the War Rule was written some time after the middle of the first century B.C., and as the reference to the 'king' of the Kittim points to the Imperial epoch (after 27 B.C.), the date of its composition should probably be placed in the last decades of the first century B.C. or at the beginning of the first century A.D.

This work should not be mistaken for a manual of military warfare pure and simple. It is a theological writing, and the war of which it treats symbolizes the eternal struggle between the spirits of Light and Darkness. The phases of its battle are fixed in advance, its plan established, and its duration predetermined. The opposing forces are equally matched and only by the intervention of 'the mighty hand of God' is the balance between them to be disturbed when he deals an 'everlasting blow' to 'Satan and all the host of his kingdom'.

1QM

I *For the M[aster. The Rule of] War on the unleashing of the attack of the sons of light against the company of the sons of darkness, the army of Satan: against the band of Edom, Moab, and the sons of Ammon, and [against the army of the sons of the East and] the Philistines, and against the bands of the Kittim of Assyria and their allies the ungodly of the Covenant*

The sons of Levi, Judah, and Benjamin, the exiles in the desert, shall battle against them in . . . all their bands when the exiled sons of light return from the Desert of the Peoples to camp in the Desert of Jerusalem; and after the battle they shall go up from there (to Jerusalem?).

[The king] of the Kittim [shall enter] into Egypt, and in his time he shall set out in great wrath to wage war against the kings of the north, that his fury may destroy and cut off the horn of [Israel].

This shall be a time of salvation for the people of God, an age of dominion for all the members of His company, and of everlasting destruction for all the company of Satan. The confusion of the sons of Japheth shall be [great] and Assyria shall fall unsuccoured. The dominion of the Kittim shall come to an end and iniquity shall be vanquished, leaving no remnant; [for the sons] of darkness there shall be no escape. [The sons of righteous]ness shall shine over all the ends of the earth; they shall go on shining until all the seasons of darkness are consumed and, at the season appointed by God, His exalted greatness shall shine eternally to the peace, blessing, glory, joy, and long life of all the sons of light.

On the day when the Kittim fall, there shall be battle and terrible carnage before the God of Israel, for that shall be the day appointed from ancient times for the battle of destruction of the sons of darkness. At that time, the assembly of gods and the hosts of men shall battle, causing great carnage; on the day of calamity, the sons of light shall battle with the company of darkness amid the shouts of a mighty multitude and the clamour of gods and men to (make manifest) the might of God. And it shall be a time of [great] tribulation for the people which God shall redeem; of all its afflictions none shall be as this, from its sudden beginning until its end in eternal redemption.

On the day of their battle against the Kittim [they shall set out for] carnage. In three lots shall the sons of light brace themselves in battle to strike down iniquity, and in three lots shall Satan's host gird itself to thrust back the company [of God. And when the hearts of the detach]ments of foot-soldiers faint, then shall the might of God fortify [the hearts of the sons of light]. And with the seventh lot, the mighty hand of God shall bring down [the army of Satan, and all] the angels of his kingdom, and all the members [of his company in everlasting destruction] . . .

. . . The priests, the Levites and the heads of [the tribes] . . . the priests as well as the Levites and the divisions of **II** the fifty-two heads of family of the congregation.

They shall rank the chief Priests below the High Priest and his vicar. And the twelve chief Priests shall minister at the daily sacrifice before God, whereas the twenty-six leaders of the priestly divisions shall minister in their divisions.

Below them, in perpetual ministry, shall be the chiefs of the Levites to the number of twelve, one for each tribe. The leaders of their divisions shall minister each in his place.

Below them shall be the chiefs of the tribes together with the heads of family of the congregation. They shall attend daily at the gates of the Sanctuary, whereas the leaders of their divisions, with their numbered men, shall attend at their appointed times, on new moons and on Sabbaths and on all the days of the year, their age being fifty years and over.

These are the men who shall attend at holocausts and sacrifices to prepare sweet-smelling incense for the good pleasure of God, to atone for all His congregation, and to satisfy themselves perpetually before Him at the table of glory. They shall arrange all these things during the season of the year of Release.

During the remaining thirty-three years of the war, the men of renown, those summoned to the Assembly, together with all the heads of family of the congregation, shall choose for themselves fighting-men for all the lands of the nations. They shall arm for themselves warriors from all the tribes of Israel to enter the army year by year when they are summoned to war. But they shall arm no man for entry into the army during the years of Release, for they are Sabbaths of rest for Israel. In the thirty-five years of service, the war shall be fought during six; the whole congregation shall fight it together.

And during the remaining twenty-nine years the war shall be divided. During the first year they shall fight against Aram-Naharaim; during the second, against the sons of Lud; during the third, against the remnant of the sons of Aram, against Uz and Hul and Togar and Mesha beyond the Euphrates; during the fourth and fifth, they shall fight against the sons of Arphakshad; during the sixth and seventh, against all the sons of Assyria and Persia and the East as far as the Great Desert; during the eighth year they shall fight against the sons of Elam; during the ninth, against the sons of Ishmael and Keturah. In the ten years which follow, the war shall be divided against all the sons of Ham according to [their clans and in their ha]bitations; and during the ten years which remain, the war shall be divided against all [the sons of Japheth in] their habitations.

[*The Rule for the trumpets of Summons and the trumpe*]*ts of Alarm according to all their duties*
. . . [the trumpets of Summons shall sound for disposal in]   **III** battle formations and to summon the foot-soldiers to advance when the gates of war shall open; and the trumpets of Alarm shall sound for massacre, and for ambush, and for pursuit when the enemy shall be smitten, and for retreat from battle.

On the trumpets calling the congregation they shall write, *The Called of God*.

On the trumpets calling the chiefs they shall write, *The Princes of God*.

On the trumpets of the levies they shall write, *The Army of God*.

On the trumpets of the men of renown and of the heads of family of the congregation gathered in the house of Assembly they shall write, *Summoned by God to the Council of Holiness*.

On the trumpets of the camps they shall write, *The Peace of God in the Camps of His Saints*.

And on the trumpets for breaking camp they shall write, *The mighty Deeds of God shall crush the Enemy, putting to Flight all those who hate Righteousness and bringing Shame on those who hate Him*.

On the trumpets for battle formations they shall write, *Formations of the Divisions of God for the Vengeance of His Wrath on the Sons of Darkness*.

On the trumpets summoning the foot-soldiers to advance towards the enemy formations when the gates of war are opened they shall write, *Reminder of Vengeance in God's appointed Time*.

On the trumpets of massacre they shall write, *The mighty Hand of God in War shall cause all the ungodly Slain to fall*.

On the trumpets of ambush they shall write, *The Mysteries of God shall undo Wickedness*.

On the trumpets of pursuit they shall write, *God has smitten all the Sons of Darkness; His Fury shall not end until they are utterly consumed.*

On the trumpets of retreat, when they retreat from battle to the formation, they shall write, *God has reassembled.*

On the trumpets of return from battle against the enemy when they journey to the congregation in Jerusalem they shall write, *Rejoicings of God in the peaceful Return.*

The Rule for the standards of the whole congregation according to their levies

On the great standard at the head of the people they shall write, *The People of God*, together with the names of Israel and Aaron, and the names of the twelve [tribes of Israel] according to the order of their precedence.

On the standards of the camp columns formed by three tribes they shall write, . . . *of God*, together with the name of the leader of the camp . . .

On the standard of the tribe they shall write, *Banner of God*, together with the name of the leader of [the tribe and the names of the chiefs of its clans].

[On the standard of the Myriad they shall write, . . . *of God*, together with] the name of the chief of the Myriad and the names of the [leaders of its Thousands].

[On the standard of the Thousand they shall write, . . . *of God*, together with the name of the chief of the Thousand and the names of the leaders of its Hundreds].

[On the standard of Hundred] . . .

IV On the standard of Merari they shall write, *The Votive-Offering of God*, together with the name of the chief of Merari and the names of the leaders of its Thousands.

On the standard of the Thousand they shall write, *The Wrath of God is kindled against Satan and against the Men of his Company, leaving no Remnant*, together with the name of the chief of the Thousand and the names of the leaders of its Hundreds.

On the standard of the Hundred they shall write, *From God comes the Might of War against all sinful Flesh*, together with the name of the chief of the Hundred and the names of the leaders of its Fifties.

On the standard of the Fifty they shall write, *The Stand of the*

Ungodly is ended by the Power of God, together with the name of the chief of the Fifty and the names of the leaders of its Tens.

On the standard of the Ten they shall write, *Praised be God on the ten-stringed Harp*, together with the name of the chief of the Ten and the names of the nine men under his command.

When they march out to battle they shall write on their standards, *Truth of God, Justice of God, Glory of God, Judgement of God*, followed by the whole ordered list of their names.

When they approach for battle they shall write on their standards, *Right Hand of God, Appointed Time of God, Tumult of God, Slain of God*, followed by the whole list of their names.

When they return from battle they shall write on their standards, *Honour of God, Majesty of God, Splendour of God, Glory of God*, together with the whole list of their names.

The Rule for the standards of the congregation

When they set out for battle they shall write, on the first standard *Congregation of God*, on the second standard *Camps of God*, on the third standard *Tribes of God*, on the fourth standard *Clans of God*, on the fifth standard *Divisions of God*, on the sixth standard *Assembly of God*, on the seventh standard *The Called of God*, on the eighth standard *Hosts of God*; and they shall write the list of their names with all their order.

When they approach for battle they shall write on their standards, *War of God, Vengeance of God, Trial of God, Reward of God, Power of God, Retributions of God, Might of God, Extermination of God for all the Nations of Vanity*; and they shall write on them the whole list of their names.

When they return from battle they shall write on their standards, *Salvation of God, Victory of God, Help of God, Support of God, Joy of God, Thanksgivings of God, Praise of God, Peace of God*.

[The measurements of the standards.] The standard of the whole congregation shall be fourteen cubits long; the standard [of the three tribes,] thirteen cubits long; [the standard of the tribe,] twelve cubits; [the standard of the Myriad], eleven cubits; [the standard of the Thousand, ten cubits; the standard of the Hundred,] nine cubits; [the standard of the Fifty, eight] cubits; the standard of the Ten, s[even cubits] . . .

V And on the sh[ield of] the Prince of all the congregation they shall write his name, together with the names of Israel, Levi and Aaron, and the names of the twelve tribes of Israel according to the order of their precedence, with the names of their twelve chiefs.

The Rule for the ordering of the battle divisions to complete a front formation when their host has reached its full number

The formation shall consist of one thousand men ranked seven lines deep, each man standing behind the other.

They shall all hold shields of bronze burnished like mirrors. The shield shall be edged with an interlaced border and with inlaid ornament, a work of art in pure gold and silver and bronze and precious stones, a many-coloured design worked by a craftsman. The length of the shield shall be two and a half cubits and its width one and a half cubits.

In their hands they shall hold a spear and a sword. The length of the spear shall be seven cubits, of which the socket and spike shall measure half a cubit. The socket shall be edged with three embossed interlaced rings of pure gold and silver and bronze, a work of art. The inlaid ornaments on both edges of the ring shall be bordered with precious stones – patterned bands worked by a craftsman – and (embossed) with ears of corn. Between the rings, the socket shall be embossed with artistry like a pillar. The spike shall be made of brilliant white iron, the work of a craftsman; in its centre, pointing towards the tip, shall be ears of corn in pure gold.

The swords shall be made of pure iron refined by the smelter and blanched to resemble a mirror, the work of a craftsman; on both sides (of their blades) pointing towards the tip, figured ears of corn shall be embossed in pure gold, and they shall have two straight borders on each side. The length of the sword shall be one and a half cubits and its width four fingers. The width of the scabbard shall be four thumbs. There shall be four palms to the scabbard (from the girdle), and it shall be attached (to the girdle) on both sides for a length of five palms (?). The hilt of the sword shall be of pure horn worked by a craftsman, with patterned bands in gold and silver and precious stones . . .

VI seven times and shall return to their positions.

And after them, three divisions of foot-soldiers shall advance and shall station themselves between the formations, and the first division shall hurl seven javelins of war towards the enemy formation. On the point of the javelins they shall write, *Shining Javelin of the Power of God*; and on the darts of the second division they shall write, *Bloody Spikes to bring down the Slain by the Wrath of God*; and on the javelins of the third division they shall write, *Flaming Blade to devour the Wicked struck down by the Judgement of God*. All these shall hurl their javelins seven times and shall afterwards return to their positions.

Then two divisions of foot-soldiers shall advance and shall station themselves between the two formations. The first division shall be armed with a spear and a shield, and the second with a shield and a sword, to bring down the slain by the judgement of God, and to bend the enemy formation by the power of God, to pay the reward of their wickedness to all the nations of vanity. And sovereignty shall be to the God of Israel, and He shall accomplish mighty deeds by the saints of his people.

Seven troops of horsemen shall also station themselves to right and to left of the formation; their troops shall stand on this (side) and on that, seven hundred horsemen on one flank and seven hundred horsemen on the other. Two hundred horsemen shall advance with the thousand men of the formation of foot-soldiers; and they shall likewise station themselves on both [flanks] of the camp. Altogether there shall be four thousand six hundred (men), and one thousand cavalrymen with the men of the army formations, fifty to each formation. The horsemen, together with the cavalry of the army, shall number six thousand: five hundred to each tribe.

The horses advancing into battle with the foot-soldiers shall all be stallions; they shall be swift, sensitive of mouth, and sound of wind, and of the required age, trained for war, and accustomed to noise and to every (kind of) sight. Their riders shall be gallant fighting men and skilled horsemen, and their age shall be from thirty to forty-five years. The horsemen of the army shall be from forty to fifty years old. They [and their mounts shall wear breastplates,] helmets, and greaves; they shall carry in their hands bucklers, and a spear [eight cubits] long. [The horsemen advancing with the foot-soldiers shall carry] bows and arrows and javelins of war. They shall all hold themselves prepared . . . of God and to spill the blood of the wicked . . .

VII   The men of the army shall be from forty to fifty years old.
  The inspectors of the camps shall be from fifty to sixty years old.
  The officers shall be from forty to fifty years old.
  The despoilers of the slain, the plunderers of booty, the cleansers of the land, the keepers of the baggage, and those who furnish the provisions shall be from twenty-five to thirty years old.

No boy or woman shall enter their camps, from the time they leave Jerusalem and march out to war until they return. No man who is lame, or blind, or crippled, or afflicted with a lasting bodily blemish, or smitten with a bodily impurity, none of these shall march out to war with them. They shall all be freely enlisted for war, perfect in spirit and body and prepared for the Day of Vengeance. And no man shall go down with them on the day of battle who is impure because of his 'fount', for the holy angels shall be with their hosts. And there shall be a space of about two thousand cubits between all their camps for the place serving as a latrine, so that no indecent nakedness may be seen in the surroundings of their camps.

When the battle formations are marshalled facing the enemy, formation facing formation, seven Priests of the sons of Aaron shall advance from the middle gates to the place between the formations. They shall be clothed in vestments of white cloth of flax, in a fine linen tunic and fine linen breeches; and they shall be girdled with fine cloth of flax embroidered with blue, purple, and scarlet thread, a many-coloured design worked by a craftsman. And on their heads they shall wear mitred turbans. These shall be battle raiment; they shall not take them into the Sanctuary.
  The first Priest shall advance before the men of the formation to strengthen their hand for battle, and the six other Priests shall hold in their hands the trumpets of Summons, and the trumpets of the Reminder, and the trumpets of Alarm (for massacre), and the trumpets of Pursuit, and the trumpets of Retreat. And when the Priests advance to the place between the formations, seven Levites shall accompany them bearing in their hands seven rams' horns; and three officers of the Levites shall walk before the

Priests and Levites. The Priests shall sound the two trumpets of Sum[mons for the gates of] war to open fifty shields (wide) and the foot-soldiers shall advance, fifty from one gate [and fifty from the other. With them shall advance] the officers of the Levites, and they shall advance with every formation according to all this R[ule].

[The Priests shall sound the trumpets, and two divisions of foot-]soldiers [shall advance] from the gate [and shall] station [themselves] between the two [formations] . . . **VIII** the trumpets shall sound to direct the slingers until they have cast seven times. Afterwards, the Priests shall sound for them the trumpets of Retreat and they shall return to the flank of the first formation to take up their position.

Then the Priests shall sound the trumpets of Summons and three divisions of foot-soldiers shall advance from the gates and shall station themselves between the formations; the horsemen shall be on their flanks, to right and to left. The Priests shall sound a sustained blast on the trumpets for battle array, and the columns shall move to their (battle) array, each man to his place. And when they have taken up their stand in three arrays, the Priests shall sound a second signal, soft and sustained, for them to advance until they are close to the enemy formation. They shall seize their weapons, and the Priests shall then blow a shrill staccato blast on the six trumpets of Massacre to direct the battle, and the Levites and all the blowers of rams' horns shall sound a mighty alarm to terrify the heart of the enemy, and therewith the javelins shall fly out to bring down the slain. Then the sound of the horns shall cease, but the Priests shall continue to blow a shrill staccato blast on the trumpets to direct the battle until they have thrown seven times against the enemy formation. And then they shall sound a soft, a sustained, and a shrill sound on the trumpets of Retreat.

It is according to this Rule that the Priests shall sound the trumpets for the three divisions. With the first throw, the [Priests] shall sound [on the trumpets] a mighty alarm to direct the ba[ttle until they have thrown seven times. Then] the Priests [shall sound] for them on the trumpets [of Retreat a soft, sustained, and a shrill sound, and they shall return] to their positions in the formation.

[Then the Priests shall blow the trumpets of Summons and the two divisions of foot-soldiers shall advance from the gates] and shall stand [between the formations. And the Priests shall then blow the trumpets of] Massacre, [and the Levites and all the blowers of rams' horns shall sound an alarm, a mighty blast, and therewith] **IX** they shall set about to bring down the slain with their hands. All the people shall cease their clamour but the Priests shall continue to blow the trumpets of Massacre to direct the battle until the enemy is smitten and put to flight; and the Priests shall blow to direct the battle.

And when they are smitten before them, the Priests shall sound the trumpets of Summons and all the foot-soldiers shall rally to them from the midst of the front formations, and the six divisions, together with the fighting division, shall take up their stations. Altogether, they shall be seven formations: twenty-eight thousand fighting men and six thousand horsemen.

All these shall pursue the enemy to destroy him in an everlasting destruction in the battle of God. The Priests shall sound for them the trumpets of Pursuit, and they shall deploy against all the enemy in a pursuit to destruction; and the horsemen shall thrust them back on the flanks of the battle until they are utterly destroyed.

And as the slain men fall, the Priests shall trumpet from afar; they shall not approach the slain lest they be defiled with unclean blood. For they are holy, and they shall not profane the anointing of their priesthood with the blood of nations of vanity.

The Rule for changes in battle order to form the position of a squa[re with towers,] a concave line with towers, a convex line with towers, a shallow convex line obtained by the advance of the centre, or [by the advance of] both flanks to terrify the enemy

The shields of the towers shall be three cubits long and their spears eight cubits. The tower shall advance from the formation and shall have one hundred shields to each side; in this [manner,] the tower shall be surrounded on three sides by three hundred shields. And it shall also have two gates, [one to the right] and one to the left.

They shall write on all the shields of the towers: on the first, *Michael*, [on the second, *Gabriel*, on the third,] *Sariel*, and on the fourth, *Raphael*. *Michael* and *Gabriel* [shall stand on the right, and *Sariel* and *Raphael* on the left] . . . they shall set an ambush to . . .

. . . **X** our camps and to keep us from all that is indecent and evil.

Furthermore, (Moses) taught us, 'Thou art in the midst of us, a mighty God and terrible, causing all our enemies to flee before [us].' He taught our generations in former times saying, 'When you draw near to battle, the Priest shall rise and speak to the people saying, "Hear, O Israel! You draw near to battle this day against your enemies. Do not fear! Do not let your hearts be afraid! Do not be [terrified], and have no fear! For your God goes with you to fight for you against your enemies that He may deliver you" ' (Deut. xx, 2–4).

Our officers shall speak to all those prepared for battle. They shall strengthen by the power of God the freely devoted of heart, and shall make all the fearful of heart withdraw; they shall fortify all the mighty men of war. They shall recount that which Thou [saidst] through Moses: 'When you go to war in your land against the oppressor who oppresses you, [you] shall blow the trumpets, and you shall be remembered before your God and shall be saved from your enemies' (Num. x, 9).

> O God of Israel, who is like Thee
>   in heaven or on earth?
> Who accomplishes deeds and mighty works like Thine?
> Who is like Thy people Israel
>   which Thou hast chosen for Thyself
>   from all the peoples of the lands;
> the people of the saints of the Covenant,
>   instructed in the laws
>   and learned in wisdom . . .
> who have heard the voice of Majesty
>   and have seen the Angels of Holiness,
> whose ear has been unstopped,
>   and who have heard profound things?
>
> [Thou, O God, hast created] the expanse of the heavens
>   and the host of heavenly lights,
> the tasks of the spirits
>   and the dominion of the Holy Ones,
> the treasury of glory
>   [and the canopy of the] clouds.
> (Thou art Creator of) the earth
>   and of the laws dividing it into desert and grassland;
> of all that it brings forth
>   and of all its fruits [according to their kinds;]
> of the circle of the seas
>   and of the gathering-place of the rivers
>   and of the divisions of the deeps;
> of the beasts and birds

and of the shape of Adam
and of the gene[rations of] his [seed];
of the confusion of tongues
and of the scattering of the peoples,
of the dwelling in clans
and of the inheritance of lands;
. . . of the sacred seasons
and of the cycles of the years
and of time everlasting.

XI   Truly, the battle is Thine! Their bodies are crushed by the might of Thy hand and there is no man to bury them.

Thou didst deliver Goliath of Gath, the mighty warrior, into the hands of David Thy servant, because in place of the sword and in place of the spear he put his trust in Thy great Name; for Thine is the battle. Many times, by Thy great Name, did he triumph over the Philistines. Many times hast Thou also delivered us by the hand of our kings through Thy lovingkindness, and not in accordance with our works by which we have done evil, nor according to our rebellious deeds.

Truly the battle is Thine and the power from Thee! It is not ours. Our strength and the power of our hands accomplish no mighty deeds except by Thy power and by the might of Thy great valour. This Thou hast taught us from ancient times, saying, *A star shall come out of Jacob, and a sceptre shall rise out of Israel. He shall smite the temples of Moab and destroy all the children of Sheth. He shall rule out of Jacob and shall cause the survivors of the city to perish. The enemy shall be his possession and Israel shall accomplish mighty deeds* (Num. xxiv, 17–19).

By the hand of Thine anointed, who discerned Thy testimonies, Thou hast revealed to us the [times] of the battles of Thy hands that Thou mayest glorify Thyself in our enemies by levelling the hordes of Satan, the seven nations of vanity, by the hand of Thy poor whom Thou hast redeemed [by Thy might] and by the fulness of Thy marvellous power. (Thou hast opened) the door of hope to the melting heart: Thou wilt do to them as Thou didst to Pharaoh, and to the captains of his chariots in the Red Sea. Thou wilt kindle the downcast of spirit and they shall be a flaming torch in the straw to consume ungodliness and never to cease till iniquity is destroyed.

From ancient times Thou hast fore[told the hour] when the might of Thy hand (would be raised) against the Kittim, saying, *Assyria shall fall by the sword of no man, the sword of no mere man shall devour him* (Isa. xxxi, 8). For Thou wilt deliver into the hands of the poor the enemies from all the lands, to humble the mighty of the peoples by the hand of those bent to the dust, to bring upon the [head of Thine enemies] the reward of the wicked, and to justify Thy true judgement in the midst of all the sons of men, and to make for Thyself an everlasting Name among the people [whom Thou hast redeemed] . . . of battles to be magnified and sanctified in the eyes of the remnant of the peoples, that they may know . . . when Thou chastisest Gog and all his assembly gathered about him . . .

For Thou wilt fight with them from heaven . . . **XII** For the multitude of the Holy Ones [is with Thee] in heaven, and the host of the Angels is in Thy holy abode, praising Thy Name. And Thou hast established in [a community] for Thyself the elect of Thy holy people. [The list] of the names of all their host is with Thee in the abode of Thy holiness; [the reckoning of the saints] is in Thy glorious dwelling-place. Thou hast recorded for them, with the graving-tool of life, the favours of [Thy] blessings and the Covenant of Thy peace, that Thou mayest reign [over them] for ever and ever and throughout all the eternal ages. Thou wilt muster the [hosts of] Thine [el]ect, in their Thousands and Myriads, with Thy Holy Ones [and with all] Thine Angels, that they may be mighty in battle, [and may smite] the rebels of the earth by Thy great judgements, and that [they may triumph] together with the elect of heaven.

For Thou art [terrible], O God, in the glory of Thy kingdom, and the congregation of Thy Holy Ones is among us for everlasting succour. We will despise kings, we will mock and scorn the mighty; for our Lord is holy, and the King of Glory is with us together with the Holy Ones. Valiant [warriors] of the angelic host are among our numbered men, and the Hero of war is with our congregation; the host of His spirits is with our foot-soldiers and horsemen. [They are as] clouds, as clouds of dew (covering) the earth, as a shower of rain shedding righteousness on all that grows on the earth.

> Rise up, O Hero!,
> Lead off Thy captives, O Glorious One!
> Gather up Thy spoils, O Author of mighty deeds!
> Lay Thy hand on the neck of Thine enemies
>   and Thy feet on the pile of the slain!
> Smite the nations, Thine adversaries,
>   and devour the flesh of the sinner with Thy sword!

Fill Thy land with glory
  and Thine inheritance with blessing!
Let there be a multitude of cattle in Thy fields,
  and in Thy palaces silver and gold and precious stones!

O Zion, rejoice greatly!
O Jerusalem, show thyself amidst jubilation!
Rejoice, all you cities of Judah;
keep your gates ever open
  that the hosts of the nations
  may be brought in!

Their kings shall serve you
  and all your oppressors shall bow down before you;
  [they shall lick] the dust [of your feet].
Shout for joy, [O daughters of] my people!
Deck yourselves with glorious jewels
  and rule over [the kingdoms of the nations!
Sovereignty shall be to the Lord]
  and everlasting dominion to Israel.

. . .

. . . **XIII** (The High Priest) shall come, and his brethren the Priests and the Levites, and all the elders of the army shall be with him; and standing, they shall bless the God of Israel and all His works of truth, and shall execrate Satan there and all the spirits of his company. Speaking, they shall say:

Blessed be the God of Israel for all His holy purpose and for His works of truth! Blessed be all those who [serve] Him in righteousness and who know Him by faith!

Cursed be Satan for his sinful purpose and may he be execrated for his wicked rule! Cursed be all the spirits of his company for their ungodly purpose and may they be execrated for all their service of uncleanness! Truly they are the company of Darkness, but the company of God is one of [eternal] Light.

[Thou art] the God of our fathers; we bless Thy Name for ever. We are the people of Thine [inheritance]; Thou didst make a Covenant with our fathers, and wilt establish it with their children throughout eternal ages. And in all Thy glorious testimonies there has been a reminder of Thy mercies among us to succour the remnant, the survivors of Thy Covenant, that they might [recount] Thy works of truth and the judgements of Thy marvellous mighty deeds.

Thou hast created us for Thyself, [O God], that we may be an everlasting people. Thou hast decreed for us a destiny of Light according to Thy truth. And the Prince of Light Thou hast appointed from ancient times to come to our support; [all the sons of righteousness are in his hand], and all the spirits of truth are under his dominion. But Satan, the Angel of Malevolence, Thou hast created for the Pit; his [rule] is in Darkness and his purpose is to bring about wickedness and iniquity. All the spirits of his company, the Angels of Destruction, walk according to the precepts of Darkness; towards them is their [inclination].

But let us, the company of Thy truth, rejoice in Thy mighty hand and be glad for Thy salvation, and exult because of Thy suc[cour and] peace. O God of Israel, who can compare with Thee in might? Thy mighty hand is with the poor. Which angel or prince can compare with Thy [redeeming] succour? [For Thou hast appointed] the day of battle from ancient times . . . [to come to the aid] of truth and to destroy iniquity, to bring Darkness low and to magnify Light . . . to stand for ever, and to destroy all the sons of Darkness . . .

. . .   **XIV**   like the fire of His wrath against the idols of Egypt.

And when they have risen from the slain to return to the camp, they shall all sing the Psalm of Return. And in the morning, they shall wash their garments, and shall cleanse themselves of the blood of the bodies of the ungodly. And they shall return to the positions in which they stood in battle formation before the fall of the enemy slain, and there they shall all bless the God of Israel. Rejoicing together, they shall praise His Name, and speaking they shall say:

> Blessed be the God of Israel
>   who keeps mercy towards His Covenant,
> and the appointed times of salvation
>   with the people He has delivered!
>
> He has called them that staggered
>   to [marvellous mighty deeds],
> and has gathered in the assembly of the nations
>   to destruction without any remnant.
> He has lifted up in judgement the fearful of heart
>   and has opened the mouth of the dumb
>   that they might praise [the mighty] works [of God].
> He has taught war [to the hand] of the feeble
>   and steadied the trembling knee;
>   he has braced the back of the smitten.

Among the poor in spirit [there is power]
    over the hard of heart,
and by the perfect of way
    all the nations of wickedness have come to an end:
    not one of their mighty men stands,
but we are the remnant [of Thy people.]

[Blessed be] Thy Name, O God of mercies,
    who hast kept the Covenant with our fathers.
In all our generations Thou hast bestowed
    Thy wonderful favours on the remnant [of Thy people]
    under the dominion of Satan.
During all the mysteries of his Malevolence
    he has not made [us] stray from Thy Covenant;
Thou hast driven his spirits [of destruction]
    far from [us],
Thou hast preserved the soul of Thy redeemed
    [when the men] of his dominion [acted wickedly].
Thou hast raised the fallen by Thy strength,
    but hast cut down the great in height
    [and hast brought down the lofty].
There is no rescue for all their mighty men
    and no refuge for their swift men;
Thou givest to their honoured men a reward of shame,
all their empty existence [hast Thou turned to nothing].

But we, Thy holy people, will praise Thy Name
    because of the works of Thy truth.
We will exalt Thy splendour because of Thy mighty deeds
    [in all the] seasons and appointed times for ever,
at the coming of day and at nightfall
    and at the departure of evening and morning.
For great [is the design of Thy glory]
    and of Thy wonderful mysteries on high
that [Thou shouldst raise up] dust before Thee
    and lay low the gods.

Rise up, rise up, O God of gods,
    raise Thyself in [might]!
May all the sons of Darkness [scatter before Thee]!
The light of Thy greatness [shall shine forth]
    [on 'go]ds' and men.
[It shall be like a fire bur]ning
    in the dark places of perdition;
it shall burn the sinners in the perdition of hell,
in an eternal blaze
    . . . in all the eternal seasons.

They shall recite there [all the] war [hy]mns. Afterwards they shall return to [their] cam[ps]. . .

XV For this shall be a time of distress for Israel, [and of the summons] to war against all the nations. There shall be eternal deliverance for the company of God, but destruction for all the nations of wickedness.

All those [who are ready] for battle shall march out and shall pitch their camp before the king of the Kittim and before all the host of Satan gathered about him for the Day [of Revenge] by the Sword of God.

Then the High Priest shall rise, with the [Priests], his brethren, and the Levites, and all the men of the army, and he shall recite aloud the Prayer in Time of War (written in the book] of the Rule concerning this time, and also all their Hymns. He shall marshal all the formations there, as is [written in the Book of War], and the priest appointed for the Day of Revenge by the voice of all his brethren shall go forward to strengthen the [hearts of the fighting men]. Speaking, he shall say:

Be strong and valiant; be warriors! Fear not! Do not be [confused and do not let your hearts be afraid!] Do not be fearful; fear them not! Do not fall back . . . for they are a congregation of wickedness and all their works are in Darkness; they tend toward Darkness. [They make for themselves] a refuge [in falsehood] and their power shall vanish like smoke. All the multitudes of their community . . . shall not be found. Damned as they are, all the substance of their wickedness shall quickly fade, like a flower in [the summer-time].

[Be brave and] strong for the battle of God! For this day is [the time of the battle of] God against all the host of Satan, [and of the judgement of] all flesh. The God of Israel lifts His hand in His marvellous [might] against all the spirits of wickedness. [The hosts of] the warrior 'gods' gird themselves for battle, [and the] formations of the Holy Ones [prepare themselves] for the Day [of Revenge] . . . **XVI** . . . For the God of Israel has called out the sword against all the nations, and He will do mighty deeds by the saints of His people.

And they shall obey all this Rule [on] the [day] when they stand before the camps of the Kittim

The Priests shall afterwards sound for them the trumpets of the Reminder, and the gates of war shall open; the foot-soldiers shall advance and the columns shall station themselves between the formations. The Priests shall sound for them the signal, 'Battle Array', and at the sound of the trumpets the columns [shall deploy] until every man is in his place. The Priests shall then sound a second signal [for them to advance], and when they are within throwing distance of the formation of the Kittim, each man shall seize his weapon of war. Then the six [Priests shall blow on] the trumpets of Massacre a shrill staccato blast to direct the battle, and the Levites and all the blowers of rams' horns shall sound [a battle alarm], a mighty clamour; and with this clamour they shall begin to bring down the slain from among the Kittim. All the people shall cease their clamour, [but the Priests shall continue to] sound the trumpets of Massacre, and battle shall be fought against the Kittim. And when [Satan] girds himself to come to the aid of the sons of darkness, and when the slain among the foot-soldiers begin to fall by the mysteries of God, and when all the men appointed for battle are put to ordeal by them, the Priests shall sound the trumpets of Summons for another formation of the reserve to advance into battle; and they shall take up their stand between the formations. And for those engaged [in battle] they shall sound the 'Retreat'.

Then the High Priest shall draw near, and standing before the formation, he shall strengthen by the power of God their hearts [and hands] in His battle. Speaking he shall say:

... **XVII** He will pay their reward with burning [fire by the hand of] those tested in the crucible. He will sharpen His weapons and will not tire until all the wicked nations are destroyed. Remember the judgement [of Nadab and Ab]ihu, sons of Aaron, by whose judgement God showed Himself holy in the eyes [of Israel. But Eleazar] and Ithamar He confirmed in an everlasting [priestly] Covenant.

Be strong and fear not; [for they tend] towards chaos and confusion, and they lean on that which is not and [shall not be. To the God] of Israel belongs all that is and shall be; [He knows] all the happenings of eternity. This is the day appointed by Him for the defeat and overthrow of the Prince of the kingdom of wickedness, and He will send eternal succour to the company of His redeemed by the might of the princely Angel of the kingdom of Michael. With everlasting light He will enlighten with joy [the children] of Israel; peace and blessing shall be with the company of God. He will raise up the kingdom of Michael in the midst of the gods, and the realm of Israel in the midst of all flesh.

Righteousness shall rejoice on high, and all the children of His truth shall jubilate in eternal knowledge.

And you, the sons of His Covenant, be strong in the ordeal of God! His mysteries shall uphold you until He moves His hand for His trials to come to an end.

After these words, the Priests shall sound to marshal them into the divisions of the formation; and at the sound of the trumpets the columns shall deploy until [every man is] in his place. Then the Priests shall sound a second signal on the trumpets for them to advance, and when the [foot-]soldiers approach throwing distance of the formation of the Kittim, every man shall seize his weapon of war. The Priests shall blow the trumpets of Massacre, [and the Levites and all] the blowers of rams' horns shall sound a battle alarm, and the foot-soldiers shall stretch out their hands against the host of the Kittim; [and at the sound of the alarm] they shall begin to bring down the slain. All the people shall cease their clamour, but the Priests shall continue to blow [the trumpets of Massacre and battle shall be fought against the Kittim.]

. . . and in the third lot . . . that the slain may fall by the mysteries of God . . .

XVIII   [In the seventh lot] when the great hand of God is raised in an everlasting blow against Satan and all the hosts of his kingdom, and when Assyria is pursued [amidst the shouts of Angels] and the clamour of the Holy Ones, the sons of Japheth shall fall to rise no more. The Kittim shall be crushed without [remnant, and no man shall be saved from among them].

[At that time, on the day] when the hand of the God of Israel is raised against all the multitude of Satan, the Priests shall blow [the six trumpets] of the Reminder and all the battle formations shall rally to them and shall divide against all the [camps of the] Kittim to destroy them utterly. [And as] the sun speeds to its setting on that day, the High Priest shall stand, together [with the Levites] who are with him and the [tribal] chiefs [and the elders] of the army, and they shall bless the God of Israel there. Speaking they shall say:

Blessed be Thy Name, O God [of gods], for Thou hast worked great marvels [with Thy people]! Thou hast kept Thy Covenant with us from of old, and hast opened to us the gates of salvation many times. For the [sake of Thy Covenant Thou hast removed our misery, in accordance with] Thy [goodness] towards us. Thou hast acted for the sake of Thy Name, O God of righteousness . . . [Thou hast worked a marvellous] miracle [for us], and from ancient times there never was anything like it. For Thou didst know the time appointed for us and it has appeared [before us] this day . . . [Thou hast shown] us [Thy merciful hand] in everlasting redemption by causing [the dominion of] the enemy to fall back for ever. (Thou hast shown us) Thy mighty hand in [a stroke of destruction in the war against all] our enemies.

And now the day speeds us to the pursuit of their multitude . . . Thou hast delivered up the hearts of the brave so that they stand no more.

For Thine is the power, and the battle is in Thy hands! . . .
XIX   For our Sovereign is holy and the King of Glory is with us; the [host of his spirits is with our foot-soldiers and horsemen. They are as clouds, as clouds of dew] covering the earth, and as a shower of rain shedding righteousness on [all that grows there].

> [Rise up, O Hero!
> Lead off Thy captives, O Glorious One!
> Gather up] Thy spoils, O Author of mighty deeds!
> Lay Thy hand on the neck of Thine enemies
>   and Thy feet [on the pile of the slain!
> Smite the nations, Thine adversaries],
>   and devour flesh with Thy sword!
> Fill Thy land with glory
>   and Thine inheritance with blessing!
> [Let there be a multitude of cattle in Thy fields,
>   and in] Thy palaces
>   [silver and gold and precious stones]!
>
> O Zion, rejoice greatly!
>   Rejoice all you cities of Judah!
> [Keep your gates ever open
>   that the] hosts of the nations
>   [may be brought in]!
> Their kings shall serve you
>   and all your oppressors shall bow down before you;
>   [they shall lick the dust of your feet.
> Shout for joy, O daughters of] my people!
> Deck yourselves with glorious jewels
>   [and rule over the kingdom of the nations!
> Sovereignty shall be to the Lord]
>   and everlasting dominion to Israel.

Then they shall gather in the camp that night to rest until the morning. And in the morning [they shall go to the place where the formation stood before the] warriors of the Kittim fell, and the multitudes of Assyria, and the hosts of all the nations [assembled] (to discover whether) the multitude of the stricken are dead (with none to bury them), those who fell there under the Sword of God. And the High Priest shall draw near, [with his vicar, and the chief Priests and the Levites] with the Prince of the battle, and all the chiefs of the formations and their numbered men; [they shall return to the positions which they held before the] slain [began to fall] from among the Kittim, and there they shall praise the God [of Israel] . . .

The War Rule from Cave 4

Of the two groups of fragments belonging to M^a, the first echoes sections from columns II, VII, XVI and XVII of 1QM, but it contains also passages without parallels there. The second unit, a poem, entitled by the editor 'The Song of Michael and of the Just', is additional to 1QM.

As for the manuscript designated M^c, its surviving lines recall 1QM VII, XVI, etc., but do not represent the same recension.

4Q491 *frs. 1–3* = *M^a*

. . . There shall be one thousand cubits between the [camp and the latrine and] no nakedness [whatever] shall be seen in their surroundings. And when they set out to prepare the battle [to cur]b [the enemy, there shall be] among them some exempted in the lot of each tribe according to their numbered men for [each] day's duty. On that day, some men from all their tribes shall set out from their camps towards the House of Meeting . . . the [Priest]s, the Levites, and all the chiefs of the camps shall go out towards them. They will pass there before . . . according to the Thousands, Hundreds, Fifties and Tens. Whoever shall not [be clean because of his 'fount' on] that [nig]ht, shall not go with them to the battle, for the holy angels shall be with their formations together. . . When the formation called up for that day's battle to pass to all. . . of the war, three formations shall stand, formations behind formations. They shall set a space between [all] the formations [and they shall go out] to battle in succession. These are the [foot-soldie]rs and beside them the [horse]men. [They shall stand between the forma]tions. And if they set up an ambush for a formation, the three ambushing formations shall be at a distance and shall not ri[se] . . . of the war and they [shall he]ar the trumpets of Alarm and the [foot-] soldiers [will begin to bring dow]n the guilty dead. Afterwards the ambush shall rise from its hiding-place arranged in formations. The re-assembly: from the right and from the left, from be[hind and from the front, f]our direction[s]. . . in the battles of annihilation. And all the formations engaged in combat with the ene[my will be in] one [place. The f]irst formation [will go out to the battle] and the second stand . . . on their post. With the completion of their time, the first shall return and rise . . . The sec[ond] . . . When the battle is joined. And the second formation shall have completed its time and they shall return and st[and on their post]. And the th[ird] . . .

And the chief Priest and his brethren, [the Priests, and] the Levites and the m[en of the orde]r [shall stand]. And the Priests shall blow the trumpets continuously . . . and a girdle of fine cloth of flax embroidered with blue, purple and scarlet threads, a many-coloured design produced by a craftsman, and a fine linen tunic and fine linen breeches and a mitred turban [on their heads. They shall not take them to the sanctuary] f[or] they are ba[ttle] raiments. According to all this rule . . .

4Q491 *fr. 11* = Mᵃ

The Song of Michael and the Just

. . . a throne of strength in the congregation of 'gods' so that not a single king of old shall sit on it, neither shall their noble men . . . my glory is incomparable, and apart from me none is exalted. None shall come to me for I dwell in . . . in heaven, and there is no . . . I am reckoned with the 'gods' and my dwelling-place is in the congregation of holiness. [My] des[ire] is not according to the flesh, [and] all that I value is in the glory of . . . [. . . the pl]ace of holiness. Whom do I count as despicable, and who is comparable to me in my glory? Who is like . . . the young (?) like me? Is there a companion who resembles me? I have . . ., and no instruction resembles [my instruction] . . . Who shall attack me when [I] op[en my mouth]? And who can deal with the issue of my lips? Who shall summon me to be destroyed by my judgement? . . . [F]or I am reckoned with the 'gods', and my glory is with the sons of the King. No pure gold or gold of Ophir . . .

$4Q493 = M^c$

. . . the battle. The Priests, sons of Aaron, shall stand before [the] formations and shall blow the trumpets of Reminder. After this, they shall open the g[ate]s for the foot-soldiers. The Priests shall blow the battle trumpets to [strike] the formations of the nations. The Priests shall depart from among the slain and stand on either side next to the . . . and they shall not profane the oil of their priesthood [by the blood of the s]lai[n]. They shall not approach any of the formations of the foot-soldiers. They shall sound a shrill blast with the trumpets of Massacre for the wa[rr]iors to go out to fight between the formations. They shall begin to wage war. When their time is completed, the trumpets of Return shall sound for them (summoning them) to come to the gates, and the second formation shall set out. According to this rule, the Le[vites] shall blow for them during (their) times (of action). When they go out, they shall blow for them the tr[umpets of Summons], and when (their time) is complete, the trumpets of Alarm, and when they return, they shall bl[ow for them the trumpets of] Retr[eat]. According to [this] sta[tute] they will blow for a[ll the formations . . .]

5. THE TEMPLE SCROLL (11QT)

❧

Discovered in 1956 in cave 11, the Temple Scroll did not emerge from semi-clandestinity until the 'Six Day War' in June 1967. It is the longest Qumran manuscript, measuring over twenty-eight feet. There are also fragments pertaining to the same document from caves 4 and 11. Originally it consisted of sixty-seven columns.

The major part of the scroll deals with the Temple (building and furniture) and cultic worship, especially sacrifices, on Sabbaths and the many feasts of the year. Most of the legislation depends, directly or indirectly, on Exodus, Leviticus, and more particularly on Deuteronomy, but there are also occasional non-biblical regulations.

The beginning of the manuscript is badly mutilated. Column I is missing. Columns III-XII are so fragmented that only a very hypothetical reconstruction, exclusively from biblical texts, is possible. I have decided not to translate them but indicate, in the summary that follows, their probable contents:

1. Covenant between God and Israel (col. II).
2. Building of the Temple, measurements of the Sanctuary, the Holy of Holies, the chambers and colonnades (cols. III-VII).
3. Description of the mercy seat, the cherubim, the veil, the table, the golden lampstand, etc. (cols. VII-XI).
4. Outline of the sacrifices and the altar (cols. XI-XII).
5. Daily, weekly and monthly sacrifices and those offered on festivals (cols. XIII-XXIX).
6. Buildings in the Temple courtyards: the stairhouse, the house of the laver, the house for sacred vessels, the slaughterhouse, etc. (cols. XXX-XXXV).
7. The three courtyards of the Temple, one for the priests, one for Jewish men over twenty years of age, and one for women and children (cols. XXXVI-XLV).
8. Purity regulations concerning the Temple and the city of the Sanctuary (cols. XLVI-XLVIII).
9. Purity regulations concerning the cities of Israel (cols. XLVIII-LI).
10. Judges and officers (col. LI).
11. Laws relating to idolatry and to sacrificial animals (cols. LI-LIII).
12. Vows and oaths (cols. LIII-LIV).

13. Laws against apostasy (cols. LIV-LV).
14. Laws relating to priests and Levites and detailed statutes of the Jewish king (cols. LVI-LIX).
15. Miscellaneous laws regarding priestly dues, idols, witnesses, the conduct of war, the rebellious son, crimes punishable by 'hanging' and incestuous relations (cols. LX-LXVI).

The sequence of subjects generally follows the Bible, but an obvious effort has been made to systematize, harmonize and re-interpret the laws. Sections complementary to Scripture include the Temple legislation (cols. III-XII, XXX-XLV), the festivals (cols. XVII-XXIX), the purity rules relative to the Temple and the city (cols. XLVI-XLVII), and the statutes of the king (cols. LVI-LIX). The aim of the redactor is to present the message of the scroll not as an interpretation of the Bible, but as an immediate divine revelation. For this purpose, not only does he formulate the supplementary legislation as directly spoken by God, but also regularly substitutes 'I' for 'the Lord=YHWH' of Scripture.

Although the view has been advanced that the Temple Scroll is not a Qumran composition, the contrary thesis has a solid foundation. The relationship between this document and the Damascus Rule is particularly striking in the case of the prohibition of royal polygamy, of marriage between uncle and niece, and of marital relations within the city of the Sanctuary (compare CD IV, 20–v, 11; XII, 1–2 with TS LVII, 16–18; LXVI, 15–17; XLV, 11–12), to name the most significant instances. Note also that the death penalty of 'hanging' (probably crucifixion) reserved for traitors appears both in TS LXIV, 6–13 and in the Nahum Commentary (cf. p. 279). Since the Damascus Rule and the Nahum Commentary are more likely to depend on the Temple Scroll than vice versa, the latter may safely be dated to the second century B.C. It may also have an antecedent history reaching back to the pre-Qumran age. Rumour has it that unpublished fragments from cave 4 dating to the mid second century B.C. quote from either the Temple Scroll itself or possibly one of its sources.

The writing is available in a magisterial edition by Yigael Yadin, who first published it in Hebrew in 1977 and subsequently, shortly before his death, in English under the title, *The Temple Scroll* I–III (Jerusalem, 1983). My translation is often indebted to Yadin's editorial work.

II [Behold, I will make a covenant.]
[For it is something dreadful that I] will do [to you.] [I myself will expel from before you] the A[morites, the Canaanites, the Hittites, the Girgashit]es, the Pe[rizzites, the Hivites and] the Jebusites. Ta[ke care not to make a cove]nant with the inhabitants of the country [which you are to] enter so that they may not prove a sn[are for you.] You must destroy their [alta]rs, [smash their]

pillars [and] cut down their [sacred trees and burn] [their] idols
[with fire]. You must not desire silver and gold so [that you may
not be ensnared by them; for that would be abominable to me].
You must [not] br[ing any abominable idol] into your house [and
come] under the ban together with it. You shall de[test and abom-
inate it], for it is under the ban. You shall not worship [another]
go[d, for YHWH, whose name is] [Jealous], is a jealous God.
Take care not to make a [covenant with the inhabitants of the
country] [so that when they whore] after [their go]ds [and] sacrifice to [them and invite you,] [you may not eat of their sacrifices
and] t[ake their daughters for your sons, and their daughters
may not whore after] their [gods] and cau[se your sons to whore
after them.] . . .*

XIII [This is what you shall offer on the altar:] t[wo y]ear[ling
lambs] without blemish [every day as a perpetual holocaust. You
shall offer the first in the morning; [and you shall offer the other
lamb in the evening; the corresponding grain-offering will be a
te]nth of fine flour mixed with [a quarter of a hin of beaten oil;
it shall be a perpetual holocaust of soothing odour, an offering
by fire] to YHWH; and the corresponding drink-offering shall
be a quart[er of a hin of] wine. [The priest who offers the holocaust shall receive the skin of] the burnt-[offering which he has
offered. You shall offer the other lamb in the even]ing with the
same grain-[offering as in the] morning and with the corresponding drink-offering as an offering by fire, a soothing odour to
YHWH . . .

On the S[abbath] days you shall offer two [yearling rams without blemish and two] **XIV** [tenths of an ephah of fine flour,
mixed with oil, for a grain-offering and the corresponding drink-
offering. This is the holocaust of every Sabbath in addition to the
perpetual holocaust and the corresponding drink-offering. On
the first day of each month you shall offer a holocaust to YHWH:
two young bulls, one ram, seven yearling rams without blemish
and a grain-offe]ring of fine flour, [three tenths of an ephah]
mix[ed with half a hin of oil, and a drink-offering, ha]lf a hin for
[each young bull and a grain-offering of fine flour mixed with
oil, two tenths of an ephah] with a third [of a hin, and wine for a
drink-offering, one third of a hin for each ram;] . . . one tenth
[of fine flour for] a grain-[offering, mixed with a quarter of a hin,
and wine, a quarter of a hi]n for each lamb . . . a soothing [odour]

---

*For the contents of the badly damaged columns III-XII, see pp. 128–9.

to YHWH on the first day of each month. This is the burnt-offering for each month for the months of the year . . . On the first day of the [first] month [the months (of the year) shall start; it shall be the first month] of the year [for you. You shall do no] work. [You shall offer a he-goat for a sin-offering.] It shall be offered by itself to expiate [for you. You shall offer a holocaust: a bullock], a ram, [seven yearli]ng ram lambs [without blemish] . . . [ad]di[tional to the bu]r[nt-offering for the new moon, and a grain-offering of three tenths of fine flour mixed with oil], half a hin [for each bullock, and wi]ne for a drink-offering, [half a hin, a soothing odour to YHWH, and two] tenths of fine flour mixed [with oil, one third of a hin. You shall offer wine for a drink-offering] one th[ird] of a hin for the ram, [an offering by fire, of soothing odour to YHWH; and one tenth of fine flour], a grain-offerin[g mixed with a quarter of a hin of oil. You shall offer wine for a drink-offering, a quarter of a hin] for each [ram] . . . lambs and for the he-g[oat] . . .   **XV**   [ea]ch day . . . seven [year]ling [lambs] and a he-[goat] . . . according to this statute. For the ordination (of the priests), one ram for each [day, and] baskets of bread for all the ra[ms of the ordination, one basket for] each [ram]. They shall divide all the rams and the baskets for the seve[n days of the ordination for each] day; according to [their] division[s, they shall offer to YHWH the right thigh] of the ram as a holocaust and [the fat covering the entrails and the] two kidneys and the fat on them [and on] the loins and the whole fat tail close to the backbone and the appendage of the liver and the corresponding grain-offering and drink-offering according to the sta[tute. They shall take one unleavened cake from the] basket and one cake of bread with oil and [one] wafer, [and they shall put it all on the fat] together with the offering of the right thigh. Those who sacrifice shall wave the rams and the baskets of bread as a wa[ve-offering be]fore YHWH. This is a holocaust, an offering by fire, of soothing odour before YHWH. [They shall burn everything on the altar over] the holocaust, to complete their ordination during the seven days of [ordination].

If the High Priest is to [minister to YHWH, whoever] has been ordained to put on the vestments in place of his father, shall offer [a bull] [fo]r all the people and another for the priests. He shall offer the one for the priests first. The elders of the priest[s] shall lay [their hands]   **XVI**   [on] its [hea]d and after them the High Priest and all the [priests. They shall slaughter] the bull [before YHWH]. The elders of the priests shall take from the blood of the bull and [place] it [with their finger on the horns of the altar] and they shall pour [the blood] around the four corners of the [altar] ledge . . . [and they shall take from its blood and pl]ace it [on his right ear lobe and on the thumb of his right hand and the big toe of his] right [foot. They shall sprinkle on him and his vestments some of the blood which was on the altar] . . . [he] shall be [holy] all his days. [He shall not go near any dead body]. He shall [not] render himself unclean [even for his father or mother,] for [he is] hol[y to YHWH, his God] . . . [He shall offer on the al]tar and burn [the fat of the first bull] . . . [all] the fat on the entrails and [the appendage of the liver and the two kidne]ys and the fat on the[m] and [the fat on] the loins, and the corresponding grain-offering and drink-[offering according to their statute,] he shall bur[n them on the altar.] It shall be [a burnt-]offering, an offering by fire, of soothing odour be[fore YHWH. The flesh of the bull], its skin and offal, they shall burn outside the [sanctuary city on a wood fire] in a place reserved for sin-offerings. There they shall bur[n it with its head and legs] together with all its entrails. They shall burn all of it there except the fat. It is a sin-[offering]. He shall take the second bull, which is for the people, and by it he shall expiate [for all the people of] the assembly, by its blood and fat. As he did with the fir[st] bull, [so he shall do] with the bull of the assembly. He shall place with his finger some of its blood on the horns of the [altar, and the remainder of] its blood, he shall sprinkle o[n the f]our corners of the altar ledge, and [its fat and] the corresponding [grain-]offering and drink-offering, he shall burn on the altar. It is a sin-offering for the assembly. **XVII** . . . They shall rejoice because expiation has been made for them . . . This day [shall] be a holy gathering for them, [an eternal rule for all their generations] wherever they dwell. They shall rejoice and . . .

[Let] them [prepare on the fourtee]nth day of the first month [between dusk and dark the Passover of YHWH]. They shall sacrifice (it) before the evening offering and shall sacrifice . . . men from twenty years of age and over shall prepare it. They shall eat it at night in the holy courts. They shall rise early and each shall go to his tent . . .

On the fifteenth day of this month (there shall be) a ho[ly] gathering. You shall do no work of labour on it. (It shall be) a seven-day feast of unleavened bread for YHWH. You shall offer on each of the[se] seven days a holocaust to YHWH: two young bulls, a ram, and seven ram lambs without blemish and a he-goat for a sin-offering and the corresponding grain-offering and drink-offering [according to the sta]tute for the young bulls, rams, l[am]bs and the he-goat. On the seventh day [(there shall be) an assembly] for [YHWH]. You shall do no work on it. **XVIII** . . . [he-]goat for a sin-offering . . . [the corresponding grain-offering and drink-]offering according to the statute; one tenth of fine flour [mixed with a quarter of a hin of oil and] a quarter of a hin of wine for a drink-offering . . . [he shall expiate] for all the guilt of the people of the assembly . . . This shall be an eternal [ru]le for you [for your generations wherever you dwell.] Then they shall offer the one ram, on[ce], on the day of the waving of the sheaf.

You shall count seven complete Sabbaths from the day of your bringing the sheaf of [the wave-offering. You shall c]ount until the morrow of the seventh Sabbath. You shall count [fifty] days. You shall bring a new grain-offering to YHWH from your homes, [a loaf of fine fl]ou[r], freshly baked with leaven. They are firstfruits to YHWH, wheat bread, twe[lve cakes, two] tenths of fine flour in each cake . . . the tribes of Israel, They shall offer **XIX** . . . their [grain-offerin]g and dr[ink-offering] according to the statute. The [priests] shall wave . . . [wave-offering with the bread of] the firstfruits. They shall b[elong to] the priests and they shall eat them in the [inner] court[yard], [as a ne]w [grain-offering], the bread of the firstfruits. Then . . . new bread from freshly ripened ears. [On this] da[y] there shall be [a holy gathering, an eter]nal [rule] for their generations. [They] shall [do] no work. It is the feast of Weeks and the feast of Firstfruits, an eterna[l] memorial.

You [shall count] seven weeks from the day when you bring the new grain-offering to YHW[H], the bread of firstfruits. Seven full Sabbaths [shall elapse un]til you have counted fifty days to the morrow of the seventh Sabbath. [You] shall [bring] new wine for a drink-offering, four hins from all the tribes of Israel, one third of a hin for each tribe.

They shall offer on this day with the wine twelve rams to YHWH; all the chiefs of the clans of Israel **XX** . . . [r]ams and the corresponding grain-offering according to the statute: two [tenths of fine flour mixed with oil, one third of a h]in of oil for a ram; with this drink-offering . . . seven yearling ram lambs and a he-[goat] . . . assembly . . . their [grain-offering and drink-offering] (shall be) according to the statute concerning young bulls and the ram . . . to YHWH. At the quarter of the day, they shall offer . . . [the r]ams and the drink-offering. They shall offer . . . fourteen yearling ram lambs . . . the burnt-offering. They shall prepare them . . . and they shall burn their fat on the altar, [the fat covering the entrails] and the fat that is on them, and [the appendage of the liver with] the kidneys he shall remove and the fat on [them], and that which is on the loins and the fat tail close to the backbone. They shall b[urn all on the altar] together with the corresponding grain-offering and drink-offering, an offering by fire, of soothing odou[r before YHWH]. They shall offer every grain-offering joined to a drink-offering according to [the statute]. They shall take a handful from [eve]ry grain-offering offered either with frankincense or dry, (this being) its [memorial portion], and burn it on the altar. They shall eat the remainder in the [in]n[er] courtyard. The priests shall e[a]t it unleavened. It shall not be eaten with leaven. It shall be ca[ten] on that day [before] sun[se]t. They shall salt all their offerings. You shall never allow the covenant of salt to fail.

They shall offer to YHWH an offering from the rams and the lambs, the right thigh, the breast, [the cheeks, the stomac]h and the foreleg as far as the shoulder bone, and they shall wave them as a wave-offering.   **XXI**   [The priests'] portions [shall] be the thigh of the offering and the breast . . . [the foreleg]s, the cheeks and the stomachs . . . [as an eternal rule, from the children of Isra]el and the shoulder remaining of the foreleg [shall be for the Levites] . . . an eternal rule for them and for their seed . . . the princes of the thousands . . . [from] the rams and from [the lambs, one ram and one ram lamb (shall belong) to the priests; to the Levites], one [ra]m, one lamb; and to every [tribe, on]e [ram], one lamb for all the tri[bes], the [twe]lve tribes of Israel. They shall eat them [on that day, in the out]er [courtyard] before YHWH.

. . . [the priest]s shall drink there first and the Levites [second] . . . the princes of the standards first . . . [men of] renown. After them the whole people, from the great to the small, shall begin to drink the new wine, They [shall not e]a[t] any un[ri]pe grapes from the vines, for [on] this [da]y they shall expiate for the *tirosh*. The children of Israel shall rejoice before YHWH, an eternal [rule] for their generations wherever they dwell. They shall rejoice on [this] d[ay for they have begun] to pour out an intoxicating drink-offering, the new wine, on the altar of YHWH, year by year.

[You sha]ll count from that day seven weeks, seven times (seven days), forty-nine days; there shall be seven full Sabbaths; until the morrow of the seventh Sabbath you shall count fifty days. You shall then offer new oil from the homes of [the tr]ibes of the ch[ildren of Is]rael, half a hin from a tribe, new beaten oil . . . oil on the altar of the holocaust, firstfruits before YHWH. **XXII** . . . [shall expi]ate with it for all the congregation before [YHWH] . . . with this oil, half a hin . . . [according to the st]atute, a holocaust, an offering by fire, of soothing [odour to YHWH] . . . [With] this oil they shall light the lamps . . . the princes of the thousands with . . . fourteen [yearling] m[ale lamb]s and the corresponding grain-offering and drink-offering . . . [for the lambs and] the rams. The Levites shall slaughter . . . [and] the priests, the sons of Aaron, [shall spri]nkle their blood [on the altar all around] . . . [and] they shall burn their fat on the altar of the [holocaust] . . . [and the corresponding grain-offering] and drink-offering, they shall burn over the fats . . . [an offering by fire, of soothing odour to] YHWH. They shall take away fr[om] . . . the right thigh and the breast . . . the cheeks and the stomach shall be the priests' portion according to the statute concerning them. (They shall give (?)) to the Levites the shoulder. Afterwards they shall bring them (the offerings) out to the children of Israel, and the children of Israel shall give the prie[st]s one ram, one lamb, and to the Levites, one ram, one lamb, and to each tribe, one ram, one lamb. They shall eat them on that day in the outer courtyard before YHWH, an eternal rule for their generations, year by year. Afterwards they shall eat from the olives and anoint themselves with the new oil, for on this day they shall expiate for [al]l [the o]il of the land before YHWH once yearly. They shall rejoice **XXIII** . . .

The High Priest shall offer the [holocaust of the Levites] first, and afterwards he shall send up in smoke the holocaust of the tribe of Judah, and w[hen he] is sending it up in smoke, they shall slaughter before him the he-goat first and he shall lift up its blood in a bowl to the altar and with his finger he shall pu[t some] of the blood to the four horns of the alta[r] of the holocaust and to the four corners of the altar ledge, and shall toss the blood towards the bas[e] of the altar ledge all around. He shall burn its fat on the altar, the fat covering the entrails and that over the entrails. The appendage of the liver with the kidneys he shall remove as well as the fat over them and on the loins. He shall send up in smoke all of them on the altar together with the corresponding grain-offering and drink-offering, an offering by fire of soothing odour to YHWH. And **XXIV** . . . the flesh, of [soothing] odour; it shall be [an offering by fire to YHWH. Thus they must do to every] young bull, and to every ram and to [every lamb] and its limbs (?) shall remain apart. The corresponding [grain-offering] and drink-offering shall be on it, an [eternal] rule for your generations before YHWH.

After this holocaust he shall offer the holocaust of the tribe of Judah separately. As he has done with the holocaust of the Levites, so shall he do with the holocaust of the children of Judah after the Levites. On the second day he shall first offer the holocaust of Benjamin and after it he shall offer the holocaust of the children of Joseph, Ephraim and Manasseh together. On the third day, he shall offer the holocaust of Reuben separately, and the holocaust of Simeon separately. On the fourth day he shall offer the holocaust of Issachar separately and the holocaust of Zebulun separately. On the fifth day he shall offer the holocaust of Gad separately and the holocaust of Asher separately. On the sixth day **XXV** [he shall offer the holocaust of Dan separately and the holocaust of Naphtali separately] . . .

In the [seventh] m[onth, on the first day of the month, you shall have] a sacred rest, a remembrance announced by a trumpet blast, a [holy] ga[thering. You shall offer a holocaust, an offering by fire, of soothing odour be]fore YHWH. You shall o[ffer on]e [young bull,] óne ram, seve[n] ye[ar]ling [lamb]s [without blemish and one he-goat for a sin-offering, and] the corresponding grain-offering and drink-offering according to the statute concerning the[m, of soothing odour to YHWH, in addition to] the perpetual [holocaus]t [and the holo]caust of the new moon. Afterwards [you shall offer] this [holocaust] at the third part of the day, an eternal rule for your generation[s wherever you dwell.] You shall rejoice on this day. On it you shall do no work. A sacred rest shall this day be for you.

The tenth of this month is the Day of Atonement. You shall mortify yourselves. For any person who does not mortify himself on this self-same day shall be cut off from his people. You shall offer on it a holocaust to YHWH: one young bull, one ram, seven ram lambs, one he-goat for a sin-offering, in addition to the sin-offering of the atonement and the corresponding grain-offering and drink-offering according to the statute concerning the young bull, the ram, the lambs and the he-goat. For the sin-offering of the atonement you shall offer two rams for holocaust. The High Priest shall offer one for himself and his father's house

XXVI ... [The High Prie]st [shall cast lots on the two goats,] o[ne] lot for YHWH and one for Azazel. He shall slaughter the goat [on] which [YHWH's lot has fallen and shall lift up] its blood in a golden bowl which is in [his ha]nd, [and do] with its blo[od as he has done with the blood of] his young bull and shall expiate with it for all the people of the assembly. He shall send up in smoke its fat and the corresponding grain- and drink-offering on the altar of the holocaust. Its flesh, skin and dung they shall burn beside his young bull. It is a sin-offering for the whole assembly. He shall expiate with it for all the people of the assembly and it shall be forgiven to them. He shall wash his hands and feet of the blood of the sin-offering and shall come to the living goat and shall confess over its head the iniquities of the children of Israel together with all their guilt, all their sins. He shall put them on the head of the goat and despatch it to Azazel in the desert by the hand of the man who is waiting ready. The goat shall bear all the iniquities of (the children of Israel). **XXVII** ... [and he shall expiate] for all the children of Israel and it shall be forgiven to them ... Afterwards he shall offer the young bull, the r[a]m, and [the lambs, according to] the [sta]tute relating to them, on the altar of the holocaust, and the [ho]locaust will be accepted for the children of Israel, an eternal rule for their generations. Once a year this day shall be for them a memorial. They shall do no work on it, for it shall be [to] them a Sabbath of sacred rest. Whoever shall do work on it or shall not mortify himself on it, shall be cut off from the midst of his people. A Sabbath of sacred rest, a holy gathering shall this day be for you. You shall sanctify it as a memorial wherever you dwell and you shall do no work.

On the fifteenth day of this month **XXVIII** ... [the corresponding] grain-offering [and drink-offering, all on] the altar, an offering by fire, of s[oothing odour to YHWH. On] the second [day:] twelve young bulls, [two rams, four]teen [lambs] and one he-goat [for a sin-offerin]g [and the corresponding gr]ai[n-offering and drink-offering] according to the statute concerning the young bulls, the ram[s], the lambs [and] the he-goat; it is an offering by fire, of soothing odour to YHWH.

On the third day eleven young bulls, two rams, fourteen lambs and one he-goat for a sin-offering and the corresponding grain-offering and drink-offering according to the statute concerning the young bulls, the rams, the lambs and the he-goat.

On the fo[ur]th day ten young bulls, two rams, fourteen yearling ram lambs and one he-goat for a sin-offering and the corresponding grain-offering and drink-offering for the young bulls, **XXIX** [the rams, the lambs and the he-goat . . . On the fifth day . . . and the corresponding grain-offering] and drink-offer[ing] . . . in the house on which I [shall cause] my name to rest . . . holocausts, [each on its] day according to the law of this statute, always from the children of Israel in addition to their free will-offerings in regard to all that they offer, their drink-offerings and all their gifts that they shall bring to me in order to be acceptable. I shall accept them and they shall be my people and I shall be for them for ever. I will dwell with them for ever and ever and will sanctify my [sa]nctuary by my glory. I will cause my glory to rest on it until the day of creation on which I shall create my sancturay, establishing it for myself for all the time according to the covenant which I have made with Jacob in Bethel.

    XXX . . . You shall make . . . for stairs, a stair[case] . . . in the house which you shall build . . . You [shall make] a staircase north of the Temple, a square house, twenty cubits from one corner to the other alongside its four corners. Its distance from the wall of the Temple shall be seven cubits on the north-west. You shall make the width of its wall four cubits . . . like the Temple and its inside from corner to corner twelv[e cubits.] (There shall be) a square column in its middle, in the centre; its width four cubits on each side around which the stairs wind . . . **XXXI** In the upper chamber of [this] ho[use you shall make a ga]te opening to the roof of the Temple and a way (shall be) made through this gate towards the entrance . . . of the Temple by which one can reach the upper chamber of the Temple. Overlay with gold [a]ll this stairhouse, its walls, its gates and its roof, from inside [and from] outside, its column and its stairs. [You] shall do everything as I tell you. You shall make a square house for the laver in the south-east, on all its sides, (each) twenty-one cubits; fifty cubits distant from the altar. The width of the wall shall be four cubits, and the height [t]wenty cubits . . . Make gates for it on the east, on the north and on the west. The width of the gates shall be four cubits and the height seven **XXXII** . . . You shall make in the wall of this house, on the inside, recesses, and in them . . . one cubit (in) width and their height four cubits above the ground. They shall be overlaid with gold on which they shall place their clothes which they have worn on arrival. Above the house of the . . . when they come to minister in the sanctuary. You shall make a trench around the laver beside its house and the trench shall go [from the house of] the laver to a cavity. It shall descend [rapid]ly to the ground where the water shall flow and disappear. It shall not be touched by any man for it is mingled with the blood of the holocaust. **XXXIII** They shall sanctify my people in the sacred vestments which . . .

You shall make a house east of the house of the [l]av[er] according to the measurement of [the house of the bas]in. Its wall shall be at a distance of seven cubits from the wall of the house of the laver. Its whole building and rafters shall be like (those of) the house of the laver. It shall have two gates on the north and the south, one opposite the other, according to the measurement of the gates of the house of the laver. Inside all the walls of this house shall have apertures, their width (and depth) two cubits each and their height four (?) with which the entrails and the feet are raised to the altar. When they have completed the sending up in smoke **XXXIV** . . . They close the wheels and . . . and tie the horns of the young bulls to the rings and . . . by the rings. Afterwards they shall slaughter them and collect [the blood] in bowls and toss it around the altar base. They shall open the wheels and strip the skin of the young bulls from their flesh and cut them up into pieces, salt the pieces, wash the entrails and the legs, salt them and send them up in smoke on the fire which is on the altar, each young bull with its pieces beside it and the corresponding grain-offering of fine flour on it, the wine of the drink-offering beside it and some of it on it. The priests, the sons of Aaron, shall send everything up in smoke on the altar, an offering by fire, of soothing odour before YHWH. You shall make chains hanging from the rafters of the twelve columns **XXXV** . . . whoever is not a priest shall die, and whoever . . . [a prie]st who shall come . . . and he is not clothed in the [holy] vest[ments in which] he was ordained, they too shall be put to death and shall not pro[fane the san]ctuary of their God, thus incurring the iniquity of mortal guilt. You shall sanctify the environs of the altar, the Temple, the laver and the colonnade and they shall be most holy for ever and ever.

You shall make a place west of the Temple, a colonnade of pillars standing around for the sin-offerings and the guilt-offerings, divided from one another, the sin-offerings of the priests, the he-goats, and the sin-offerings of the people and their guilt-offerings. None of these shall be mingled one with another, for their places shall be divided from one another in order that the priests may not err concerning all the sin-offerings of the people, and all the rams (?) of the guilt-offerings, (thus) incurring sin of guilt.

The birds for the altar: he shall prepare turtle doves   **XXXVI** . . . from the corner of . . . [to the corne]r of the gat[e, one hundred and twenty cubits.] The gate (shall be) forty [cubits] wide. Each side shall be [according to this measurement. The wid]th of [its wa]ll shall be seven cubits, [and] its [height forty]-five [cubits to the raft]ers of [its] roof. The width of its ch[ambers] (shall be) twenty-six cubits from corner to corner. The gates of entrance and exit: the gate shall be fourteen cubits wide and [tw]enty-eight cubits high from the threshold to the lintel. The height of the rafters above the lintel shall be fourteen cubits. (The gate shall be) roofed with a panelling of cedar wood overlaid with pure gold. Its doors shall be overlaid with fine gold.

From the corner of the gate to the second angle of the courtyard, (there shall be) one hundred and twenty cubits. Thus shall be the measurement of all these gates of the inner courtyard. The gates shall lead inside into the courtyard.   **XXXVII**   You shall make [in]side the court[yard] seats for the priests, and tables in front of the seats, in the inner colonnade by the outer wall of the courtyard, places made for the priests and their sacrifices, for the firstfruits and the tithes, for their peace-offering sacrifices which they shall sacrifice. The sacrifices of the peace-offerings of the children of Israel shall not be mingled with the sacrifices of the priests.

In the four corners of the courtyard you shall make for them a place for cooking-stoves where they shall seethe their sacrifices [and] sin-offerings.   **XXXVIII**   . . . There they shall eat . . . the bird, the turtle dove and the young pigeons . . .

You shall make a second [co]urtyard aro[u]nd [the in]ner [courtyard], one hundred cubits wide, and four hundred and eighty cubits long on the east side, and thus shall be the width and length of all its sides: to the south, to the west and to the north. Its wall shall be [fo]ur cubits wide and twenty-eight cubits high. Chambers shall be made in the wall outside and between each   chamber   there   shall   be   three-[and-a-half cubits]   **XXXIX**   . . . that all the congregation of the children of Israel may bow down before me . . . No woman shall come there, nor a child until the day that he has fulfilled the rule . . . [and has paid for] himself [a ransom] to Y H W H, half a shekel, an eternal rule, a memorial wherever they dwell. The shekel (consists of) twenty gerahs.

When they shall collect from him the half-shekel . . . to me. Afterwards they shall enter from the age of twenty . . . The na[mes of the g]ates of this [co]urtyard sha[ll b]e according to the nam[es of] the children of Is[ra]el: Simeon, Levi and Judah in the east; Reuben, Joseph and Benjamin in the south; Issachar, Zebulun and Gad in the west; Dan, Naphtali and Asher in the north. Between each gate the measurement (shall be): from the north-eastern corner to the gate of Simeon, ninety-nine cubits, and the gate twenty-eight cubits. From this gate of Simeon to the gate of Levi, ninety-nine cubits, and the gate, twenty-eight cubits. From the gate of Levi to the gate of Judah **XL** . . . You shall make a third courtyard . . . to their daughters and to the strangers who [were] born . . . [wi]de around the middle courtyard . . . in length about one thousand six [hundred] cubits from one corner to the next. Each side shall be according to this measurement: on the east, the south, the west and the no[rt]h. The wall shall be seven cubits wide and forty-nine cubits high. Chambers shall be made between its gates along the foundation as far up as its 'crowns' (= crenellations: Yadin). There shall be three gates in the east, three in the south, three in the west and three in the north. The gates shall be fifty cubits wide and their height seventy cubits. Between one gate and another there shall be three hundred and sixty cubits. From the corner to the gate of Simeon, three hundred and sixty cubits. From the gate of Simeon to the gate of Levi, likewise. From the gate of Levi to the gate of Judah, likewise three [hundred and] sixty (cubits). **XLI** . . . From the gate of Issachar [to the gate of Zebulun, three] hundred [and sixty] cubits. From the gate of Zebulun to the gate of Gad, three hundred and sixty cubits. From the ga[te of] Gad to the northern corner, three hundred and sixty cubits. From this corner to the gate of Dan: three hundred and sixty cubits. Thus from the gate of Dan to the gate of Naphtali, three hundred and sixty cubits. From the gate of Naphtali to the gate of Asher, three hundred and sixty cubits. From the gate of Asher to the eastern corner, three hundred and sixty cubits. The gates shall jut outwards from the wall of the courtyard seven cubits, and extend inwards from the wall to the courtyard thirty-six cubits. The entrance of the gate shall be fourteen cubits wide and twenty-eight cubits high up to the lintel. The rafters at the door-ways (?) shall be of cedar wood and overlaid with gold. The doors shall be overlaid with pure gold. Between each gate inwards you shall make store-houses, **XLII**   [rooms and colonnades.]

The room shall be ten cubits wide, twenty cubits long, and four[teen] cubits high . . . with cedar wood. The wall shall be two cubits wide. On the outside there shall be storehouses. [The storehouse shall be ten cubits wide and] twenty cubits [long]. The wall shall be two cubits wide [and fourteen cubits high] up to the lintel. Its entrance shall be three cubits wide. [You shall make in this way] all the storehouses and the [corresponding] rooms. The colon[nade] . . . shall be ten cubits [wi]de. Between each gate [you shall make eight]een storehouses and the corresponding eight[een] rooms . . .

You shall make a staircase next to the walls of the gates towards the colonnade. Winding stairs shall go up to the second and third colonnades and to the roof. You shall build storehouses and corresponding rooms and colonnades as on the ground floor. The second and the third (levels) shall follow the measurement of the lower one. On the roof of the third you shall make pillars roofed with rafters from one pillar to the next (providing) a place for tabernacles. The (pillars) shall be eight cubits high and the tabernacles shall be made on their (roof) each year at the feast of the Tabernacles for the elders of the congregation, for the princes, the heads of the fathers' houses of the children of Israel, the captains of the thousands, the captains of the hundreds, who will ascend and dwell there until the sacrificing of the holocaust of the festival which is the feast of the Tabernacles, each year. Between each gate there shall be   **XLIII**   . . . on the days of the firstfruits of the corn, of the w[ine (*tirosh*) and the oil, and at the festival of the offering of] wood. On these days (the tithe) shall be eaten. They shall not put aside anything from it from one year to another. For they shall eat it in this manner. From the feast of the Firstfruits of the corn of wheat they shall eat the corn until the next year, until the feast of the Firstfruits, and (they shall drink) the wine from the day of the festival of Wine until the next year, until the day of the festival of the Wine, and (they shall eat) the oil from its festival, until the next year, until the festival, the day of offering the new oil on the altar. Whatever is left (to last beyond) their festivals shall be sanctified by being burnt with fire. It shall no longer be eaten for it is holy. Those who live within a distance of three days' walk from the sanctuary shall bring whatever they can bring. If they cannot carry it, they shall sell it for money and buy with it corn, wine, oil, cattle and sheep, and shall eat them on the days of the festivals. On working days they shall not eat from this in their weariness for it is holy. On the holy days it shall be eaten, but it shall not be eaten on working days. **XLIV** . . .

You shall allot [the rooms and the corresponding chambers. From the gate of Simeo]n to the gate of Judah shall be for the priests . . . All that is to the right and to the left of the gate of Levi, you shall allo[t] to Aaron, your brother, one hundred and eight rooms and corresponding chambers and two tabernacles which are on the roof. (You shall allot) to the sons of Judah (the area) from the gate of Judah to the corner: fifty-four rooms and corresponding chambers and the tabernacle that is over them. (You shall allot) to the sons of Simeon (the area) from the gate of Simeon to the second corner: their rooms, the corresponding chambers and tabernacles. (You shall allot) to the sons of Reuben (the area) from the corner which is beside the sons of Judah to the gate of Reuben: fifty-two rooms and the corresponding chambers and tabernacles. (The area) from the gate of Reuben to the gate of Joseph (you shall allot) to the sons of Joseph, to Ephraim and Manasseh. (The area) from the gate of Joseph to the gate of Benjamin (you shall allot) to the sons of Kohath from the Levites. (The area) from the gate of Benjamin to the western corner (you shall allot) to the sons of Benjamin. (The area) from this corner to the gate of Issachar (you shall allot) to the sons of Issachar. (The area) from the gate (of Issachar) **XLV** . . . the second (= incoming) [priestly course] shall enter on the left . . . and the first (= outgoing) shall leave on the right. They shall not mingle with one another nor their vessels. [Each] priestly course shall come to its place and they shall stay there. One shall arrive and the other leave on the eighth day. They shall clean the rooms, one after the other, when the first (priestly course) leaves. There shall be no mingling there.

No man who has had a nocturnal emission shall enter the sanctuary at all until three days have elapsed. He shall wash his garments and bathe on the first day and on the third day he shall wash his garments and bathe, and after sunset he shall enter the sanctuary. They shall not enter my sanctuary in their impure uncleanness and render it unclean. No man who has had sexual intercourse with his wife shall enter anywhere into the city of the sanctuary where I cause my name to abide, for three days. No blind man shall enter it in all his days and shall not profane the city where I abide, for I, YHWH, abide amongst the children of Israel for ever and ever.

Whoever is to purify himself of his flux shall count seven days for his purification. He shall wash his garments on the seventh day and bathe his whole body in running water. Afterwards he shall enter the city of the sanctuary. No one unclean through contact with a corpse shall enter there until he has purified himself. No leper nor any man smitten (in his body) shall enter there until he has purified himself and has offered . . .   **XLVI**   . . . [No] unclean bird shall fly over [my] sanctua[ry] . . . the roofs of the gates . . . the outer courtyard . . . be in my sanctuary for ever and ever all the time that I [abide] among them.

You shall make a terrace roundabout, outside the outer court- yard, fourteen cubits wide like the entrances of all the gates. You shall make twelve steps (leading) to it by which the children of Israel shall ascend there to enter my sanctuary.

You shall make a one-hundred-cubits-wide ditch around the sanctuary which shall divide the holy sanctuary from the city so that no one can rush into my sanctuary and defile it. They shall sanctify my sanctuary and hold it in awe because I abide among them.

You shall make for them latrines outside the city where they shall go out, north-west of the city. These shall be roofed houses with holes in them into which the filth shall go down. It shall be far enough not to be visible from the city, (at) three thousand cubits.

You shall make three areas to the east of the city, divided from one another, where the lepers, those suffering from a flux and men who have had a (nocturnal) emission   **XLVII**   . . . Their cities [shall be] pure . . . for ever. The city which I will sanctify, causing my name and [my] sanctuar[y] to abide [in it], shall be holy and pure of all impurity with which they can become impure. Whatever is in it shall be pure. Whatever enters it shall be pure: wine, oil, all food and all moistened (food) shall be clean. No skin of clean animals slaughtered in their cities shall be brought there (to the city of the sanctuary). But in their cities they may use them for any work they need. But they shall not bring them to the city of my sanctuary, for the purity of the skin corre- sponds to that of the flesh. You shall not profane the city where I cause my name and my sanctuary to abide. For it is in the skins (of animals) slaughtered in the sanctuary that they shall bring their wine and oil and all their food to the city of my sanctuary. They shall not pollute my sanctuary with the skins of animals slaughtered in their country which are tainted (= unfit for the Temple). You cannot render any city among your cities as pure as my city, for the purity of the skin of the animal corresponds to the purity of its flesh. If you slaughter it in my sanctuary, it shall be pure for my sanctuary, but if you slaughter it in your cities, it shall be pure (only) for your cities. Whatever is pure for the sanctuary, shall be brought in skins (fit) for the sanctuary, and you shall not profane my sanctuary and my city where I abide with tainted skins.

XLVIII ... [the cormorant, the stork, every ki]nd of [heron,] the hoop[oe and the bat] ...

You may eat [the following] flying [insects]: every kind of great locust, every kind of long-headed locust, every kind of green locust, and every kind of desert locust. These are among the flying insects which you may eat: those which walk on four legs and have legs jointed above their feet to leap with them on the ground and wings to fly with them. You shall not eat the carcass of any bird or beast but may sell it to a foreigner. You shall not eat any abominable thing, for you are a holy people to YHWH, your God.

You are the sons of YHWH, your God. You shall not gash yourselves or shave your forelocks in mourning for the dead, nor shall you tattoo yourselves, for you are a holy people to YHWH, your God. You shall not profane your land.

You shall not do as the nations do; they bury their dead everywhere, they bury them even in their houses. Rather you shall set apart areas in the midst of your land where you shall bury your dead. Between four cities you shall designate an area for burial. In every city you shall set aside areas for those stricken with leprosy, with plague and with scab, who shall not enter your cities and profane them, and also for those who suffer from a flux; and for menstruating women, and women after child birth, so that they may not cause defilement in their midst by their impure uncleanness. The leper suffering from chronic leprosy or scab, who has been pronounced unclean by the priest **XLIX** ... with cedar wood, hyssop and ... your cities with the plague of leprosy and they shall be unclean.

If a man dies in your cities, the house in which the dead man has died shall be unclean for seven days. Whatever is in the house and whoever enters the house shall be unclean for seven days. Any food on which water has been poured shall be unclean, anything moistened shall be unclean. Earthenware vessels shall be unclean and whatever they contain shall be unclean to every clean man. The open (vessels) shall be unclean to every Israelite (with) whatever is moistened in them.

On the day when the body is removed from there, they shall cleanse the house of all pollution of oil, wine and water moisture. They shall rub its (the house's) floor, walls and doors and shall wash with water the bolts, doorposts, thresholds and lintels. On the day when the body is removed from there, they shall purify the house and all its utensils, hand-mills and mortars, all utensils of wood, iron and bronze and all utensils capable of purification. Clothes, sacks and skins shall be washed. As for the people, whoever has been in the house or has entered the house shall bathe in water and shall wash his clothes on the first day. On the third day they shall sprinkle purifying water on them and shall bathe. They shall wash their garments and all the utensils in the house.

On the seventh day they shall sprinkle (them) a second time. They shall bathe, wash their clothes and utensils and shall be clean by the evening of (the impurity contracted) from the dead so as to (be fit to) touch their pure things. As for a man who has not been rendered unclean on account of L . . . they have been unclean. No longer . . . until they have sprinkled (them) the second [time] on the seventh day and shall be clean by the evening at sunset.

Whoever touches the bone of a dead person in the fields, or one slain by the sword, or a dead body or the blood of a dead person, or a tomb, he shall purify himself according to the rule of this statute. But if he does not purify himself according to the statute of this law, he is unclean, his uncleanness being still in him. Whoever touches him must wash his clothes, bathe and shall be clean by the evening.

If a woman is with child and it dies in her womb, as long as it is dead in her, she shall be unclean like a tomb. Any house that she enters shall be unclean with all its utensils for seven days. Whoever touches it shall be unclean till the evening. If anyone enters the house with her, he shall be unclean for seven days. He shall wash his clothes and bathe in water on the first (day). On the third day he shall sprinkle and wash his clothes and bathe. On the seventh day he shall sprinkle a second time and wash his clothes and bathe. At sunset he shall be clean.

As for all the utensils, clothes, skins and all the materials made of goat's hair, you shall deal with them according to the statute of this law. All earthenware vessels shall be broken for they are unclean and can no more be purified ever.

All creatures that teem on the ground you shall proclaim unclean: the weasel, the mouse, every kind of lizard, the wall gecko, the sand gecko, the great lizard and the chameleon. Whoever touches them dead **LI** . . . [and whatever com]es out of the[m] . . . [shall be] unclean [to you.] You shall [not] render yourselves unclean by th[em. Whoever touches them] dead shall be unclean un[til the] evening. He shall wash his clothes and bathe [in water and at] sun[set] he shall be clean. Whoever carries any of their bones, their carcass, skin, flesh or claw shall wash his clothes and bathe in water. After sunset he shall be clean. You shall forewarn the children of Israel about all the impurities.

They shall not render themselves unclean by those of which I tell you on this mountain and they shall not be unclean.

For I, YHWH, abide among the children of Israel. You shall sanctify them and they shall be holy. They shall not render themselves abominable by anything that I have separated for them as unclean and they shall be holy.

You shall establish judges and officers in all your towns and they shall judge the people with just judgement. They shall not be partial in (their) judgement. They shall not accept bribes, nor shall they twist judgement, for the bribe twists judgement, overturns the works of justice, blinds the eyes of the wise, produces great guilt, and profanes the house by the iniquity of sin. Justice and justice alone shall you pursue that you may live and come to inherit the land that I give you to inherit for all days. The man who accepts bribes and twists just judgement shall be put to death. You shall not fear to execute him.

You shall not do in your land as the nations do. Everywhere they sacrifice, plant sacred trees, erect sacred pillars and set up carved stones to bow down before them and build for them **LII** . . . You shall not plant [any tree as a sacred tree beside my altar to be made by you.] You shall not erect a sacred pillar [that is hateful to me.] You shall not make anywhere in your land a carved stone to bow down before it. You shall not sacrifice to me any cattle or sheep with a grave blemish, for they are abominable to me. You shall not sacrifice to me any cattle or sheep or goat that is pregnant, for this would be an abomination to me. You shall not slaughter a cow or a ewe and its young on the same day, neither shall you kill a mother with her young.

Of all the firstlings born to your cattle or sheep, you shall sanctify for me the male animals. You shall not use the firstling of your cattle for work, nor shall you shear the firstling of your small cattle. You shall eat it before me every year in the place that I shall choose. Should it be blemished, being lame or blind or (afflicted with) any grave blemish, you shall not sacrifice it to me. It is within your towns that you shall eat it. The unclean and the clean among you together (may eat it) like a gazelle or a deer. It is the blood alone that you shall not eat. You shall spill it on the ground like water and cover it with dust. You shall not muzzle an ox while it is threshing. You shall not plough with an ox and an ass (harnessed) together. You shall not slaughter clean cattle or sheep or goat in any of your towns, within a distance of three days' journey from my sanctuary. It is rather in my sanctuary that you shall slaughter it, making of it a holocaust or peace-offering. You shall eat and rejoice before me in the place on which I choose to set my name. Every clean animal with a blemish, you shall eat it within your towns, away from my sanctuary at a distance of thirty stadia. You shall not slaughter it close to my sanctuary for its flesh is tainted. You shall not eat in my city, which I sanctify by placing my name in it, the flesh of cattle, sheep or goat which has not entered my sanctuary. They shall sacrifice it there, toss its blood to the base of the altar of holocaust and shall burn its fat. **LIII** [When I extend your frontiers as I have told you, and if the place where I have chosen to set my name is too distan]t, and you say, 'I will eat meat', because you [l]ong for it, [whatever you desire,] you may eat, [and you may slau]gh[ter] any of your small cattle or cattle which I give you according to my blessing. You may eat it within your towns, the clean and the unclean together, like gazelle or deer (meat). But you shall firmly abstain from eating the blood. You shall spill it on the ground like water and cover it with dust. For the blood is the life and you shall not eat the life with the flesh so that it may be well with you and with your sons after you for ever. You shall do that which is correct and good before me, for I am YHWH, your God.

But all your devoted gifts and votive donations you shall bring when you come to the place where I cause my name to abide, and you shall sacrifice (them) there before me as you have devoted and vowed them with your mouth. When you make a vow, you shall not tarry in fulfilling it, for surely I will require it of you and you shall become guilty of a sin. You shall keep the word uttered by your lips, for your mouth has vowed freely to perform your vow.

When a man makes a vow to me or swears an oath to take upon himself a binding obligation, he must not break his word. Whatever has been uttered by his mouth, he shall do it.

When a woman makes a vow to me, or takes upon herself a binding obligation by means of an oath in her father's house, in her youth, if her father hears of her vow or the binding obligation which she has taken upon herself and remains silent, all her vows shall stand, and her binding obligation which she has taken upon herself shall stand. If, however, her father definitely forbids her on the day that he hears of it, none of her vows or binding obligations which she has taken upon herself shall stand, and I will absolve her because (her father) has forbidden her   **LIV**   [when he] h[eard of them. But if he annuls them after] the da[y that he has] hea[rd of them, he shall bear] her guilt: [her] fa[ther has annulled them. Any vow] or binding oath (made by a woman) [to mortify herself,] her husband may confi[rm it] or annul it on the day that he hears of it, and I will absolve her.

But any vow of a widow or a divorced woman, whatever she has taken upon herself shall stand in conformity with all that her mouth has uttered.

Everything that I command you today, see to it that it is kept. You shall not add to it, nor detract from it.

If a prophet or a dreamer appears among you and presents you with a sign or a portent, even if the sign or the portent comes true, when he says, 'Let us go and worship other gods whom you have not known!', do not listen to the words of that prophet or that dreamer, for I test you to discover whether you love YHWH, the God of your fathers, with all your heart and soul. It is YHWH, your God, that you must follow and serve, and it is him that you must fear and his voice that you must obey, and you must hold fast to him. That prophet or dreamer shall be put to death for he has preached rebellion against YHWH, your God, who brought you out of the land of Egypt and redeemed you from the house of bondage, to lead you astray from the path that I have commanded you to follow. You shall rid yourself of this evil.

If your brother, the son of your father or the son of your mother, or your son, or your daughter, or the wife of your bosom, or your friend who is like your own self, (seeks to) entice you secretly, saying, 'Let us go and worship other gods whom you have not known', neither you, (nor your fathers) **LV** . . . [never again to do such an evil thing among you.] If in on[e of your cities in which I] give you to dw[ell] you hear this said: 'Men, [s]ons of [Beli]al have arisen in your midst and have led astray all the inhabitants of their city saying, "Let us go and worship gods whom you have not known!",' you shall inquire, search and investigate carefully. If the matter is proven true that such an abomination has been done in Israel, you shall surely put all the inhabitants of that city to the sword. You shall place it and all who are in it under the ban, and you shall put the beasts to the sword. You shall assemble all the booty in (the city) square and shall burn it with fire, the city and all the booty, as a whole-offering to YHWH, your God. It shall be a ruin for ever and shall never be rebuilt. Nothing from that which has been placed under the ban shall cleave to your hand so that I may turn from my hot anger and show you compassion. I will be compassionate to you and multiply you as I told your fathers, provided that you obey my voice, keeping all my commandments that I command you today, to do that which is correct and good before YHWH, your God.

If among you, in one of your towns that I give you, there is found a man or a woman who does that which is wrong in my eyes by transgressing my covenant, and goes and worships other gods, and bows down before them, or before the sun or the moon, or all the host of heaven, if you are told about it, and you hear about this matter, you shall search and investigate it carefully. If the matter is proven true that such an abomination has been done in Israel, you shall lead out that man or that woman and stone him (to death) with stones.

LVI . . . [You shall go to the Levitical priests o]r to the [j]u[dges then in office]; you shall seek their guidance and [they] shall pro[nounce on] the matter for which [you have sought their guidance, and they shall procl]aim the(ir) judgement to you. You shall act in conformity with the law that they proclaim to you and the saying that they declare to you from the book of the Law. They shall issue to you a proclamation in truth from the place where I choose to cause my name to abide. Be careful to do all that they teach you and act in conformity with the decision that they communicate to you. Do not stray from the law which they proclaim to you to the right or to the left. The man who does not listen but acts arrogantly without obeying the priest who is posted there to minister before me, or to the judge, that man shall die. You shall rid Israel of evil. All the people shall hear of it and shall be awe-stricken, and none shall ever again be arrogant in Israel.

When you enter the land which I give you, take possession of it, dwell in it and say, 'I will appoint a king over me as do all the nations around me!', you may surely appoint over you the king whom I will choose. It is from among your brothers that you shall appoint a king over you. You shall not appoint over you a foreigner who is not your brother. He (the king) shall definitely not acquire many horses, neither shall he lead the people back to Egypt for war to acquire many horses and much silver and gold, for I told you, 'You shall never again go back that way'. He shall not acquire many wives that they may not turn his heart away from me. He shall not acquire very much silver and gold.

When he sits on the throne of his kingdom, they shall write for him this law from the book which is before the priests. **LVII** This is the law [that they shall write for him] . . . [They shall count,] on the day that they appoint hi[m] king, the sons of Israel from the age of twenty to sixty years according to their standard (units). He shall install at their head captains of thousands, captains of hundreds, captains of fifties and captains of tens in all their cities. He shall select from among them one thousand by tribe to be with him: twelve thousand warriors who shall not leave him alone to be captured by the nations. All the selected men whom he has selected shall be men of truth, God-fearers, haters of unjust gain and mighty warriors. They shall be with him always, day and night. They shall guard him from anything sinful, and from any foreign nation in order not to be captured by them. The twelve princes of his people shall be with him, and twelve from among the priests, and from among the Levites twelve. They shall sit together with him to (proclaim) judgement and the law so that his heart shall not be lifted above them, and he shall do nothing without them concerning any affair.

He shall not marry as wife any daughter of the nations, but shall take a wife for himself from his father's house, from his father's family. He shall not take another wife in addition to her, for she alone shall be with him all the time of her life. But if she dies, he may marry another from his father's house, from his family. He shall not twist judgement; he shall take no bribe to twist a just judgement and shall not covet a field or a vineyard, any riches or house, or anything desirable in Israel. He shall (not) rob **LVIII** . . .

When the king hears of any nation or people intent on plundering whatever belongs to Israel, he shall send for the captains of thousands and the captains of hundreds posted in the cities of Israel. They shall send with him (the captain) one tenth of the people to go with him (the king) to war against their enemies, and they shall go with him. But if a large force enters the land of Israel, they shall send with him one fifth of the warriors. If a king with chariots and horses and a large force (comes), they shall send with him one third of the warriors, and the two (remaining) divisions shall guard their city and their boundaries so that no marauders invade their land. If the war presses him (the king) hard, they shall send to him half of the people, the men of the army, but the (other) half of the people shall not be severed from their cities.

If they triumph over their enemies, smash them, put them to the sword and carry away their booty, they shall give the king his tithe of this, the priests one thousandth and the Levites one hundreth from everything. They shall halve the rest between the combatants and their brothers whom they have left in their cities.

If he (the king) goes to war against his enemies, one fifth of the people shall go with him, the warriors, all the mighty men of valour. They shall avoid everything unclean, everything shameful, every iniquity and guilt. He shall not go until he has presented himself before the High Priest who shall inquire on his behalf for a decision by the Urim and Tummim. It is at his word that he shall go and at his word that he shall come, he and all the children of Israel who are with him. He shall not go following his heart's counsel until he (the High Priest) has inquired for a decision by the Urim and Tummim. He shall (then) succeed in all his ways on which he has set out according to the decision which **LIX** . . . and they shall disperse them in many lands and they shall become a h[orror], a by-word, a mockery. With a heavy yoke and in extreme want, they shall there serve gods made by human hands, of wood and stone, silver and gold. During this time their cities shall become a devastation, a laughing-stock and a wasteland, and their enemies shall devastate them. They shall sigh in the lands of their enemies and scream because of the heavy yoke. They shall cry out but I will not listen; they shall scream but I will not answer them because of their evil doings. I will hide my face from them and they shall become food, plunder and prey. None shall save them because of their wickedness, because they have broken my covenant and their soul has loathed my law until they have incurred every guilt. Afterwards they will return to me with all their heart and all their soul, in conformity with all the words of this law and I will save them from the hand of their enemies and redeem them from the hand of those who hate them, and I will bring them to the land of their fathers. I will redeem them, and increase them and exult over them. I will be their God and they shall be my people.

The king whose heart and eyes have gone astray from my commandments shall never have one to sit on the throne of his fathers, for I will cut off his posterity for ever so that it shall no more rule over Israel. But if he walk after my rules and keep my commandments and do that which is correct and good before me, no heir to the throne of the kingdom of Israel shall be cut off from among his sons for ever. I will be with him and will save him from the hand of those who hate him and from the hand of those who seek his life. I will place all his enemies before him and he shall rule over them according to his pleasure and they shall not rule over him. I will set him on an upward, not on a downward, course, to be the head and not the tail, that the days of his kingdom may be lengthened greatly for him and his sons after him.

LX . . . and all their wave-offerings. All their firstling male [bea]sts and all . . . of their beasts and all their holy gifts which they shall sanctify to me together with all their holy gifts of praise and a proportion of their offering of birds, wild animals and fish, one thousandth of their catch, and all that they shall devote, and the proportion of the booty and the plunder.

To the Levites shall belong the tithe of the corn, the wine and the oil that they have sanctified to me first; the shoulder from those who slaughter a sacrifice and a proportion of the booty, the plunder and the catch of birds, wild animals and fish, one hundredth; the tithe from the young pigeons and from the honey one fiftieth. To the priests shall belong one

hundredth of the young pigeons, for I have chosen them from
all your tribes to attend on me and minister (before me) and
bless my name, he and his sons always. If a Levite come from
any town anywhere in Israel where he sojourns to the place
where I will choose to cause my name to abide, (if he come)
with an eager soul, he may minister like his brethren the Levites
who attend on me there. He shall have the same share of food
with them, besides the inheritance from his father's family.

When you enter the land which I give you, do not learn to
practise the abominations of those nations. There shall be
found among you none who makes his son or daughter pass
through fire, nor an augur or a soothsayer, a diviner or a
sorcerer, one who casts spells or a medium, or wizards or
necromancers. For they are an abomination before me, all who
practise such things, and it is because of these abominations
that I drive them out before you. You shall be perfect towards
YHWH, your God. For these nations that   **LXI**   . . . to ut[ter
a word] in [my] n[ame which I have n]ot comman[ded him to]
utter, or wh[o speaks in the name of oth]er go[ds], that prophet
shall be put to death. If you say in your heart, 'How shall we
know the word which YHWH has not uttered?', when the
word uttered by the prophet in the name of YHWH is not
fulfilled and does not come true, that is not a word that I have
uttered. The prophet has spoken arrogantly; do not fear him.

A single witness may not come forward against a man in the
matter of any iniquity or sin which he has committed. It is on
the evidence of two witnesses or three witnesses that a case can
be established. If a malicious witness comes forward against a
man to testify against him in a case of a crime, both disputants
shall stand before me and before the priests and the Levites
and before the judges then in office, and the judges shall
inquire, and if the witness is a false witness who has testified
falsely against his brother, you shall do to him as he proposed
to do to his brother. You shall rid yourselves of evil. The rest
shall hear of it and shall be awe-stricken and never again shall
such a thing be done in your midst. You shall have no mercy
on him: life for life, eye for eye, tooth for tooth, hand for
hand, foot for foot.

When you go to war against your enemies, and you see
horses and chariots and an army greater than yours, be not
afraid of them, for I am with you who brought you out of the
land of Egypt. When you approach the battle, the priest shall

come forward to speak to the army and say to them, 'Hear, Israel, you approach . . .' . . . **LXII** [and another man shall use its fruit. If any man has betrothed a woman but has not yet married her, he shall return] home. Otherwise he may die in the war and another man may take her. [The] of[ficers shall continue] to address the army and say, 'If any man is afraid and has lost heart, he shall go and return. Otherwise he may render his kinsmen as faint-hearted as himself.'

When the judges have finished addressing the army, they shall appoint army captains at the head of the people.

When you approach a city to fight it, (first) offer it peace. If it seeks peace and opens (its gates) to you, then all the people found in it shall become your forced labourers and shall serve you. If it does not make peace with you, but is ready to fight a war against you, you shall besiege it and I will deliver it into your hands. You shall put all its males to the sword, but the women, the children, the beasts and all that is in the city, all its booty, you may take as spoil for yourselves. You may enjoy the use of the booty of your enemies which I give you. Thus shall you treat the very distant cities, those which are not among the cities of these nations. But in the cities of the peoples which I give you as an inheritance, you shall not leave alive any creature. Indeed you shall utterly exterminate the Hittites, the Amorites, the Canaanites, the Hivites, the Jebusites, the Girgashites and the Perizzites as I have commanded you, that they may not teach you to practise all the abominations that they have performed to their gods.

LXIII . . . [a heifer with which] he has not worked, which [has not drawn the yoke. The elders of] that city [shall bring down] the heifer to a ravine with an ever-flowing stream which has never been sown or cultivated, and there they shall break its neck.

The priests, the sons of Levi, shall come forward, for I have chosen them to minister before me and bless my name, and every dispute and every assault shall be decided by their word. All the elders of the city nearest to the body of the murdered man shall wash their hands over the head of the heifer whose neck has been broken in the ravine. They shall declare, 'Our hands did not shed this blood, nor did our eyes see it happen. Accept expiation for thy people Israel whom thou hast redeemed, O Y H W H, and do not permit the guilt of innocent blood to rest among thy people, Israel. Let this blood be expiated for them.' You shall rid Israel (of the guilt) of innocent blood, and you shall do that which is correct and good before YHWH, your God.

When you go to war against your enemies, and I deliver them into your hands, and you capture some of them, if you see among the captives a pretty woman and desire her, you may take her to be your wife. You shall bring her to your house, you shall shave her head, and cut her nails. You shall discard the clothes of her captivity and she shall dwell in your house, and bewail her father and mother for a full month. Afterwards you may go to her, consummate the marriage with her and she will be your wife. But she shall not touch whatever is pure for you for seven years, neither shall she eat of the sacrifice of peace-offering until seven years have elapsed. Afterwards she may eat. **LXIV** . . . [the firstfruits of his virility; he has the right of the first-born.]

If a man has a disobedient and rebellious son who refuses to listen to his father and mother, nor listens to them when they chastise him, his father and mother shall take hold of him and bring him to the elders of his city, to the gate of his place. They shall say to the elders of his town, 'This son of ours is disobedient and rebellious; he does not listen to us; he is a glutton and a drunkard.' All the men of his city shall stone him with stones and he shall die, and you shall rid yourselves of evil. All the children of Israel shall hear of it and be awe-stricken. If a man slanders his people and delivers his people to a foreign nation and does evil to his people, you shall hang him on a tree and he shall die. On the testimony of two witnesses and on the testimony of three witnesses he shall be put to death and they shall hang him on the tree. If a man is guilty of a capital crime and flees (abroad) to the nations, and curses his people, the children of Israel, you shall hang him also on the tree, and he shall die. But his body shall not stay overnight on the tree. Indeed you shall bury him on the same day. For he who is hanged on the tree is accursed of God and men. You shall not pollute the ground which I give you to inherit. If you see your kinsman's ox or sheep or donkey straying, do not neglect them; you shall indeed return them to your kinsman. If your kinsman does not live near you, and you do not know who he is, you shall bring the animal to your house and it shall be with you until he claims (it). **LXV** . . .

[Wh]en a bird's nest happens to lie before you by the roadside, on any tree or on the ground, with fledglings or eggs, and the hen is sitting on the fledglings or the eggs, you shall not take the hen with the young. You shall surely let the hen escape and take only the young so that it may be well with you and your days shall be prolonged. When you build a new house, you shall construct a parapet on the roof so that you do not bring blood-guilt on your house if anyone should fall from it.

When a man takes a wife, has sexual intercourse with her and takes a dislike to her, and brings a baseless charge against her, ruining her reputation, and says, 'I have taken this woman, approached her, and did not find the proof of virginity in her', the father or the mother of the girl shall take the girl's proof of virginity and bring it to the elders at the gate. The girl's father shall say to the elders, 'I gave my daughter to be this man's wife; he has taken a dislike to her and has brought a baseless charge against her saying, "I have not found the proof of virginity in your daughter." Here is the proof of my daughter's virginity.' They shall spread out the garment before the elders of that city. The elders of that city shall take that man and chastise him. They shall fine him one hundred pieces of silver which they shall give to the father of the girl, because he (the husband) has tried to ruin the reputation of an Israelite virgin. He shall not   **LXVI** . . . [When a virgin betrothed to a man is found by another man in the city and he lies with her, they shall bring both of them to the gate] of that city and stone them with stones and they shall be put to death: the girl because she has not shouted (for help, although she was) in the city, and the man because he has dishonoured his neighbour's wife. You shall rid yourselves of evil. If the man has found the woman in the fields in a distant place hidden from the city, and raped her, only he who has lain with her shall be put to death. To the girl they shall do nothing since she has committed no crime worthy of death. For this affair is like that of a man who attacks his neighbour and murders him. For it was in the fields that he found her and the betrothed girl shouted (for help), but none came to her rescue.

When a man seduces a virgin who is not betrothed, but is suitable to him according to the rule, and lies with her, and he is found out, he who has lain with her shall give the girl's father fifty pieces of silver and she shall be his wife. Because he has dishonoured her, he may not divorce her all his days.

A man shall not take his father's wife and shall not lift his father's skirt. A man shall not take the wife of his brother and shall not lift the skirt of his brother, the son of his father or the son of his mother, for this is unclean. A man shall not take his sister, the daughter of his father or the daughter of his mother, for this is abominable. A man shall not take his father's sister or his mother's sister, for this is immoral. A man shall not take the daughter of his brother or the daughter of his sister for this is abominable. (A man) shall not take   **LXVII**   ...

6. THE WICKED AND THE HOLY (4Q181)

❦

The first fragment of a document from cave 4 (4Q181), which its editor has left untitled, describes in a manner similar to Community Rule IV the respective destinies of the damned and the chosen. See J. M. Allegro, A. A. Anderson, *DJD* V, Oxford, 1968, pp. 79–80; cf. J. Strugnell, *Revue de Qumrân*, 1970, pp. 254–5; J. T. Milik, *Journal of Jewish Studies*, 1972, pp. 114–18.

. . . for guilt with the congregation of his people, for it has wallowed in the sin of the sons of men; (and it was appointed) for great judgements and evil diseases in the flesh according to the mighty deeds of God and in accordance with their wickedness. In conformity with their congregation of uncleanness, (they are to be separated) as a community of wickedness until (wickedness) ends.

In accordance with the mercies of God, according to His goodness and wonderful glory, He caused some of the sons of the world to draw near (Him) . . . to be counted with Him in the com[munity of the 'g]ods' as a congregation of holiness in service for eternal life and (sharing) the lot of His holy ones . . . each man according to his lot which He has cast for . . . for eternal life . . .

7. CURSES OF SATAN AND HIS LOT
(4Q286–7, 4Q280–82)

⌁

J. T. Milik published two fragments from cave 4 in 1972, containing liturgical curses. One of these, designated as 4Q286–7, and provisionally entitled 'Blessings (and Curses)', is paralleled by War Rule XIII and Community Rule II. The other (4Q280–2) depends mainly on Community Rule II, but reveals Satan's specific name, *Melkiresha'* (My king is wickedness), the counterpart of *Melkizedek* (My king is justice), chief of the Army of Light (cf. below, pp. 262–3, 300–301). See Milik, *Journal of Jewish Studies*, 1972, pp. 126–35.

Blessings and Curses (4Q286-7)

. . . council of the Community shall all say together, Amen, amen.

Afterwards [they] shall damn Satan and all his guilty lot. They shall answer and say, Cursed be [S]atan in his hostile design, and damned in his guilty dominion. Cursed be all the spirits of his [lo]t in their wicked design, and damned in their thoughts of unclean impurity. For they are the lot of darkness and their visitation is for eternal destruction. Amen, amen.

Cursed be the Wicke[d One in all . . .] of his dominions, and may all the sons of Satan be damned in all the works of their service until their annihilation [for ever, Amen, amen.]

And [they shall continue to say: Be cursed, Ang]el of Perdition and Spir[it of Dest]ruction, in all the thoughts of your g[uilty] inclination [and all your abomina]ble [plots] and [your] wicked design, [and] may you be [da]mned . . . Amen, am[en.]

[Cursed be a]ll those who practi[se] their [wicked designs] and establish [in their heart] your (evil) devices, [plotting against Go]d'[s Covenant] . . . to exchange the judgemen[ts of truth for folly.]

Melkiresha' (4Q280–82)

[May God set him apart] for evil from the midst of the Sons of Li[ght because he has turned away from following Him.

And they shall continue saying: Be cur]sed, Melkiresha', in all the thou[ghts of your guilty inclination. May] God [deliver you up] for torture at the hands of the vengeful Avengers. May God not heed [when] you call on Him. [May He raise His angry face] towards you. May there be no (greeting of) 'Peace' for you in the mouth of all those who hold fast to the Father[s. May you be cursed] with no remnant, and damned without escape.

Cursed be those who practi[se their wicked designs] and [es]tablish in their heart your (evil) devices, plotting against the Covenant of God. . ., seers of [His] truth.

[Who]ever refuses to enter [His Covenant, walking in the stubbornness of his heart] . . .

B. HYMNS, LITURGIES AND WISDOM POETRY

8. THE THANKSGIVING HYMNS (1QH)

The Hymns Scroll was published by E. L. Sukenik in 1954–5 (*The Dead Sea Scrolls of the Hebrew University*, Jerusalem). It has suffered a good deal of deterioration and the translator has difficulty, not only in making sense of the poems, but also in determining where one ends and the other begins.

I have counted twenty-five compositions similar to the biblical Psalms. They are all hymns of thanksgiving, individual prayers as opposed to those intended for communal worship, expressing a rich variety of spiritual and doctrinal detail. But the two fundamental themes running through the whole collection are those of salvation and knowledge. The sectary thanks God continually for having been saved from the 'lot' of the wicked, and for his gift of insight into the divine mysteries. He, a 'creature of clay', has been singled out by his Maker to receive favours of which he feels himself unworthy and he alludes again and again to his frailty and total dependence on God.

Whereas some of the Hymns give expression to thoughts and sentiments common to all the members of the sect, others, particularly nos. 1, 2, and 7–11, appear to refer to the experiences of a teacher abandoned by his friends and persecuted by his enemies. Several scholars tend to ascribe the authorship of these to the Teacher of Righteousness, and even consider that he may be responsible for all the Hymns. But although this hypothesis is not impossible, no sure conclusion can yet be reached.

Nor are we in a position to date any particular composition. The most we can say is that the collection as such probably attained its final shape during the last pre-Christian century.

Philo's account of the banquet celebrated by the contemplative Essenes, or Therapeutae, on the Feast of Pentecost may indicate the use to which the Hymns were put. He reports that when the President of the meeting had ended his commentary on the Scriptures, he rose and chanted a hymn, either one of his own making or an old one, and after him each of his brethren did likewise (*The Contemplative Life*, § 80). Similarly, it is probable that the psalms of this Scroll were recited by the Guardian and newly initiated members at the Feast of the Renewal of the Covenant. Hymn 21 expressly refers to the oath of the Covenant, and Hymn 22 appears to be a poetic commentary on the liturgy of the

entry into the Community. Indeed, the relative poverty of principal
themes may be due to the fact that all this poetry was intended for a
special occasion and its inspirational scope thereby limited.

I

I . . .
Thou art long-suffering in Thy judgements
   and righteous in all Thy deeds.

By Thy wisdom [all things exist from] eternity,
   and before creating them Thou knewest their works
   for ever and ever.
[Nothing] is done [without Thee]
   and nothing is known unless Thou desire it.

Thou hast created all the spirits
   [and hast established a statute] and law
   for all their works.
Thou hast spread the heavens for Thy glory
   and hast [appointed] all [their hosts]
   according to Thy will;
the mighty winds according to their laws
   before they became angels [of holiness]
   . . . and eternal spirits in their dominions;
the heavenly lights to their mysteries,
   the stars to their paths,
[the clouds] to their tasks,
   the thunderbolts and lightnings to their duty,
and the perfect treasuries (of snow and hail)
   to their purposes,
. . . to their mysteries.

Thou hast created the earth by Thy power
   and the seas and deeps [by Thy might].
Thou hast fashioned [all] their [inhabi]tants
   according to Thy wisdom,
   and hast appointed all that is in them
   according to Thy will.

[And] to the spirit of man
   which Thou hast formed in the world,
[Thou hast given dominion over the works of Thy hands]
   for everlasting days and unending generations.
. . . in their ages
Thou hast allotted to them tasks
   during all their generations,

and judgement in their appointed seasons
   according to the rule [of the two spirits.
For Thou hast established their ways]
   for ever and ever,
[and hast ordained from eternity]
   their visitation for reward and chastisements;
Thou hast allotted it to all their seed
   for eternal generations and everlasting years . . .
In the wisdom of Thy knowledge
   Thou didst establish their destiny before ever they were.
All things [exist] according to [Thy will]
   and without Thee nothing is done.

These things I know
   by the wisdom which comes from Thee,
for Thou hast unstopped my ears
   to marvellous mysteries.

And yet I, a shape of clay
   kneaded in water,
a ground of shame
   and a source of pollution,
a melting-pot of wickedness
   and an edifice of sin,
a straying and perverted spirit
   of no understanding,
   fearful of righteous judgements,
what can I say that is not foreknown,
   and what can I utter that is not foretold?
All things are graven before Thee
   on a written Reminder
   for everlasting ages,
and for the numbered cycles
   of the eternal years
   in all their seasons;
they are not hidden or absent from Thee.

What shall a man say
   concerning his sin?
And how shall he plead
   concerning his iniquities?
And how shall he reply
   to righteous judgement?
For thine, O God of knowledge,
   are all righteous deeds
   and the counsel of truth;
but to the sons of men is the work of iniquity

and deeds of deceit.

It is Thou who hast created breath for the tongue
    and Thou knowest its words;
Thou didst establish the fruit of the lips
    before ever they were.
Thou dost set words to measure
    and the flow of breath from the lips to metre.
Thou bringest forth sounds
    according to their mysteries,
and the flow of breath from the lips
    according to its reckoning,
that they may tell of Thy glory
    and recount Thy wonders
in all Thy works of truth
    and [in all Thy] righteous [judgements];
and that Thy Name be praised
    by the mouth of all men,
and that they may know Thee
    according to their understanding
    and bless Thee for ever.

By Thy mercies and by Thy great goodness,
Thou hast strengthened the spirit of man
    in the face of the scourge,
and hast purified [the erring spirit]
    of a multitude of sins,
that it may declare Thy marvels
    in the presence of all Thy creatures.
[I will declare to the assembly of the simple]
    the judgements by which I was scourged,
and to the sons of men, all Thy wonders
    by which Thou hast shown Thyself mighty [in me
    in the presence of the sons of Adam].

Hear, O you wise men, and meditate on knowledge;
    O you fearful, be steadfast!
Increase in prudence, [O all you simple];
    O just men, put away iniquity!
Hold fast [to the Covenant],
    O all you perfect of way;
[O all you afflicted with] misery,
    be patient and despise no righteous judgement!
. . .

[but the foo]lish of heart
    shall not comprehend these things.
. . .

II . . . Upon my [uncircumcised] lips
   Thou hast laid a reply.
Thou hast upheld my soul,
   strengthening my loins and restoring my power;
my foot has stood in the realm of ungodliness.
I have been a snare to those who rebel,
   but healing to those of them who repent,
prudence to the simple,
   and steadfastness to the fearful of heart.
To traitors Thou hast made of me
   a mockery and scorn,
but a counsel of truth and understanding
   to the upright of way.
I have been iniquity for the wicked,
   ill-repute on the lips of the fierce,
   the scoffers have gnashed their teeth.
I have been a byword to traitors,
   the assembly of the wicked has raged against me;
they have roared like turbulent seas
   and their towering waves have spat out mud and slime.
But to the elect of righteousness
   Thou hast made me a banner,
and a discerning interpreter of wonderful mysteries,
   to try [those who practise] truth
   and to test those who love correction.
To the interpreters of error I have been an opponent,
   [but a man of peace] to all those who see truth.
To all those who seek smooth things
   I have been a spirit of zeal;
like the sound of the roaring of many waters
   so have [all] the deceivers thundered against me;
   [all] their thoughts were devilish [schemings].

They have cast towards the Pit the life of the man
   whose mouth Thou hast confirmed,
and into whose heart
   Thou hast put teaching and understanding,
that he might open a fountain of knowledge
   to all men of insight.
They have exchanged them for lips of uncircumcision,
   and for the foreign tongue
   of a people without understanding,
   that they might come to ruin in their straying.

2

I thank Thee, O Lord,
   for Thou hast placed my soul
   in the bundle of the living,
and hast hedged me about
   against all the snares of the Pit.

Violent men have sought after my life
   because I have clung to Thy Covenant.
For they, an assembly of deceit,
   and a horde of Satan,
know not that my stand
   is maintained by Thee,
and that in Thy mercy Thou wilt save my soul
   since my steps proceed from Thee.
From Thee it is
   that they assail my life,
that Thou mayest be glorified
   by the judgement of the wicked,
and manifest Thy might through me
   in the presence of the sons of men;
for it is by Thy mercy that I stand.

And I said, Mighty men
   have pitched their camps against me,
and have encompassed me
   with all their weapons of war.
They have let fly arrows
   against which there is no cure,
and the flame of (their) javelins
   is like a consuming fire among trees.
The clamour of their shouting
   is like the bellowing of many waters,
like a storm of destruction
   devouring a multitude of men;
as their waves rear up,
   Naught and Vanity spout upward to the stars.
But although my heart melted like water,
   my soul held fast to Thy Covenant,
and the net which they spread for me
   has taken their own foot;
they have themselves fallen
   into the snares which they laid for my life.
But my foot remains upon level ground;
   apart from their assembly I will bless Thy Name.

3

I thank Thee, O Lord,
  for Thou hast [fastened] Thine eye upon me.
Thou hast saved me from the zeal
  of lying interpreters,
and from the congregation of those
  who seek smooth things.
Thou hast redeemed the soul of the poor one
  whom they planned to destroy
    by spilling his blood because he served Thee.

Because [they knew not]
  that my steps were directed by Thee,
they made me an object of shame and derision
  in the mouth of all the seekers of falsehood.
But Thou, O my God, hast succoured
  the soul of the poor and the needy
    against one stronger than he;
Thou hast redeemed my soul
  from the hand of the mighty.
Thou hast not permitted their insults to dismay me
  so that I forsook Thy service
    for fear of the wickedness of the [ungodly],
or bartered my steadfast heart for folly
. . .

4

III . . .
  They caused [me] to be
    like a ship on the deeps of the [sea],
and like a fortified city
  before [the aggressor],
[and] like a woman in travail
  with her first-born child,
upon whose belly pangs have come
  and grievous pains,
filling with anguish her child-bearing crucible.

For the children have come to the throes of Death,
  and she labours in her pains who bears a man.
For amid the throes of Death
  she shall bring forth a man-child,
and amid the pains of Hell
  there shall spring from her child-bearing crucible
  a Marvellous Mighty Counsellor;

and a man shall be delivered from out of the throes.

When he is conceived
   all wombs shall quicken,
and the time of their delivery
   shall be in greivous pains;
they shall be appalled
   who are with child.
And when he is brought forth
   every pang shall come upon the child-bearing crucible.

And they, the conceivers of Vanity,
   shall be prey to terrible anguish;
the wombs of the Pit
   shall be prey to all the works of horror.
The foundations of the wall shall rock
   like a ship upon the face of the waters;
the heavens shall roar
   with a noise of roaring,
and those who dwell in the dust
   as well as those who sail the seas
   shall be appalled by the roaring of the waters.

All their wise men
   shall be like sailors on the deeps,
for all their wisdom shall be swallowed up
   in the midst of the howling seas.
As the Abysses boil
   above the fountains of the waters,
the towering waves and billows shall rage
   with the voice of their roaring;
and as they rage,
   [Hell and Abaddon] shall open
[and all] the flying arrows of the Pit
   shall send out their voice to the Abyss.

And the gates [of Hell] shall open
   [on all] the works of Vanity;
and the doors of the Pit shall close
   on the conceivers of wickedness;
and the everlasting bars shall be bolted
   on all the spirits of Naught.

5

I thank Thee, O Lord,
   for Thou hast redeemed my soul from the Pit,
and from the hell of Abaddon

Thou hast raised me up to everlasting height.

I walk on limitless level ground,
and I know there is hope for him
   whom Thou hast shaped from dust
   for the everlasting Council.
Thou hast cleansed a perverse spirit of great sin
   that it may stand with the host of the Holy Ones,
and that it may enter into community
   with the congregation of the Sons of Heaven.
Thou hast allotted to man an everlasting destiny
   amidst the spirits of knowledge,
that he may praise Thy Name in a common rejoicing
   and recount Thy marvels before all Thy works.

And yet I, a creature of clay,
   what am I?
Kneaded with water,
   what is my worth and my might?
For I have stood in the realm of wickedness
   and my lot was with the damned;
the soul of the poor one was carried away
   in the midst of great tribulation.
Miseries of torment dogged my steps
while all the snares of the Pit were opened
   and the lures of wickedness were set up
   and the nets of the damned (were spread) on the waters;
while all the arrows of the Pit
   flew out without cease,
   and striking, left no hope;
while the rope beat down in judgement
   and a destiny of wrath (fell) upon the abandoned
   and a venting of fury upon the cunning.
It was a time of the wrath of all Satan
   and the bonds of death tightened without any escape.

The torrents of Satan shall reach
   to all sides of the world.
In all their channels
   a consuming fire shall destroy
   every tree, green and barren, on their banks;
unto the end of their courses
   it shall scourge with flames of fire,
and shall consume the foundations of the earth
   and the expanse of dry land.
The bases of the mountains shall blaze
   and the roots of the rocks shall turn

to torrents of pitch;
it shall devour as far as the great Abyss.

The torrents of Satan shall break into Abaddon,
and the deeps of the Abyss shall groan
amid the roar of heaving mud.
The land shall cry out because of the calamity
fallen upon the world,
and all its deeps shall howl.
And all those upon it shall rave
and shall perish amid the great misfortune.
For God shall sound His mighty voice,
and His holy abode shall thunder
with the truth of His glory.
The heavenly hosts shall cry out
and the world's foundations
shall stagger and sway.
The war of the heavenly warriors shall scourge the earth;
and it shall not end before the appointed destruction
which shall be for ever and without compare.

6

I thank Thee, O Lord,
for Thou art as a fortified wall to me,
and as an iron bar against all destroyers
. . .

Thou hast set my feet upon rock . . .
that I may walk in the way of eternity
and in the paths which Thou hast chosen
. . .

7

IV . . .
I thank Thee, O Lord,
for Thou hast illumined my face by Thy Covenant,
. . .
I seek Thee,
and sure as the dawn
Thou appearest as [perfect Light] to me.
Teachers of lies [have smoothed] Thy people [with words],
and [false prophets] have led them astray;
they perish without understanding
for their works are in folly.
For I am despised by them

and they have no esteem for me
    that Thou mayest manifest Thy might through me.
They have banished me from my land
    like a bird from its nest;
all my friends and brethren are driven far from me
    and hold me for a broken vessel.

And they, teachers of lies and seers of falsehood,
    have schemed against me a devilish scheme,
to exchange the Law engraved on my heart by Thee
    for the smooth things (which they speak) to Thy people.
And they withhold from the thirsty the drink of Knowledge,
    and assuage their thirst with vinegar,
that they may gaze on their straying,
    on their folly concerning their feast-days,
    on their fall into their snares.

But Thou, O God,
    dost despise all Satan's designs;
it is Thy purpose that shall be done
    and the design of Thy heart
    that shall be established for ever.

As for them, they dissemble,
    they plan devilish schemes.
They seek Thee with a double heart
    and are not confirmed in Thy truth.
A root bearing poisoned and bitter fruit
    is in their designs;
they walk in stubbornness of heart
    and seek Thee among idols,
and they set before them
    the stumbling-block of their sin.
They come to inquire of Thee
    from the mouth of lying prophets deceived by error
who speak [with strange] lips to Thy people,
    and an alien tongue,
that they may cunningly turn
    all their works to folly.

For [they hearken] not [to] Thy [voice],
    nor do they give ear to Thy word;
of the vision of knowledge they say, 'It is unsure',
    and of the way of Thy heart, 'It is not (the way)'.
But Thou, O God, wilt reply to them,
chastising them in Thy might
    because of their idols
    and because of the multitude of their sins,

that they who have turned aside from Thy Covenant
  may be caught in their own designs.
Thou wilt destroy in Judgement
  all men of lies,
  and there shall be no more seers of error;
for in Thy works is no folly,
  no guile in the design of Thy heart.
But those who please Thee
  shall stand before Thee for ever;
those who walk in the way of Thy heart
  shall be established for evermore.

Clinging to Thee, I will stand.
I will rise against those who despise me
  and my hand shall be turned
  against those who deride me;
for they have no esteem for me
  [that Thou mayest] manifest Thy might through me.
Thou hast revealed Thyself to me in Thy power
  as perfect Light,
  and Thou has not covered my face with shame.
All those who are gathered in Thy Covenant
  inquire of me,
and they hearken to me who walk in the way of Thy heart,
  who array themselves for Thee
  in the Council of the holy.

Thou wilt cause their law to endure for ever
  and truth to go forward unhindered,
and Thou wilt not allow them to be led astray
  by the hand of the damned
  when they plot against them.
Thou wilt put the fear of them into Thy people
  and (wilt make of them) a hammer
  to all the peoples of the lands,
that at the Judgement they may cut off
  all those who transgress Thy word.

Through me Thou hast illumined
  the face of the Congregation
  and hast shown Thine infinite power.
For Thou hast given me knowledge
  through Thy marvellous mysteries,
and hast shown Thyself mighty within me
  in the midst of Thy marvellous Council.
Thou hast done wonders before the Congregation
  for the sake of Thy glory,

that they may make known Thy mighty deeds
   to all the living.

But what is flesh (to be worthy) of this?
What is a creature of clay
   for such great marvels to be done,
whereas he is in iniquity from the womb
   and in guilty unfaithfulness until his old age?
Righteousness, I know, is not of man,
   nor is perfection of way of the son of man:
to the Most High God belong all righteous deeds.
The way of man is not established
   except by the spirit which God created for him
   to make perfect a way for the children of men,
that all His creatures may know
   the might of His power,
and the abundance of His mercies
   towards all the sons of His grace.

As for me, shaking and trembling seize me
   and all my bones are broken;
my heart dissolves like wax before fire
   and my knees are like water
   pouring down a steep place.
For I remember my sins
   and the unfaithfulness of my fathers.
When the wicked rose against Thy Covenant
   and the damned against Thy word,
I said in my sinfulness,
   'I am forsaken by Thy Covenant.'
But calling to mind the might of Thy hand
   and the greatness of Thy compassion,
I rose and stood,
   and my spirit was established
   in face of the scourge.

I lean on Thy grace
   and on the multitude of Thy mercies,
for Thou wilt pardon iniquity,
   and through Thy righteousness
   [Thou wilt purify man] of his sin.
Not for his sake wilt Thou do it,
   [but for the sake of Thy glory].
For Thou hast created the just and the wicked
. . . **V** . . .

8

I thank Thee, O Lord,
   for Thou hast not abandoned me
   whilst I sojourned among a people [burdened with sin].

[Thou hast not] judged me
   according to my guilt,
   nor hast Thou abandoned me
   because of the designs of my inclination;
but Thou hast saved my life from the Pit.
Thou hast brought [Thy servant deliverance]
   in the midst of lions destined to the guilty,
and of lionesses which crush the bones of the mighty
   and drink the blood of the brave.

Thou hast caused me to dwell with the many fishers
   who spread a net upon the face of the waters,
   and with the hunters of the children of iniquity;
Thou hast established me there for justice.
Thou hast confirmed the counsel of truth in my heart
   and the waters of the Covenant for those who seek it.
Thou hast closed up the mouth of the young lions
   whose teeth are like a sword,
   and whose great teeth are like a pointed spear,
   like the venom of dragons.
All their design is for robbery
   and they have lain in wait;
but they have not opened their mouth against me.

For Thou, O God, hast sheltered me
   from the children of men,
and hast hidden Thy Law [within me]
   against the time when Thou shouldst reveal
   Thy salvation to me.
For Thou hast not forsaken me
   in my soul's distress,
and Thou hast heard my cry
   in the bitterness of my soul;
and when I groaned,
   Thou didst consider my sorrowful complaint.
Thou hast preserved the soul of the poor one
   in the den of lions
   which sharpened their tongue like a sword.
Thou hast closed up their teeth, O God,
   lest they rend the soul of the poor and needy.
Thou hast made their tongue go back
   like a sword to its scabbard

[lest] the soul of Thy servant [be blotted out].

Thou hast dealt wondrously with the poor one
  to manifest Thy might within me
  in the presence of the sons of men.
Thou hast placed him in the melting-pot,
  [like gold] in the fire,
and like silver refined
  in the melting-pot of the smelters,
  to be purified seven times.
The wicked and fierce have stormed against me
  with their afflictions;
  they have pounded my soul all day.
But Thou, O my God,
  hast changed the tempest to a breeze;
Thou hast delivered the soul of the poor one
  like [a bird from the net
  and like] prey from the mouth of lions.

9

I thank Thee (corrected: Blessed art Thou) O Lord,
  for Thou hast not abandoned the fatherless
  or despised the poor.
For Thy might [is boundless]
  and Thy glory beyond measure
  and wonderful Heroes minister to Thee;
yet [hast Thou done marvels] among the humble
  in the mire underfoot,
  and among those eager for righteousness,
causing all the well-loved poor
  to rise up together from the trampling.

But I have been [iniquity to] those who contend with me,
dispute and quarrelling to my friends,
wrath to the members of my Covenant
and murmuring and protest to all my companions.

[All who have ea]ten my bread
  have lifted their heel against me,
and all those joined to my Council
  have mocked me with wicked lips.
The members of my [Covenant] have rebelled
  and have murmured round about me;
they have gone as talebearers
  before the children of mischief
  concerning the mystery which Thou hast hidden in me.

And to show Thy great[ness] through me,
  and because of their guilt,
Thou hast hidden the fountain of understanding
  and the counsel of truth.

They consider but the mischief of their heart;
[with] devilish [schemings] they unsheath
  a perfidious tongue
  from which ever springs the poison of dragons.
And like (serpents) which creep in the dust,
  so do they let fly [their poisonous darts],
  viper's [venom] against which there is no charm;
and this has brought incurable pain,
  a malignant scourge
  within the body of Thy servant,
causing [his spirit] to faint
  and draining his strength
  so that he maintains no firm stand.

They have overtaken me in a narrow pass without escape
  and there is no [rest for me in my trial].
They sound my censure upon a harp
  and their murmuring and storming upon a zither.
Anguish [seizes me]
  like the pangs of a woman in travail,
  and my heart is troubled within me.
I am clothed in blackness
  and my tongue cleaves to the roof [of my mouth];
[for I fear the mischief of] their heart
  and their inclination (towards evil)
  appears as bitterness before me.
The light of my face is dimmed to darkness
  and my radiance is turned to decay.

For Thou, O God, didst widen my heart,
  but they straiten it with affliction
  and hedge me about with darkness.
I eat the bread of wailing
  and drink unceasing tears;
truly, my eyes are dimmed by grief,
  and my soul by daily bitterness.
[Groaning] and sorrow encompass me
  and ignominy covers my face.
My bread is turned into an adversary
  and my drink into an accuser;
it has entered into my bones
  causing my spirit to stagger

and my strength to fail.
According to the mysteries of sin,
  they change the works of God by their transgression.

Truly, I am bound with untearable ropes
  and with unbreakable chains.
A thick wall [fences me in],
  iron bars and gates [of bronze];
my [prison] is counted with the Abyss
  as being without [any escape]
. . .

[The torrents of Satan] have encompassed my soul
  [leaving me without deliverance]
. . .

10

VI . . .
  Thou hast unstopped my ears
    [to the correction] of those who reprove with justice
  . . .
  [Thou hast saved me] from the congregation of [vanity]
    and from the assembly of violence;
  Thou hast brought me into the Council of . . .
    [and hast purified me of] sin.
  And I know there is hope
    for those who turn from transgression
    and for those who abandon sin
  . . .
  and to walk without wickedness
    in the way of Thy heart.
  I am consoled for the roaring of the peoples,
    and for the tumult of k[ing]doms when they assemble;
  [for] in a little while, I know,
    Thou wilt raise up survivors among Thy people
    and a remnant within Thine inheritance.
  Thou wilt purify and cleanse them of their sin
    for all their deeds are in Thy truth.
  Thou wilt judge them in Thy great lovingkindness
    and in the multitude of Thy mercies
    and in the abundance of Thy pardon,
    teaching them according to Thy word;
  and Thou wilt establish them in Thy Council
    according to the uprightness of Thy truth.

  Thou wilt do these things for Thy glory

and for Thine own sake,
to [magnify] the Law and [the truth
and to enlighten] the members of Thy Council
in the midst of the sons of men,
that they may recount Thy marvels
for everlasting generations
and [meditate] unceasingly upon Thy mighty deeds.
All the nations shall acknowledge Thy truth,
and all the people Thy glory.

For Thou wilt bring Thy glorious [salvation]
to all the men of Thy Council,
to those who share a common lot
with the Angels of the Face.
And among them shall be no mediator to [invoke Thee],
and no messenger [to make] reply;
for . . .
They shall reply according to Thy glorious word
and shall be Thy princes in the company [of the Angels].

They shall send out a bud [for ever]
like a flower [of the fields],
and shall cause a shoot to grow
into the boughs of an everlasting Plant.
It shall cover the whole [earth] with its shadow
[and its crown] (shall reach) to the [clouds];
its roots (shall go down) to the Abyss
[and all the rivers of Eden shall water its branches].
. . .
A source of light
shall become an eternal ever-flowing fountain,
and in its bright flames
all the [sons of iniquity] shall be consumed;
[it shall be] a fire to devour all sinful men
in utter destruction.

They who bore the yoke of my testimony
have been led astray [by teachers of lies],
[and have rebelled] against the service of righteousness.
Whereas Thou, O my God, didst command them
to mend their ways
[by walking] in the way of [holiness]
where no man goes who is uncircumcised
or unclean or violent,
they have staggered aside from the way of Thy heart
and languish in [great] wretchedness.
A counsel of Satan is in their heart

[and in accordance with] their wicked design
    they wallow in sin.

[I am] as a sailor in a ship
    amid furious seas;
their waves and all their billows
    roar against me.
[There is no] calm in the whirlwind
    that I may restore my soul,
no path that I may straighten my way
    on the face of the waters.
The deeps resound to my groaning
    and [my soul has journeyed] to the gates of death.

But I shall be as one who enters a fortified city,
    as one who seeks refuge behind a high wall
    until deliverances (comes);
    I will [lean on] Thy truth, O my God.
For Thou wilt set the foundation on rock
    and the framework by the measuring-cord of justice;
and the tried stones [Thou wilt lay]
    by the plumb-line [of truth],
to [build] a mighty [wall] which shall not sway;
    and no man entering there shall stagger.

For no enemy shall ever invade [it
    since its doors shall be] doors of protection
    through which no man shall pass;
and its bars shall be firm
    and no man shall break them.
No rabble shall enter in with their weapons of war
    until all the [arrows] of the war of wickedness
    have come to an end.

And then at the time of Judgement
    the Sword of God shall hasten,
and all the sons of His truth shall awake
    to [overthrow] wickedness;
all the sons of iniquity shall be no more.
The Hero shall bend his bow;
the fortress shall open on to endless space
and the everlasting gates shall send out weapons of war.
They shall be mighty
    from end to end [of the earth
and there shall be no escape]
    for the guilty of heart [in their battle];
they shall be utterly trampled down
    without any [remnant.

There shall be no] hope
   in the greatness [of their might],
   no refuge for the mighty warriors;
for [the battle shall be] to the Most High God
. . .

Hoist a banner,
   O you who lie in the dust!
O bodies gnawed by worms,
   raise up an ensign for [the destruction of wickedness]!
[The sinful shall] be destroyed
   in the battles against the ungodly.

The scourging flood when it advances
   shall not invade the stronghold
. . .

VII . . . As for me, I am dumb . . .
[my arm] is torn from its shoulder
   and my foot has sunk into the mire.
My eyes are closed by the spectacle of evil,
   and my ears by the crying of blood.
My heart is dismayed by the mischievous design,
   for Satan is manifest in their (evil) inclination.
All the foundations of my edifice totter
   and my bones are pulled out of joint;
my bowels heave like a ship in a violent tempest
   and my heart is utterly distressed.
A whirlwind engulfs me
   because of the mischief of their sin.

11

I thank Thee, O Lord,
   for Thou hast upheld me by Thy strength.
Thou hast shed Thy Holy Spirit upon me
   that I may not stumble.

Thou hast strengthened me
   before the battles of wickedness,
and during all their disasters
   Thou hast not permitted that fear
   should cause me to desert Thy Covenant.
Thou hast made me like a strong tower, a high wall,
   and hast established my edifice upon rock;
eternal foundations
   serve for my ground,
and all my ramparts are a tried wall

which shall not sway.

Thou hast placed me, O my God,
   among the branches of the Council of Holiness;
Thou hast [established my mouth] in Thy Covenant,
   and my tongue is like that of Thy disciples;
   whereas the spirit of disaster is without a mouth
   and all the sons of iniquity without a reply;
   for the lying lips shall be dumb.
For Thou wilt condemn in Judgement
   all those who assail me,
distinguishing through me
   between the just and the wicked.
For Thou knowest the whole intent of a creature,
   Thou discernest every reply,
and Thou hast established my heart
   [on] Thy teaching and truth,
directing my steps into the paths of righteousness
   that I may walk before Thee
   in the land [of the living],
into paths of glory and [infinite] peace
   which shall [never] end.
For Thou knowest the inclination of Thy servant,
that I have not relied [upon the works of my hands]
   to raise up [my heart],
nor have I sought refuge
   in my own strength.
I have no fleshly refuge,
[and Thy servant has] no righteous deeds
   to deliver him from the [Pit of no] forgiveness.
But I lean on the [abundance of Thy mercies]
   and hope [for the greatness] of Thy grace,
that Thou wilt bring [salvation] to flower
   and the branch to growth,
providing refuge in (Thy) strength
   [and raising up my heart].

[For in] Thy righteousness
   Thou hast appointed me for Thy Covenant,
and I have clung to Thy truth
   and [gone forward in Thy ways].

Thou hast made me a father to the sons of grace,
   and as a foster-father to men of marvel;
they have opened their mouths like little babes . . .
   like a child playing in the lap of its nurse.
Thou hast lifted my horn above those who insult me,

    and those who attack me
    [sway like the boughs] (of a tree);
my enemies are like chaff before the wind,
    and my dominion is over the sons [of iniquity,
For] Thou hast succoured my soul, O my God,
    and hast lifted my horn on high.
And I shall shine in a seven-fold light
    in [the Council appointed by] Thee for Thy glory;
for Thou art an everlasting heavenly light to me
    and wilt establish my feet
    [upon level ground for ever].

12

I [thank Thee, O Lord],
    for Thou hast enlightened me through Thy truth.
In Thy marvellous mysteries,
and in Thy lovingkindness to a man [of vanity,
and] in the greatness of Thy mercy to a perverse heart
    Thou hast granted me knowledge.

Who is like Thee among the gods, O Lord,
    and who is according to Thy truth?
Who, when he is judged,
    shall be righteous before Thee?
For no spirit can reply to Thy rebuke
    nor can any withstand Thy wrath.

Yet Thou bringest all the sons of Thy truth
    in forgiveness before Thee,
[to cleanse] them of their faults
    through Thy great goodness,
and to establish them before Thee
    through the multitude of Thy mercies
    for ever and ever.

For Thou art an eternal God;
    all Thy ways are determined for ever [and ever]
    and there is none other beside Thee.
And what is a man of Naught and Vanity
    that he should understand Thy marvellous mighty deeds?
. . .

13

[I thank] Thee, O God,
    for Thou hast not cast my lot
    in the congregation of Vanity,

nor hast Thou placed my portion
   in the council of the cunning.

[Thou hast] led me to Thy grace and forgiveness
. . . **VIII** . . .

14

I [thank Thee, O Lord,
   for] Thou hast placed me beside a fountain of streams
      in an arid land,
and close to a spring of waters
   in a dry land,
and beside a watered garden
   [in a wilderness].

[For Thou didst set] a plantation
   of cypress, pine, and cedar for Thy glory,
trees of life beside a mysterious fountain
   hidden among the trees by the water,
and they put out a shoot
   of the everlasting Plant.
But before they did so, they took root
   and sent out their roots to the watercourse
that its stem might be open to the living waters
   and be one with the everlasting spring.

And all [the beasts] of the forest
   fed on its leafy boughs;
its stem was trodden by all who passed on the way
   and its branches by all the birds.
And all the [trees] by the water rose above it
   for they grew in their plantation;
but they sent out no root to the watercourse.

And the bud of the shoot of holiness
   for the Plant of truth
      was hidden and was not esteemed;
and being unperceived,
   its mystery was sealed.
Thou didst hedge in its fruit, [O God],
   with the mystery of mighty Heroes
   and of spirits of holiness
   and of the whirling flame of fire.
No [man shall approach] the well-spring of life
or drink the waters of holiness
   with the everlasting trees,

or bear fruit with [the Plant] of heaven,
who seeing has not discerned,
   and considering has not believed
   in the fountain of life,
who has turned [his hand against] the everlasting [bud].

And I was despised by tumultuous rivers
   for they cast up their slime upon me.

But Thou, O my God, hast put into my mouth
   as it were rain for all [those who thirst]
   and a fount of living waters which shall not fail.
When they are opened they shall not run dry;
they shall be a torrent [overflowing its banks]
   and like the [bottom]less seas.
They shall suddenly gush forth
   which were hidden in secret,
[and shall be like the waters of the Flood
   to every tree], both the green and the barren;
   to every beast and bird [they shall be an abyss.
The trees shall sink like] lead in the mighty waters,
   fire [shall burn among them]
and they shall be dried up;
but the fruitful Plant
   [by the] everlasting [spring
shall be] an Eden of glory
   [bearing] fruits [of life].

By my hand Thou hast opened for them
   a well-spring and ditches,
[that all their channels] may be laid out
   according to a certain measuring-cord,
and the planting of their trees
   according to the plumb-line of the sun,
that [their boughs may become
   a beautiful] Branch of glory.
When I lift my hand to dig its ditches
   its roots shall run deep into hardest rock
   and its stem . . . in the earth;
   in the season of heat it shall keep its strength.
But if I take away my hand
   it shall be like a thistle [in the wilderness];
its stem shall be like nettles in a salty land,
   and thistles and thorns shall grow from its ditches,
   and brambles and briars.
Its border [trees] shall be like the wild grapevine
   whose foliage withers before the heat,

and its stem shall not be open to [the spring].

[Behold, I am] carried away with the sick;
    [I am acquainted] with scourges.
I am forsaken in [my sorrow] . . .
    and without any strength.
For my sore breaks out in bitter pains
    and in incurable sickness impossible to stay;
[my heart laments] within me
    as in those who go down to Hell.
My spirit is imprisoned with the dead
    for [my life] has reached the Pit;
my soul languishes [within me]
    day and night without rest.

My wound breaks out like burning fire
    shut up in [my bones],
whose flames devour me for days on end,
    diminishing my strength for times on end
    and destroying my flesh for seasons on end.
The pains fly out [towards me]
    and my soul within me languishes even to death.
My strength has gone from my body
    and my heart runs out like water;
my flesh is dissolved like wax
    and the strength of my loins is turned to fear.

My arm is torn from its socket
    [and I can] lift my hand [no more];
My [foot] is held by fetters
    and my knees slide like water;
    I can no longer walk.
I cannot step forward lightly,
    [for my legs and arms] are bound by shackles
    which cause me to stumble.
The tongue has gone back which Thou didst make
    marvellously mighty within my mouth;
    it can no longer give voice.
[I have no word] for my disciples
    to revive the spirit of those who stumble
    and to speak words of support to the weary.
My circumcised lips are dumb.
  . . .

IX . . .
    [For] the throes of death [encompass me]
        and Hell is upon my bed;
    my couch utters a lamentation

[and my pallet] the sound of a complaint.
My eyes are like fire in the furnace
   and my tears like rivers of water;
my eyes grow dim with waiting,
   [for my salvation] is far from me
   and my life is apart from me.

But behold,
   from desolation to ruin,
   and from the pain to the sore,
   and from the travail to the throes,
my soul meditates on Thy marvellous works.
In Thy mercies Thou hast not cast me aside;
season by season, my soul shall delight
   in the abundance of mercy.
I will reply to him who slanders me
   and I will rebuke my oppressor;
I will declare his sentence unjust
   and declare Thy judgement righteous.

For I know by Thy truth,
   and I choose Thy judgement upon me:
I delight in my scourges
   for I hope for Thy lovingkindness.
Thou hast put a supplication
   in the mouth of Thy servant
and Thou hast not threatened my life
   nor rejected my peace.
Thou hast not failed my expectation,
   but hast upheld my spirit in face of the scourge.

For it is Thou who hast founded my spirit
   and Thou knowest my intent;
   in my distress Thou hast comforted me.
I delight in forgiveness,
   and am consoled for the former transgression;
for I know there is hope in Thy grace
   and expectation in Thy great power.
For no man can be just in Thy judgement
   or [righteous in] Thy trial.
Though one man be more just than another,
   one person [more] wise [than another],
one mortal more glorious
   than another creature [of clay],
   yet is there no power to compare with Thy might.
There is no [bound] to Thy glory,
   and to Thy wisdom, no measure;

[to Thy truth] there is no . . .
  and all who forsake it . . .

. . .
  and my oppressor shall [not] prevail against me.
I will be a stumbling-block to [those who swallow me up,
  and a snare to] all those who battle against me;
[I will be for my enemies a] cause of shame,
  and a cause of disgrace
  to those who murmur against me.
For Thou, O my God . . .
  Thou wilt plead my cause;
for it is according to the mystery of Thy wisdom
  that Thou hast rebuked me.

Thou wilt conceal the truth until [its] time,
  [and righteousness] until its appointed moment.
Thy rebuke shall become my joy and gladness,
  and my scourges shall turn to [eternal] healing
  and everlasting [peace].
The scorn of my enemies shall become a crown of glory,
  and my stumbling (shall change) to everlasting might.

For in Thy . . .
  and my light shall shine forth in Thy glory.
For as a light from out of the darkness,
  so wilt Thou enlighten me.
[Thou wilt bring healing to] my wound,
  and marvellous might in place of my stumbling,
  and everlasting space to my straitened soul.
For Thou art my refuge, my high mountain,
  my stout rock and my fortress;
in Thee will I shelter
  from all the [designs of ungodliness,
for Thou wilt succour me] with eternal deliverance.

For Thou hast known me from (the time of) my father,
  [and hast chosen me] from the womb.
[From the belly of] my mother
  Thou hast dealt kindly with me,
and from the breast of her who conceived me
  have Thy mercies been with me.
[Thy grace was with me] in the lap of her who reared me,
  and from my youth Thou hast illumined me
  with the wisdom of Thy judgement.

Thou hast upheld me with certain truth;
  Thou hast delighted me with Thy Holy Spirit

and [hast opened my heart] till this day.
Thy just rebuke accompanies my [faults]
   and Thy safeguarding peace delivers my soul.
The abundance of (Thy) forgiveness is with my steps
   and infinite mercy accompanies Thy judgement of me.
Until I am old Thou wilt care for me;
   for my father knew me not
   and my mother abandoned me to Thee.
For Thou art a father
   to all [the sons] of Thy truth,
and as a woman who tenderly loves her babe,
   so dost Thou rejoice in them;
and as a foster-father bearing a child in his lap
   so carest Thou for all Thy creatures.

15

[I thank Thee, O Lord]

. . .

X . . . and nothing exists except by Thy will;
none can consider [Thy deep secrets]
   or contemplate Thy [mysteries].

What then is man that is earth,
   that is shaped [from clay] and returns to the dust,
that Thou shouldst give him to understand such marvels
   and make known to him the counsel of [Thy truth]?

Clay and dust that I am,
   what can I devise unless Thou wish it,
   and what contrive unless Thou desire it?
What strength shall I have
   unless Thou keep me upright,
and how shall I understand
   unless by (the spirit) which Thou hast shaped for me?
What can I say unless Thou open my mouth
   and how can I answer unless Thou enlighten me?
Behold, Thou art Prince of gods
   and King of majesties,
Lord of all spirits,
   and Ruler of all creatures;
nothing is done without Thee,
   and nothing is known without Thy will.
Beside Thee there is nothing,
   and nothing can compare with Thee in strength;
in the presence of Thy glory there is nothing,

and Thy might is without price.

Who among Thy great and marvellous creatures
   can stand in the presence of Thy glory?
   How then can he who returns to his dust?
For Thy glory's sake alone hast Thou made all these things.

16

Blessed art Thou, O Lord,
   God of mercy [and abundant] grace,
for Thou hast made known [Thy wisdom to me
   that I should recount] Thy marvellous deeds,
   keeping silence neither by day nor [by night]!

[For I have trusted] in Thy grace.
In Thy great goodness,
   and in [the multitude of Thy mercies]
. . .
For I have leaned on Thy truth
. . .
[And unless] Thou rebuke,
   there is no stumbling;
unless Thou foreknow it,
   [there is no] scourge;
   [nothing is done without] Thy [will].

[I will cling to Thy ways]
   according to my knowledge [of Thy] truth;
contemplating Thy glory
   I will recount Thy wonderful works,
and understanding [Thy goodness
   I will lean on the] multitude of Thy mercies
   and hope for Thy forgiveness.

For Thou Thyself hast shaped [my spirit]
   and established me [according to Thy will];
and Thou hast not placed my support in gain,
   [nor does] my [heart delight in riches];
   Thou hast given me no fleshly refuge.
The might of warriors [rests] on abundant delights,
   [and on plenty of corn] and wine and oil;
   they pride themselves in possessions and wealth.
[But the righteous is like a] green [tree]
   beside streams of water,
   bringing forth leaves and multiplying its branches;
for [Thou hast chosen them

    from among the children of] men
    that they may all grow fat from the land.

Thou wilt give to the children of Thy truth
    [unending joy and] everlasting [gladness],
and according to the measure of their knowledge,
    so shall they be honoured one more than another.

And likewise for the son of man . . .
    Thou wilt increase his portion
    in the knowledge of Thy truth,
and according to the measure of his knowledge,
    so shall he be honoured . . .
[For the soul] of Thy servant has loathed [riches] and gain,
    and he has not [desired] exquisite delights.
My heart rejoices in Thy Covenant
    and Thy truth delights my soul.
I shall flower [like the lily]
    and my heart shall be open to the everlasting fountain;
    my support shall be in the might from on high.
But . . .
    and withers like a flower before [the heat].
My heart is stricken with terror,
    and my loins with trembling;
my groaning goes down to the Abyss,
    and is shut up in the chambers of Hell.
I am greatly afraid when I hear of Thy judgement
    of the mighty Heroes,
and of Thy trial of the host
    of Thy Holy Ones
. . . **XI** . . .

17

I thank Thee, my God,
    for Thou hast dealt wondrously to dust,
    and mightily towards a creature of clay!
I thank Thee, I thank Thee!

What am I, that Thou shouldst [teach] me
    the counsel of Thy truth,
and give me understanding
    of Thy marvellous works;
that Thou shouldst lay hymns of thanksgiving
    within my mouth
    and [praise] upon my tongue,
and that of my circumcised lips

(Thou shouldst make) a seat of rejoicing?

I will sing Thy mercies,
  and on Thy might I will meditate all day long.
I will bless Thy Name evermore.
I will declare Thy glory in the midst of the sons of men
  and my soul shall delight in Thy great goodness.

I know that Thy word is truth,
  and that righteousness is in Thy hand;
that all knowledge is in Thy purpose,
  and that all power is in Thy might,
  and that every glory is Thine.
In Thy wrath are all chastisements,
  but in Thy goodness is much forgiveness
  and Thy mercy is towards the sons of Thy goodwill.
For Thou hast made known to them
  the counsel of Thy truth,
and hast taught them Thy marvellous mysteries.

For the sake of Thy glory
  Thou hast purified man of sin
that he may be made holy for Thee,
  with no abominable uncleanness
  and no guilty wickedness;
that he may be one [with] the children of Thy truth
  and partake of the lot of Thy Holy Ones;
that bodies gnawed by worms may be raised from the dust
  to the counsel [of Thy truth],
and that the perverse spirit (may be lifted)
  to the understanding [which comes from Thee];
that he may stand before Thee
  with the everlasting host
  and with [Thy] spirits [of holiness],
to be renewed together with all the living
  and to rejoice together with them that know.

18

I thank Thee, my God!
I praise Thee, my Rock!
. . .

For Thou hast made known to me the counsel of Thy truth
  [and hast taught me Thy marvellous mysteries;]
. . .
  and hast revealed Thy [wonders] to me.

I have beheld [Thy deeds towards the children] of grace,
   and I know [that] righteousness is Thine,
that in Thy mercies there is [hope for me],
   but without Thy grace [destruction] without end.
But a fountain of bitter mourning opens for me,
   [and my tears fall down].
Distress is not hidden from my eyes
   when I think of the (evil) inclinations of man,
of his return [to dust,
   and of his leaning] towards sin and the sorrow of guilt.
They enter my heart and reach into my bones
   to . . .
   and to meditate in sorrowful meditation.
I will groan with the zither of lamentation
   in all grief-stricken mourning and bitter complaint
until iniquity and [wickedness] are consumed
   and the disease-bringing scourge is no more.
Then will I play on the zither of deliverance
   and the harp of joy,
[on the tabors of prayer] and the pipe of praise
   without end.

Who among all Thy creatures
   is able to recount [Thy wonders]?
May Thy Name be praised
   by the mouth of all men!
May they bless Thee for ever
   in accordance with [their understanding],
and proclaim Thee with the voice of praise
   in the company of [the Sons of Heaven]!
There shall be neither groaning nor complaint
   and wickedness [shall be destroyed for ever];
Thy truth shall be revealed in eternal glory
   and everlasting peace.

Blessed art [Thou, O my Lord],
who hast given to [Thy servant]
   the knowledge of wisdom
that he may comprehend Thy wonders,
   and recount Thy . . .
   in Thy abundant grace!
Blessed art Thou,
   O God of mercy and compassion,
for the might of Thy [power]
   and the greatness of Thy truth,
and for the multitude of Thy favours
   in all Thy works!

Rejoice the soul of Thy servant with Thy truth
   and cleanse me by Thy righteousness.
Even as I have hoped in Thy goodness,
   and waited for Thy grace,
so hast Thou freed me from my calamities
   in accordance with Thy forgiveness;
and in my distress Thou hast comforted me
   for I have leaned on Thy mercy.

Blessed art Thou, O Lord,
   for it is Thou who hast done these things!
Thou hast set [hymns of praise]
   within the mouth of Thy servant,
and hast established for me a response of the tongue.
. . .

19

XII . . .
I will praise Thy Name among them that fear Thee.
Bowing down in prayer I will beg Thy favours
   [from generation to generation]
   and from season to season without end:

when light emerges from [its dwelling-place],
and when the day reaches its appointed end
   in accordance with the laws
   of the Great Light of heaven;
when evening falls and light departs
   at the beginning of the dominion of darkness,
at the hour appointed for night,
and at its end when morning returns
   and (the shadows) retire to their dwelling-place
   before the approach of light;
always;
   at the genesis of every period
   and at the beginning of every age
   and at the end of every season,
according to the statute and signs
   appointed to every dominion
   by the certain law from the mouth of God,
by the precept which is and shall be
   for ever and ever without end.
Without it nothing is nor shall be,
   for the God of knowledge established it
   and there is no other beside Him.

I, the Master, know Thee O my God,
  by the spirit which Thou hast given to me,
and by Thy Holy Spirit I have faithfully hearkened
  to Thy marvellous counsel.
In the mystery of Thy wisdom
  Thou hast opened knowledge to me,
and in Thy mercies
  [Thou hast unlocked for me] the fountain of Thy might.
. . .

Before Thee no man is just . . .
[that he may] understand all Thy mysteries
  or give answer [to Thy rebuke.
But the children of Thy grace
  shall delight in] Thy correction
  and watch for Thy goodness,
for in Thy mercies [Thou wilt show Thyself to them]
  and they shall know Thee;
at the time of Thy glory
  they shall rejoice.
[Thou hast caused them to draw near]
  in accordance [with their knowledge],
and hast admitted them
  in accordance with their understanding,
and in their divisions they shall serve Thee
  throughout their dominion
[without ever turning aside] from Thee
  or transgressing Thy word.

Behold, [I was taken] from dust
  [and] fashioned [out of clay]
as a source of uncleanness,
  and a shameful nakedness,
a heap of dust,
  and a kneading [with water,]
. . .
  and a house of darkness,
  a creature of clay returning to dust,
returning [at the appointed time
  to dwell] in the dust whence it was taken.

How than shall dust reply [to its Maker,
  and how] understand His [works]?
How shall it stand before Him who reproves it?
. . .
  [and the Spring of] Eternity,
the Well of Glory

and the Fountain of Knowledge.
Not even [the wonderful] Heroes [can] declare all Thy glory
  or stand in face of Thy wrath,
and there is none among them
  that can answer Thy rebuke;
for Thou art just and none can oppose Thee.
How then can (man) who returns to his dust?

I hold my peace;
  what more shall I say than this?
I have spoken in accordance with my knowledge,
  out of the righteousness given to a creature of clay.
And how shall I speak unless Thou open my mouth;
  how understand unless Thou teach me?
How shall I seek Thee unless Thou uncover my heart,
  and how follow the way that is straight
  unless [Thou guide me?
How shall my foot] stay on [the path
  unless Thou] give it strength;
and how shall I rise . . .

20

XIII . . .
  All these things [Thou didst establish in Thy wisdom.
  Thou didst appoint] all Thy works
    before ever creating them:
  the host of Thy spirits
    and the Congregation [of Thy Holy Ones,
  the heavens and all] their hosts
    and the earth and all it brings forth.
  In the seas and deeps . . .
    . . . and an everlasting task;
  for Thou hast established them from before eternity.

  And the work of . . .
    and they shall recount Thy glory
    throughout all Thy dominion
  For Thou hast shown them that
    which they had not [seen
  by removing all] ancient things
    and creating new ones,
  by breaking asunder things anciently established,
    and raising up the things of eternity.
  For [Thou art from the beginning]
    and shalt endure for ages without end.

And Thou hast [appointed] all these things
   in the mysteries of Thy wisdom
   to make known Thy glory [to all].

[But what is] the spirit of flesh
   that it should understand all this,
and that it should comprehend
   the great [design of Thy wisdom]?
What is he that is born of woman
   in the midst of all Thy terrible [works]?
He is but an edifice of dust,
   and a thing kneaded with water,
whose beginning [is sinful iniquity],
   and shameful nakedness,
   [and a fount of uncleanness],
and over whom a spirit of straying rules.
If he is wicked he shall become [a sign for] ever,
   and a wonder to (every) generation,
   [and an object of horror to all] flesh.

By Thy goodness alone is man righteous,
   and with Thy many mercies [Thou strengthenest him].
Thou wilt adorn him with Thy splendour
   and wilt [cause him to reign amid] many delights
   with everlasting peace and length of days.
[For Thou hast spoken],
   and Thou wilt not take back Thy word.

And I, Thy servant
   I know by the spirit which Thou hast given to me
   [that Thy words are truth],
and that all Thy works are righteousness,
   and that Thou wilt not take back Thy word
. . . **XIV** . . .

21

[Blessed art Thou,] O Lord
   who hast given understanding
   to the heart of [Thy] servant
that he may . . .
   and resist [the works] of wickedness
   and bless [Thy Name always
and that he may choose all] that Thou lovest
   and loathe all that Thou [hatest]

. . .

[For Thou hast divided men] into good and evil
   in accordance with the spirits of their lot;
[in accordance with] their [divisions
   do they accomplish] their task.
And I know through the understanding
   which comes from Thee,
that in Thy goodwill towards [ashes
   Thou hast shed] Thy Holy Spirit [upon me]
   and thus drawn me near to understanding of Thee.
And the closer I approach,
   the more am I filled with zeal
   against all the workers of iniquity
   and the men of deceit.

For none of those who approach Thee
   rebels against Thy command,
nor do any of those who know Thee
   alter Thy words;
for Thou art just,
   and all Thine elect are truth.
Thou wilt blot out all wickedness [and sin] for ever,
   and Thy righteousness shall be revealed
   before the eyes of all Thy creatures.

I know through Thy great goodness;
and with an oath I have undertaken
   never to sin against Thee,
nor to do anything evil in Thine eyes.
And thus do I bring into community
   all the men of my Council.

I will cause each man to draw near
   in accordance with his understanding,
and according to the greatness of his portion
   so will I love him.
I will not honour an evil man,
   nor consider [the bribes of the wicked];
I will [not] barter Thy truth for riches,
   nor one of Thy precepts for bribes.
But according as [Thou drawest a man near to Thee,
   so will I love] him,
and according as Thou removest him far from Thee,
   so will I hate him;
and none of those who have turned [from] Thy [Covenant]
   will I bring into the Council [of Thy truth].

22

[I thank] Thee, O Lord,
    as befits the greatness of Thy power
    and the multitude of Thy marvels for ever and ever.

[Thou art a merciful God] and rich in [favours],
    pardoning those who repent of their sin
    and visiting the iniquity of the wicked.
[Thou delightest in] the free-will offering [of the righteous]
    but iniquity Thou hatest always.
Thou hast favoured me, Thy servant,
    with a spirit of knowledge,
[that I may choose] truth [and goodness]
    and loathe all the ways of iniquity.
And I have loved Thee freely
    and with all my heart;
[contemplating the mysteries of] Thy wisdom
    [I have sought Thee].
For this is from Thy hand
    and [nothing is done] without [Thy will].
. . . **XV** . . .

I have loved Thee freely
    and with all my heart and soul
I have purified . . .
    [that I might not] turn aside from any of Thy commands.
I have clung to the Congregation . . .
    that I might not be separated from any of Thy laws.

I know through the understanding which comes from Thee
    that righteousness is not in a hand of flesh,
    [that] man [is not master of] his way
    and that it is not in mortals to direct their step.
I know that the inclination of every spirit
    [is in Thy hand];
Thou didst establish [all] its [ways] before ever creating it,
    and how can any man change Thy words?
Thou alone didst [create] the just
    and establish him from the womb
    for the time of goodwill,
that he might hearken to Thy Covenant
    and walk in all (Thy ways),
and that [Thou mightest show Thyself great] to him
    in the multitude of Thy mercies,
and enlarge his straitened soul to eternal salvation,
    to perpetual and unfailing peace.
Thou wilt raise up his glory

from among flesh.

But the wicked Thou didst create
   for [the time] of Thy [wrath],
Thou didst vow them from the womb
   to the Day of Massacre,
   for they walk in the way which is not good.
They have despised [Thy Covenant]
   and their souls have loathed Thy [truth];
they have taken no delight in all Thy commandments
   and have chosen that which Thou hatest.

[For according to the mysteries] of Thy [wisdom],
   Thou hast ordained them for great chastisements
   before the eyes of all Thy creatures,
that [for all] eternity
   they may serve as a sign [and a wonder],
and that [all men] may know Thy glory
   and Thy tremendous power.

But what is flesh
   that it should understand [these things]?
   And how should [a creature of] dust direct his steps?
It is Thou who didst shape the spirit
   and establish its work [from the beginning];
   the way of all the living proceeds from Thee.
I know that no riches equal Thy truth,
   and [have therefore desired
   to enter the Council of] Thy holiness.
I know that Thou hast chosen them before all others
   and that they shall serve Thee for ever.
Thou wilt [take no bribe for the deeds of iniquity],
   nor ransom for the works of wickedness;
for Thou art a God of truth
   and [wilt destroy] all iniquity [for ever,
and] no [wickedness] shall exist before Thee.
. . .

XVI . . .
   Because I know all these things
      my tongue shall utter a reply.
Bowing down and [confessing all] my transgressions,
     I will seek [Thy] spirit [of knowledge];
cleaving to Thy spirit of [holiness],
     I will hold fast to the truth of Thy Covenant,
that [I may serve] Thee in truth and wholeness of heart,
     and that I may love [Thy Name].

Blessed art Thou, O Lord,
   Maker [of all things and mighty in] deeds:
   all things are Thy work!
Behold, Thou art pleased to favour [Thy servant],
   and hast graced me with Thy spirit of mercy
   and [with the radiance] of Thy glory.
Thine, Thine is righteousness,
   for it is Thou who hast done all [these things]!

I know that Thou hast marked the spirit of the just,
   and therefore I have chosen to keep my hands clean
   in accordance with [Thy] will;
the soul of Thy servant [has loathed]
   every work of iniquity.
And I know that man is not righteous
   except through Thee,
and therefore I implore Thee
   by the spirit which Thou hast given [me]
   to perfect Thy [favours] to Thy servant [for ever],
purifying me by Thy Holy Spirit,
   and drawing me near to Thee by Thy grace
   according to the abundance of Thy mercies

. . .

[Grant me] the place [of Thy lovingkindness]
   which [Thou hast] chosen for them that love Thee
   and keep [Thy commandments,
that they may stand] in Thy presence [for] ever.

. . .

Let no scourge [come] near him
   lest he stagger aside from the laws of Thy Covenant.

. . .

I [know, O Lord,
   that Thou art merciful] and compassionate,
   [long]-suffering and [rich] in grace and truth,
   pardoning transgression [and sin].
Thou repentest of [evil against them that love Thee]
   and keep [Thy] commandments,
[that] return to Thee with faith
   and wholeness of heart
. . . to serve Thee
   [and to do that which is] good in Thine eyes.
Reject not the face of Thy servant
. . .   **XVII**   . . .

23

. . .

As Thou hast said by the hand of Moses,
   Thou forgivest transgression, iniquity, and sin,
   and pardonest rebellion and unfaithfulness.

For the bases of the mountains shall melt
   and fire shall consume the deep places of Hell,
but Thou wilt deliver
   all those that are corrected by Thy judgements,
that they may serve Thee faithfully
   and that their seed may be before Thee for ever.
   Thou wilt keep Thine oath
   and wilt pardon their transgression;
   Thou wilt cast away all their sins.
Thou wilt cause them to inherit all the glory of Adam
   and abundance of days.

24

[I give Thee thanks]
   because of the spirits which Thou hast given to me!
I [will bring forth] a reply of the tongue
   to recount Thy righteous deeds,
and the forbearance . . .
   and the works of Thy mighty right hand,
   and [the pardon] of the sins of the forefathers.
[I will bow down] and implore Thy mercy
   [on my sins and wicked] deeds,
   and on the perversity of [my heart],
for I have wallowed in uncleanness,
   and have [turned aside] from the counsel [of Thy truth]
and I have not laboured . . .

[For] Thine, Thine is righteousness,
   and an everlasting blessing be upon Thy Name!
[According to] Thy righteousness,
   let [Thy servant] be redeemed
   [and] the wicked be brought to an end.

For I have understood that [it is Thou
   who dost establish] the path of whomsoever Thou choosest;
Thou dost hedge him in with [true] discernment
   that he may not sin against Thee,
and that his humility [may bear fruit]
   through Thy chastisement.

[Thou dost purify] his heart in [Thy trials].
[Preserve] Thy servant, [O God], lest he sin against Thee,
   or stagger aside from any word of Thy will.
Strengthen the [loins of Thy servant
   that he may] resist the spirits [of falsehood,
that] he may walk in all that Thou lovest,
   and despise all that Thou loathest,
   [that he may do] that which is good in Thine eyes.
[Destroy] their [dominion] in my bowels,
   for [within] Thy servant is a spirit of [flesh].

25

[I thank Thee, O Lord,
   for] Thou didst shed [Thy] Holy Spirit upon Thy Servant
. . .

XVIII   . . .
   they are confirmed in [the ears] of Thy servant for ever
   . . . [to announce] Thy marvellous tidings

   . . .

Withdraw not Thy hand . . .
   that he may be confirmed in Thy Covenant
   and stand before Thee [for ever].

[For Thou, O my God,] didst open a [fountain]
   in the mouth of Thy Servant.
Thou didst engrave by the measuring-cord
   [Thy mysteries] upon his tongue,
[that] out of his understanding
   [he might] preach to a creature,
and interpret these things
   to dust like myself.

Thou didst open [his fountain]
   that he might rebuke the creature of clay for his way,
and him who is born of woman
  for the guilt of his deeds;
that he might open [the fount of] Thy truth
   to a creature whom Thou upholdest by Thy might;
[that he might be], according to Thy truth,
   a messenger [in the season] of Thy goodness;
that to the humble he might bring
   glad tidings of Thy great mercy,
[proclaiming salvation]
   from out of the fountain [of holiness
   to the contrite] of spirit,

and everlasting joy to those who mourn.

. . .

[How] shall I look,
   unless Thou open my eyes?
Or hear,
   [unless Thou unstop my ears]?
My heart is astounded,
for to the uncircumcised ear
   a word has been disclosed,
and a heart [of stone
   has understood the right precepts].

I know it is for Thyself
   that Thou hast done these things, O God;
for what is flesh
   [that Thou shouldst act] marvellously [towards it]?
It is Thy purpose to do mightily
   and to establish all things for Thy glory.
[Thou hast created] the host of knowledge
   to declare (Thy) mighty deeds to flesh,
   and the right precepts to him that is born [of woman].
Thou hast [caused the perverse heart to enter]
   into a Covenant with Thee,
and hast uncovered the heart of dust
that it may be preserved from evil
   and saved from the snares of Judgement
   in accordance with Thy mercies.

And I, a creature [of clay
   kneaded with water,
a heap of dust]
   and a heart of stone,
for what am I reckoned to be worthy of this?
For into an ear of dust [Thou hast put a new word]
   and hast engraved on a heart of [stone] things everlasting.
Thou hast caused [the straying spirit] to return
   that it may enter into a Covenant with Thee,
and stand [before Thee for ever]
   in the everlasting abode,
illumined with perfect Light for ever,
   with [no more] darkness,
   [for un]ending [seasons of joy]
   and un[numbered] ages of peace.

. . .

9. APOCRYPHAL PSALMS (11QPs^a)

The incomplete Psalms Scroll from cave 11 (11QPs^a), published by J. A. Sanders (*DJD* IV, Oxford, 1965), contains six non-canonical poems interspersed among the canonical Psalms. One of these figures as Ps. cli in the Greek Psalter, and four further compositions have been preserved in Syriac translation.

In Ps. 151 A and B or Syriac Ps. I, the story of the election of David, the shepherd boy, as ruler of Israel, and his victory over Goliath, are poetically retold. Ps. 154 or Syr. Ps. II is a sapiential hymn, the beginning and the end of which are extant only in Syriac. Ps. 155 or Syr. Ps. III is an amalgam of an individual complaint and thanksgiving. Part of it is an alphabetic acrostic, i.e. the lines begin with consecutive letters of the Hebrew alphabet. *Plea for Deliverance* is an individual thanksgiving hymn, the beginning of which is lost. The *Zion Psalm* is another alphabetic acrostic hymn praising Jerusalem. Finally, the *Psalm of the Creation* is a further sapiential hymn.

A midrashic account of the poetic activities of David is inserted in column XXVII of 11QPs^a, crediting him with 4,050 compositions, subdivided into psalms, songs for the daily holocaust, songs for the Sabbath sacrifice, songs for festivals and songs for exorcism. The fifty-two Sabbaths and the 354 days indicate that the author envisaged the solar year of the Qumran calendar.

The figure of 4,050 should be viewed against the equally prolific literary achievement claimed for Solomon in 1 Kings v, 12 (3,000 proverbs and 1,005 songs according to the Hebrew text; 3,000 proverbs and 5,000 songs according to the Septuagint). As for Josephus, he attributes to Solomon 1,005 *books* of poems and 3,000 *books* of parables (*Antiquities* viii, 44).

Only this catalogue, written in prose, is definitely sectarian. The psalms themselves probably belong to the second century B.C. at the latest, but they may even date to the third century B.C.

Psalm 151A

XXVIII Hallelujah. Of David, son of Jesse.
  1 I was smaller than my brothers, and younger than the sons of my father.
     He made me shepherd of his flock, and a ruler over his kids.

2 My hands have made a pipe and my fingers a lyre.
I have rendered glory to the Lord; I have said so in my soul.
3 The mountains do not testify to him, and the hills do not tell
(of him).
The trees praise my words and the flocks my deeds.
4 For who can tell and speak of, and recount the works of the
Lord?
God has seen all, he has heard all, and he listens to all.
5 He sent his prophet to anoint me, Samuel to magnify me.
My brothers went out to meet him, beautiful of figure, beautiful of appearance.
6 They were tall of stature with beautiful hair, yet the Lord did
not choose them.
7 He sent and took me from behind the flock, and anointed me
with holy oil
as a prince of his people, and a ruler among the sons of his
Covenant.

Psalm 151B

The first display of David's power after God's prophet had
anointed him.
1 Then I saw the Philistine taunting [from the enemy lines] . . .

Syriac Psalm II

1 **XVIII** [Glorify God with a great voice. Proclaim his majesty
in the congregation of the many.
2 Glorify his name amid the multitude of the upright and
recount his greatness with the faithful.
3 Join] your souls to the good and to the perfect to glorify the
Most High.
4 Assemble together to make known his salvation
and be not slow in making known his strength, and his majesty
to all the simple.
5 For wisdom is given to make known the glory of the Lord
and to recount the greatness of his deeds. She is made known
to man;
7 to declare his strength to the simple, and to give insight into
his greatness to those without understanding,
8 they who are far from her gates, who have strayed from her
entrances.

9 For the Most High is the Lord of Jacob, and his majesty is over all his works.

10 And a man who glorifies the Most High is accepted by him as one bringing an offering,

11 as one offering he-goats and calves, as one causing the altar to grow fat on a multitude of burnt offerings,
as an agreeable incense by the hand of the righteous.

12 From the doors of the righteous her voice is heard, and from the congregation of the devout her song.

13 When they eat their fill, she is mentioned, and when they drink in community together.

14 Their meditation is on the Law of the Most High, and their words are for making known his strength.

15 How far from the wicked is her word, and her knowledge from the insolent.

16 Behold the eyes of the Lord have compassion on the good,

17 and his mercy is great over those who glorify him; from an evil time he saves [their] souls.

18 [Bless] the Lord who redeems the humble from the hand of the str[angers]
[and deliv]ers [the perfect from the hand of the wicked;]

19 [who lifts up a horn out of Ja]cob, and a judge [out of Israel].

20 [He shall spread his tent in Zion, and dwell for ever in Israel.]

Syriac Psalm III

1 **XXIV** Lord, I have called to Thee, hear me.

2 I have spread out my hands towards Thy holy dwelling-place.

3 Turn Thine ear and grant me my request,

4 and my plea, do not withhold from me.

5 Construct my soul and do not cast it away,

6 and do not leave it alone before the wicked.

7 May the true judge turn from me the rewards of evil.

8 Lord, do not judge me according to my sins,
for no living man is righteous before Thee.

9 Lord, cause me to understand Thy Law and teach me Thy judgements.

10 And the multitude shall hear of Thy deeds, and peoples shall honour Thy glory.

11 Remember me and forget me not, and bring me not to unbearable hardships.

12 Put away from me the sin of my youth, and may my sins not
be remembered against me.

13 Lord, cleanse me from the evil plague, and let it not return
to me.

14 Dry up its roots within me, and permit not its leaves flourish
in me.

15 Lord, Thou art glory; therefore my plea is fulfilled before
Thee.

16 To whom shall I cry and he will grant it to me? What more
can the po[wer] of the sons of men do?

17 From before Thee, O Lord, comes my trust.
I cried to the Lord and he answered me; he healed the
brokenness of my heart.

18 I was sleepy [and I] slept; I dreamt and also [I awoke].

19 [Lord, Thou didst support me when my heart was stricken,
and I called upon the Lor]d [my saviour].

20 Now I will see their shame; I have relied on Thee, and I will
not be ashamed. (Render glory for ever and ever.)

21 Redeem Israel, Thy pious one, O Lord, and the house of
Jacob, Thine elect.

Prayer for Deliverance

XIX For no worm thanks Thee, nor a maggot recounts Thy
lovingkindness.

Only the living thank Thee, all they whose feet totter, thank Thee,
when Thou makest known to them Thy lovingkindness, and
causest them to understand Thy righteousness.

For the soul of all the living is in Thy hand; Thou hast given
breath to all flesh.

Lord, do towards us according to Thy goodness, according to
the greatness of Thy mercies, and according to the greatness of
Thy righteous deeds.

The Lord listens to the voice of all who love his name and does
not permit his lovingkindness to depart from them.

Blessed be the Lord, doer of righteous deeds, who crowns his
pious ones with lovingkindness and mercies.

My soul shouts to praise Thy name, to praise with jubilation
Thy mercies;

to announce Thy faithfulness; there is no limit to Thy praises.

I belonged to death because of my sins, and my iniquities had
sold me to Sheol.

But Thou didst save me, O Lord, according to the greatness of Thy mercies, according to the greatness of Thy righteous deeds.

I, too, have loved Thy name, and have taken refuge in Thy shadow.

When I remember Thy power, my heart is strengthened and I rely on Thy mercies.

Forgive my sins, O Lord, and purify me of my iniquity.

Grant me a spirit of faithfulness and knowledge; let me not be dishonoured in ruin.

Let Satan not dominate me, nor an unclean spirit; let pain and the evil inclination not possess my bones.

For Thou, O Lord, art my praise, and I hope in Thee every day.

My brethren rejoice with me and the house of my father is astounded by Thy graciousness.

. . . forever I will rejoice in Thee.

Apostrophe to Zion

XXII I will remember you, O Zion, for a blessing;
with all my might I love you;
your memory is to be blessed forever.
Your hope is great, O Zion;
Peace and your awaited salvation will come.
Generation after generation shall dwell in you,
and generations of the pious shall be your ornament.
They who desire the day of your salvation
shall rejoice in the greatness of your glory.
They shall be suckled on the fullness of your glory,
and in your beautiful streets they shall make tinkling sounds.
You shall remember the pious deeds of your prophets,
and shall glorify yourself in the deeds of your pious ones.
Cleanse violence from your midst;
lying and iniquity, may they be cut off from you.
Your sons shall rejoice within you,
and your cherished ones shall be joined to you.
How much they have hoped in your salvation,
and how much your perfect ones have mourned for you?
Your hope, O Zion, shall not perish,
and your expectation will not be forgotten.
Is there a just man who has perished?
Is there a man who has escaped his iniquity?

Man is tried according to his way,
each is repaid according to his deeds.
Your oppressors shall be cut off from around you, O Zion,
and all who hate you shall be dispersed.
Your praise is pleasing, O Zion;
it rises up in all the world.
Many times I will remember you for a blessing;
I will bless you with all my heart.
You shall attain to eternal righteousness,
and shall receive blessings from the noble.
Take the vision which speaks of you,
and the dreams of the prophets requested for you.
Be exalted and increase O Zion;
Praise the Most High, your Redeemer!
May my soul rejoice in your glory!

Hymn to the Creator

XXVI   The Lord is great and holy; the Most Holy for generation and generation.

Majesty goes before him, and after him abundance of many waters.

Lovingkindness and truth are about his face; truth and judgement and righteousness are the pedestal of his throne.

He divides light from obscurity; he establishes the dawn by the knowledge of his heart.

When all his angels saw it, they sang, for he showed them that which they had not known.

He crowns the mountains with fruit, with good food for all the living.

Blessed be the master of the earth with his power, who establishes the world by his wisdom.

By his understanding he stretched out the heaven, and brought forth [wind] from his st[ores].

He made [lightnings for the rai]n, and raised mist from the end [of the earth].

An Account of David's Poems

XXVII   David son of Jesse was wise and brilliant like the light of the sun; (he was) a scribe, intelligent and perfect in all his ways before God and men.

YHWH gave him an intelligent and brilliant spirit, and he wrote 3,600 psalms and 364 songs to sing before the altar for the daily perpetual sacrifice, for all the days of the year; and 52 songs for the Sabbath offerings; and 30 songs for the New Moons, for Feast days and for the Day of Atonement.

In all, the songs which he uttered were 446, and 4 songs to make music on behalf of those stricken (by evil spirits).

In all, they were 4,050.

All these he uttered through prophecy which was given him from before the Most High.

10. LAMENTATIONS (4Q179, 4Q501)

◇◆◇

Several fragments of a poem inspired by the biblical Book of Lamentations have been preserved in cave 4 (4Q179). Only fragment 2 offers a text long enough for intelligible translation. See J. M. Allegro, A. A. Anderson, *DJD* v, pp. 75–7; cf. J. Strugnell, *Revue de Qumrân*, 1970, pp 250–52.

A second work (4Q501) has appeared in M. Baillet, *DJD* VII, pp. 79–80. Both texts are dated to the second half of the first century B.C.

4Q179

. . .

[How] solitary [lies] the city,

. . .

the princess of all the peoples is desolate
like a forsaken woman;
and all her [dau]ghters are forsak[en]
[like] a forsaken woman;
like a woman hurt and forsaken
by her [husband].
All her palaces and [her] wal[ls] are
like a barren woman;
and like a sheltered woman,
all [her] paths;
[all her] . . .
like a woman of bitterness,
and all her daughters are like women
mourning for [their] hus[bands];
[all her] . . . like women
deprived of their only children.
Weep, weep, Jer[usalem]

. . .

[her tears flow] upon her cheeks
because of her sons . . .

4Q501

Give not our inheritance to strangers,
  nor our (hard-earned) property to foreigners.
Remember that we are [the forsaken of Thy people
  and the forsaken of Thine inheritance.
Remember the desolate children of Thy Covenant . . .
T[hy] freely devoted . . .;
they err with no one to bring them back;
  they are broken with none to bind them;
  [they are bent down with none to ra]ise them up.
The damned of Thy people have surrounded me
  with their lying tongues.
They have been turned . . .
  and Thy boughs to the progeny of a woman.
Look and see the shame of the sons of [Thy people (?),
  for] our skin [is burning]
and feverish heat has seized us
  because of their reviling tongue.

11. THE WORDS OF THE HEAVENLY LIGHTS
(4Q504)

⤙⤚

Preserved in three fragmentary manuscripts from cave 4 (4Q504), 'The Words of the Heavenly Lights' are collective prayers full of biblical reminiscences for the days of the week. The Sabbath and the fourth day are expressly mentioned in the surviving text. The editor of the document, M. Baillet (*DJD* VII, 1982, pp. 137–75), attributes to it an exaggeratedly early date, the mid second century B.C.

I . . . Amen! Amen!

. . . **II** . . . We pray Thee, O Lord, do in accordance with Thyself, in accordance with the greatness of Thy might, Thou who didst pardon our fathers when they rebelled against Thy saying. Thou wert angry with them so as to wish to destroy them, but because of Thy love for them and for the sake of Thy Covenant – for Moses had atoned for their sin – and in order that Thy great might and the abundance of Thy mercy might be known to everlasting generations, Thou didst take pity on them. So let Thine anger and wrath against all [their] sin turn away from Thy people Israel.

Remember Thy marvels which Thou didst to the poor of the nations. For we were called by Thy Name . . . to [cause] us [to repent] with all (our) heart and soul and to plant Thy Law in our heart [that we might never depart from it, straying neither] to right nor to left. For Thou wilt heal us of foolishness and of blindness and confusion [of heart . . . Behold] we were sold because of our iniquities but despite our offences Thou didst call us . . . Thou wilt save us from sinning against Thee . . . and to make us understand the testimonies . . .

III . . . Behold, all the nations are as nothing beside Thee, they are counted as void and nought before Thee. We have called on Thy Name alone. Thou hast created us for Thy glory and made us Thy children in the sight of all the nations. For Thou hast named Israel 'My son, my first born', and hast chastised us as a man chastises his son. Thou hast brought us up throughout the years of our generations [by means of] evil diseases, famine, thirst, pestilence, and the sword . . . of Thy Covenant. Because Thou hast chosen us [from all] the earth [to be Thy people,] therefore hast Thou poured out Thine anger [and jealousy] upon us in all the fury of Thy wrath. Thou hast caused [the scourge] of Thy [plagues] to cleave to us of which Moses wrote, and Thy servants the Prophets, that Thou wouldst send evil against us in the last days . . .

IV . . . Thy dwelling-place . . . a resting-place in Jerus[alem, the city which] Thou hast [chosen] from all the earth that Thy [Name] might remain there for ever. For Thou hast loved Israel above all the peoples. Thou hast chosen the tribe of Judah and hast established Thy Covenant with David that he might be as a princely shepherd over Thy people and sit before Thee on the throne of Israel for ever. All the nations have seen Thy glory; Thou who hast sanctified Thyself in the midst of Thy people Israel. They brought their offering to Thy great Name, silver and gold and precious stones together with all the treasures of their lands, that they might glorify Thy people, and Zion Thy holy city, and the House of Thy majesty. And there was neither adversary nor misfortune, but peace and blessing . . . and they ate and were satisfied and grew fat . . .

V . . . [they forsook] the fount of living waters . . . and served a strange god in their land. Also, their land was ravaged by their enemies; for Thy fury and the heat of Thy wrath overflowed, in the fire of Thy jealousy, making of it a desert where no man could go and return. Yet notwithstanding all this, Thou didst not reject the seed of Jacob, neither didst Thou cast away Israel to destruction, breaking Thy Covenant with them. For Thou alone art a living God and there is none beside Thee. Thou didst remember Thy Covenant, Thou who didst rescue us in the presence of all the nations, and didst not forsake us amid the nations. Thou wert gracious towards Thy people Israel in all the lands to which Thou didst banish them, that they might remember to return to Thee and to hearken to Thy voice [according to] all Thou hadst commanded by the hand of Moses Thy servant.

For Thou hast shed Thy Holy Spirit upon us, bringing upon us Thy blessings, that we might seek Thee in our distress [and mur]mur (prayers) in the ordeal of Thy chastisement. We have entered into distress, have been [stri]cken and tried by the fury of the oppressor. For we also have tired God with our iniquity, we have wearied the Rock with [our] sins. [But] in order that we may profit, Thou hast not wearied us who leadest [us] in the way in [which we must walk. But] we have not heeded . . .

VI . . . [Thou hast taken away] all our transgressions and hast purified us of our sin for Thine own sake. Thine, Thine is righteousness, O Lord, for it is Thou who hast done all this! Now, on the day when our heart is humbled, we expiate our iniquity and the iniquity of our fathers, together with our unfaithfulness and rebellion. We have not rejected Thy trials and scourges; our soul has not despised them to the point of breaking Thy Covenant despite all the distress of our soul. For Thou, who hast sent our enemies against us, strengthenest our heart that we may recount Thy mighty deeds to everlasting generations. We pray Thee O Lord, since Thou workest marvels from everlasting to everlasting, to let Thine anger and wrath retreat from us. Look on [our affliction] and trouble and distress, and deliver Thy people Israel [from all] the lands, near and far, [to which Thou hast banished them], every man who is inscribed in the Book of Life . . . serve Thee and give thanks to [Thy holy Name] . . . from those who vex them . . .

VII . . . who deliverest us from all distress. Amen! [Amen!]

hymns for the sabbath day

> Give thanks . . .
> [Bless] His holy Name always
> . . . all the angels of the holy firmament
> . . . [above] the heavens,
> the earth and all its deep places,
> the great [Abyss] and Abaddon
> and the waters and all that is [in them.]
> [Let] all His creatures [bless Him] always
> for everlasting [ages. Amen! Amen!]
> . . . bless His holy Name.
> Sing to God . . .

Fr. 3

II . . . Blessed be the God who has given us rest. [Amen], amen. [Prayer on the] fourth [da]y. Remember, O Lord . . .

Fr. 4

II . . . We know these through Thy Ho[ly] Spirit which Thou hast granted us. [Have mercy on us] and remember us not for the iniquities of the men of old in all their evi[l] dealings, [nor] their stiff necks. Thou redeem us and, [pray,] forgive our iniquities and [our] s[ins].

Fr. 6

II . . . Remember, pray, that we are Thy people and that Thou hast carried us marvellously [on the wings of] eagles and hast brought us towards Thee. And like an eagle which rouses its nestlings and hovers over [its young], spreads out its wings, takes one and carries it on [its pinions], so we dwell apart and are not reckoned among the nations and . . . Thou art in our midst in the pillar of fire and the cloud [of] Thy [holi]ness walking before us, and as it were Thy glory in our mid[st] . . .

Fr. 8 recto

II . . . [Rememb]er, O Lo[r]d that . . . Thou hast fashioned A[dam], our [f]ather in the likeness of [Thy] glory; Thou didst breathe [a breath of life] into his nostrils and with understanding a knowledge [Thou didst give him] . . . Thou didst make [him] to rule [over the Gar]den of Eden which Thou didst plant . . . and to walk in the land of glory . . . he guarded. And Thou didst enjoin him not to st[ray . . .] . . . he is flesh and to dust [he will return (?)] . . . And Thou, Thou knowest . . . for everlasting generations . . . a living God and Thy hand . . . man in the ways of . . . [to fill the] earth with [vi]olence and to shed [innocent blood] . . .

12. SONGS FOR THE HOLOCAUST OF THE SABBATH
(4Q400–407, 11Q5–6)

⊷⊶

Fragments of a document concerned with heavenly worship were first published by J. Strugnell under the title, 'The Angelic Liturgy', *Congress Volume Oxford*, Supplements to Vetus Testamentum vii, Leiden, 1960, pp. 318–45. The full material, viz. eight manuscripts from cave 4 (4Q400–407), small fragments from cave 11 and a large fragment from Masada, has recently been edited by Carol Newsom (*Songs of the Sabbath Sacrifice: A Critical Edition*, Harvard Semitic Studies 27, Atlanta, 1985). The songs contain angelic praises of God assigned to the first thirteen sabbaths, i.e. the first quarter, of the solar year. They imply the simultaneity of the heavenly and earthly worship. Although often obscure, the poems depict the celestial sanctuary, the throne-chariot, the various groups participating in the angelic liturgy; they also include the words of the benedictions sung by the seven archangels.

The main source of inspiration is the book of Ezekiel, especially chapters i and x for the throne-chariot and xl–xlviii for the heavenly sanctuary.

The songs include nothing that can be dated. On the basis of the script and on general grounds the composition is said to belong to the first century B.C.

The *Merkabah*, or divine throne-chariot, was a central subject in ancient and medieval Jewish esotericism and mysticism. Hence this early post-biblical manifestation of the speculation is of considerable historical importance for the study of the so-called *Merkabah* mysticism and of the *Hekhaloth* (heavenly palaces) literature. It is noteworthy that the Mishnah prohibits the use of Ezekiel's passage on the chariot as a prophetic reading in synagogue (*Megillah* iv, 10) or even its discussion in private, unless with a sage already familiar with the subject (*Hagigah* ii, 1).

The presence of this Qumran document in the fortress of Masada is best explained by assuming either that some Essenes joined the revolutionaries and took with them some of their manuscripts, or that the rebels occupied the Qumran area after its evacuation by the Community and subsequently transferred Essene manuscripts to their final place of resistance.

4Q400

[To the Master. Song of the holocaust of the] first [Sabba]th, on the fourth of the first month.

Praise [the God of . . .] the 'gods' (= *elohim*) of supreme holiness; in [his] divine [kingship, rejoice. For he has established] supreme holiness among the everlastingly holy, to be for him the priests of [the inner Temple in his royal sanctuary], ministers of the Presence in his glorious innermost Temple chamber. In the congregation of all the gods (= *elim*) of [knowledge, and in the councils of all the spirits of] God, he engraved his precepts for all the spiritual works, and [his glorious] judgements [for all who lay the foundations of] knowledge, the people (endowed with) his glorious understanding, the 'gods' who are close to knowledge . . . of eternity and from the fountain of holiness to the sanctuary of supreme [holiness] . . . prie[sts of the inner Temple, ministers of the Presence of the [most] holy King. . . . his glory. They shall grow in strength decree by decree to be seven [eternal councils. For he fo]unded them [for] himself as the most [holy, who minister in the h]oly of holies . . . do not endure [those who per]vert the way. There is [n]othing impure in their holy gifts. He engraved for them [precepts relating to ho]ly gifts; by them, all the everlastingly holy shall sanctify themselves. He shall purify the [luminously] pure [to rewar]d all those who render their way crooked. Their expiations shall obtain his good will for all those who repent from sin. . . . knowledge among the priests of the inner Temple, and from their mouth (proceed) the teachings of the holy with the judgements of [his glory] . . . his [gra]ces for everlasting merciful forgivenesses. In his zealous vengeance . . . he has established for himself as priests of the inner Temple, the most holy . . . of gods, the priests of the highest heights who are near [to] . . .

4Q400 2

wonderfully to extol Thy glory among the divine beings of knowledge, and the praises of Thy kingship among the most holy. They are glorified amid all the camps of the 'gods' and feared by companies of men. They recount his royal majesty according to their knowledge and exalt [his glory in all] his royal heavens. In all the highest heights [they shall sing] marvellous psalms according to all [their understanding, and the glorious splendour] of the King of the 'gods' they shall recount on their stations . . . for what shall we be counted among them? For what shall our priesthood be counted in their dwellings? [How shall our] ho[liness compare with their supreme] holiness? How does the offering of our tongue of dust compare with the knowledge of the divine [beings] . . .

Masada Fragment 1, 1–7=4Q402 4, 11–15

. . . wonderful new works. all these he has done wonder[fully with all the eternally hidden things] . . . all the words of knowledge; for from the God of knowledge (comes) all that exists for ever, [and from] his [plan]s (come) all the eternally appointed. He produces the former things in their appointed times, and the latter things in their seasons. None among those who know the [wonderfully] revealed things can comprehend them before he makes them. When he makes them, none of [the doers of righteous]ness can understand his plan; for they are his glorious works. Before they come into being, (they derived) [from] his [pla]n.

[For the Master. So]ng of the holocaust of the sixth Sabbath on the ninth of the [second] month.

[Praise the G]od of gods, you inhabitants of the highest heights. . . . [h]oly of holies and exalt his glory . . . [kn]owledge of the everlasting gods . . .

4Q403 1i, 1–29=Masada Fragment

[Psalm of exaltation (uttered) by the tongue] of the third of the sovereign Princes, an exaltation . . . He shall exalt the God of the angels on high seven times with seven wonderful exaltations.

Psalm of praise (uttered) by the tongue of the four[th] to the Mighty One above all the [gods], seven wonderful mighty deeds. He shall praise the God of mighty deeds seven times with seven words of [marvellous] prais[e].

Psalm of thanksgiving (uttered) by the tongue of the fifth to the [K]in[g] of glory with its seven wonderful thanksgivings. He shall thank the God of glory se[ven times with se]v[en wor]ds of wonderful thanksgivings.

[Psalm of] exultation (uttered) by the tongue of the sixth to [the] God of goodness with its seven [wonderful] exultations. He shall exult before the Ki[ng of] goodness seven times with sev[en words of] wonderful exultation.

Psalm of [singing (uttered) by the t]ongue of the seventh of the [sovereign] Prin[ces], a powerful song [to the Go]d of ho[liness] with its se[ven] marvellous [songs]. He shall sing [to] the Kin[g of ho]liness seven times with [seven w]ords of [wonderful] so[ngs; sev]en psa[lms (singing) his blessings; sev]en [psalm]s of magnification of [his righteousness; seven psalms] of exaltation of [his] kingshi[p; seven] psalms of [praises of his glory; sev]en p[salms of thanksgivings for his marvellous deeds]; [seven psalms of ex]ul[tation of] his power; seven [psalms singin]g his holiness; . . . [seven times with seven wonderful words, words of . . .]

In the glo[ri]ous name of God, [the first of] the sov[erei]gn Princes sha[ll bless] all the . . . [with seven wonderful words blessing all] their [councils] in [his holy] sanctuary [with sev]en wonderful wo[rd]s, [and he shall bless those who kn]ow the everlasting things.

[In the name of] his truth, [the second of the sovereign Princes shall bless] all [their] sta[tions with] se[ven] wonderful word[s and he shall bless with] seven [wonderful] words. [He shall bless all those who exalt the] King with seven g[lor]iou[s] w[ords of his] marvels, [all the] eternally pure.

[In the name of] his exalted kingship, the third [of the sovereign Princes shall bless all who are lif]ted up [in kn]owledge with se[ven w]ords of exal[ta]tion . . . [of his true kn]ow[ledge], he shall bless with seven marvellous words; and he shall bless all [who are destined] for righteousness [with seven] wonderful [w]ords.

In the name of the King's majesty, [the fourth] of the [sovereign] Princes shall bless with seven [majestic] words [all who] walk [up]rightly. He shall bless all the gods [close to] true knowledge [with seve]n righteous words (for gaining) [his gl]o[rious] favours.

In the name of [the majesty] of his marvellous deeds, the fifth [sovereign] Prince shall bless with seven [words] of his exalted truth [all who] . . . purity. [He shall bless] all who eagerly do his will with seven [marvellous words. And he shall bless] all who confess him with seven majestic [wor]ds that they may thank [him for ever].

In the name of [the mighty deeds of] the gods the sixth sovereign Prince shall bless with seven words of his marvellous mighty deeds all who are mighty in wisdom. He shall bless all the perfect of way with seven marvellous words to be in attendance for [ever].

He shall bless all who wait for him with seven marvellous words that they may obtain the return of his [gracious] favours.

In the name of his holiness, the seventh of the sovereign Princes shall bless with seven words of his marvellous holiness all the holy founders of kno[wledge. He shall bless] all who exalt his statutes with sev[en] marvellous [wo]rds (which shall be for them) stout shields. He shall bless all [who are destined for] righteousness [and always] forever [pra]ise his glorious kingship with seven [marvellous words] for everlasting peace.

In [the name of his holiness] all the [sovereign] Princes [shall bless together] the God of the divine beings [in] all their sevenfold t[estimonies]. They shall bless those destined for righteousness and all the blessed . . . the eter[na]ll[y ble]ssed for them.

Blessed be [the] Lo[r]d, the Kin[g of] all, who is above all blessing and p[raise. He shall bless all the holy] who bless [him, and proclaim him righ]te[ous] in the name of his glory. [And he shall b]less all who are blessed for ever.

4Q403 *1 i, 30–46*

For the Master. Song of the holocaust of the seventh Sabbath on the sixteenth of the month.

Praise the most high God, O you high among all the gods of knowledge.

Let the holy ones of the 'gods' sanctify the King of glory, who sanctifies by his holiness all his holy ones.

Princes of the praises of all the 'gods', praise the God of majestic praises,

For in the splendour of praises is the glory of his kingship.

In it are (contained) the praises of all the 'gods' together with the splendour of all [his] king[ship].

Exalt his exaltation on high, O 'gods', above the gods on high, and his glorious divinity above all the highest heights.

For he [is the God of gods], of all the Princes on high, and the King of king[s] of all the eternal councils.

By a discerning good-will (expressed by) the words of his mouth a[ll the gods on high] come into being,

at the opening of his lips all the eternal spirits, by his discerning good-will, all his creatures in their undertakings.

Exult O you who exult [in his knowledge with] an exultation among the wonderful 'gods';

utter his glory with the tongue of all who utter knowledge;

may his wonderful exultation be in the mouth of all who utter [his knowledge].

[For he] is the God of all who exult in everlasting knowledge, and the Judge through his might of all the spirits of understanding.

Celebrate all celebrating gods the King of majesty, for all the gods of knowledge celebrate his glory,

and all the spirits of righteousness celebrate his truth, and seek acceptance of their knowledge by the judgements of his mouth,

and of their celebrations when his mighty hand executes (?) judgements of reward.

Sing to the God of power with an offering of the princely spirit, a song of divine joy,

and a jubilation among all the holy, a wonderful song for eter-[nal] rejoicing.

With these shall praise all the f[oundations of the hol]y of holies,

the pillars bearing the highest abode, and all the corners of its structure.

Sing to the Go[d who is a]wesome in strength . . .

to extol together the splendid firmament, the supreme purity of [his] holy sanctuary.

[Praise] him, divine spirits, prai[sing for ever and] ever the firmament of the highest heavens,

all . . . and its walls, a[l]l its [struc]ture, its shape.

[The spi]rits of the hol[y] of holies, the living 'gods', [the spir]its of [et]ernal holiness above all the holy [ones];

. . . marvellous marvel, majesty and beauty and marvel.

[Gl]ory is in the perfect light of knowledge . . . in all the marvellous sanctuaries.

The divine spirits surround the dwelling of the King of truth and righteousness; all its walls . . .

4Q403 1ii, 18–29

For the Master. Song of the holocaust for the eighth Sabbath on the tw[enty]-third [of the second month].

[Praise the God of all the highest heights, all the holy ones for ever] and ever,

they who are second among the priests of the inner Temple, the second council in the wonderful dwelling, with seven words of . . . eternally.

Extol him, O sovereign Princes, in his marvellous portion, praise [the God of gods, O you seven priesthoods of his inner Temple].

. . . height, the seven wonderful domains by the precept concerning his sanctuaries.

The sovereign Princes of the [wonderful] priest[hood] . . . the seven priest[hoods] in the wonderful sanctuary for seven councils of holiness . . . the Prince, the angels of the King in the wonderful dwellings. The knowledge of their understanding is for seven . . . Prince from the priest of the inner Temple. The Princes of the congregation of the King in the assembly of . . . and praises of exaltation to the King of glory and a tower of . . . for the God of gods, the King of purity. The offering of their tongues . . . the seven mysteries of knowledge in the wonderful mystery of the seven domains [of] the Ho[ly of holies] . . . [The tongue of the first shall be seven times stronger than the tongue of the second; the tongue of the second shall be] seven times [stronger] than that of the third: [the to]ngue of the thi[rd shall be] seven tim[es] stronger [than that of the fourth; the tongue of the fourth shall be seven times stronger than the tongue of the fifth: the tongue of the fifth shall be seven times stronger than the tongue of] the sixth; the tongu[e of the sixth shall be seven times stronger than the] t[ongue of the seventh; the tongue of the seventh . . .

4Q405 14–15 i

. . . tongue of blessing from the likeness [of the gods] issues a [v]oice of blessing for the King of those who exalt, and their wonderful praise is for the God of gods . . . their many-coloured . . . and they sing . . . the vestibules by which they enter, the spirits of the most holy inner Temple . . . [And the likene]ss of the living 'gods' is engraved on the vestibules by which the King enters, luminous spiritual figures . . . [K]ing, figures of a glorious l[ight, wonderful] spirits; [amo]ng the spirits of splendour there are works of (art of) marvellous colours, figures of the living 'gods' . . . [in the] glorious innermost Temple chambers, the structure of [the most ho]ly [sanctuary] in the innermost chambers of the King, design[s of 'go]ds' . . . likeness of . . . most holy . . . [the Temple] chambers of the Ki[ng] . . .

4Q405 19ABCD

The figures of the 'gods' shall praise him, [the most] h[oly] spirits . . . of glory; the floor of the marvellous innermost chambers, the spirits of the eternal gods, all . . . fi[gures of the innermost] chamber of the King, the spiritual works of the marvellous firmament are purified with salt, [spi]rits of knowledge, truth [and] righteousness in the holy of [ho]lies, [f]orms of the living 'gods', forms of the illuminating spirits. All their [works (of art)] are marvellously linked, many-coloured [spirits], artistic figures of the 'gods', engraved all around their glorious bricks, glorious figures on b[ri]cks of splendour and majes[ty]. All their works (of art) are living 'gods', and their artistic figures are holy angels. From beneath the marvellous inner[most chambers] comes a sound of quiet silence: the 'gods' bless . . .

4Q405 20 ii 21–22

For the Mas[ter. Song of the holocaust of] the twelfth [S]abbath [on the twenty-first of the third month.]

[Praise the God of . . . w]onder, and exalt him . . . of glory in the te[nt of the God of] knowledge. The [cheru]bim prostrate themselves before him and bless. As they rise, a whispered divine voice [is heard], and there is a roar of praise. When they drop their wings, there is a [whispere]d divine voice. The cherubim bless the image of the throne-chariot above the firmament, [and] they praise [the majes]ty of the luminous firmament beneath his seat of glory. When the wheels advance, angels of holiness come and go. From between his glorious wheels there is as it were a fiery vision of most holy spirits. About them, the appearance of rivulets of fire in the likeness of gleaming brass, and a work of . . . radiance in many-coloured glory, marvellous pigments, clearly mingled. The spirits of the living 'gods' move perpetually with the glory of the marvellous chariot(s). The whispered voice of blessing accompanies the roar of their advance, and they praise the Holy One on their way of return. When they ascend, they ascend marvellously, and when they settle, they stand still. The sound of joyful praise is silenced and there is a whispered blessing of the 'gods' in all the camps of God. And the sound of praise . . . from among all their divisions . . . and all their numbered ones praise, each in his turn.

4Q405 23i

... his whole-offering. The 'gods' praise him [when they take] up their station, and all the s[pirits of] the clear firm[am]ent rejoice in his glory. A sound of blessing (is heard) from all his divisions speaking of the firmaments of his glory, and his gates praise with a resounding voice. When the gods of knowledge enter by the doors of glory, and when the holy angels depart towards their realm, the entrance doors and the gates of exit proclaim the glory of the King, blessing and praising all the spirits of God when they depart and enter by the gates. None among them skips over a precept, nor do they ... against the saying of the King ... They run not away from the path, nor slip away from his domain. They are neither too high for his commission nor too lowly. For he shall be compassionate in the realm of his furious, destr[oying ange]r; He will not judge in the provinces of his glorious wrath. The fear of the King of 'gods' is awe-inspiring to [al]l the 'gods', [and they undertake] all his commissions by virtue of his true order, and they go ...

4Q405 23ii

... At their marvellous stations are spirits, many-coloured like the work of a weaver, splendid engraved figures. In the midst of a glorious appearance of scarlet, colours of the most holy spiritual light, they hold to their holy station before [the K]ing, spirits of [pure] colours in the midst of an appearance of whiteness. The likeness of the glorious spirit is like a work (of art) of sparkling fine gold. All their pattern is clearly mingled like the work (of art) of a weaver. These are the Princes of those marvellously clothed for service, the Princes of the kingdom, the kingdom of the holy ones of the King of holiness in all the heights of the sanctuaries of his glorious kingdom. The Princes in charge of offerings have tongues of knowledge, [and] they bless the God of knowledge among all his glorious works ...

11Q5–6

... their [mar]vellous marvels by the power of the God of [eter]nity; and they shall exalt the mighty deeds of the G[od] ... From the four foundations of the marvellous firmament they shall pr[oclaim] soundlessly (?) a divine oracle . . . wall. They bless and praise the God of gods . . .

13. LITURGICAL PRAYER (1Q**34** AND **34**bis)

The following fragments, published by J. T. Milik *(DJD* I, Oxford, 1955, pp. 152–5), belong to a collection of prayers for Jewish festivals. The title of the present section is lost, but reference to the Renewal of the Covenant seems to indicate that we have here another part of the sect's Pentecostal liturgy.

I . . . Thou wilt cause the wicked to be our ransom and the unfaithful to be our redemption. [Thou wilt] blot out all our oppressors and we shall praise Thy Name for ever [and ever]. For this hast Thou created us and [to say to Thee] this: Blessed art Thou . . .

II . . . the Great Light (of heaven) for the [day]time, [and the Little Light (of heaven) for the night] . . . without transgressing their laws, . . . and their dominion is over all the world.

But the seed of man did not understand all that Thou caused them to inherit; they did not discern Thee in all Thy words and wickedly turned aside from every one. They heeded not Thy great power and therefore Thou didst reject them. For wickedness pleases Thee not, and the ungodly shall not be established before Thee.

But in the time of Thy goodwill Thou didst choose for Thyself a people. Thou didst remember Thy Covenant and [granted] that they should be set apart for Thyself from among all the peoples as a holy thing. And Thou didst renew for them Thy Covenant (founded) on a glorious vision and the words of Thy Holy [Spirit], on the works of Thy hands and the writing of Thy Right Hand, that they might know the foundations of glory and the steps towards eternity . . . [Thou didst raise up] for them a faithful shepherd . . .

14. PRAYERS FOR FESTIVALS (4Q507-9)

Three badly worn manuscripts from cave 4 (4Q507-9) partly correspond to the foregoing fragments from cave 1 (1Q34 and 34bis). They have preserved prayers for festivals, two of which are explicitly associated with the Day of Atonement and the Day of the Firstfruits. The editor, M. Baillet (*DJD* VII, Oxford, 1982, pp. 175–215), dates them to the beginning of the first century A.D.

4Q507

Fr. 1

We are (encompassed) by iniquity since the womb, and since the breast by guilt. While we live, we walk in iniquity . . .

4Q508

Fr. 1 (cf. 1Q34bis)

[And the righteous . . . to grow fat thanks to the clouds of heaven and the produce of the land, to distingui]sh the righteous from the wicked. And Thou shalt make of the wicked our expiation, and by the upright Thou shalt destroy all our oppressors. And we will praise Thy na[m]e for ever and ever. For [Thou hast created us for this and we answer Thee with this; Blessed be . . .

Fr. 2 (cf. 1Q34bis)

. . . Prayer for the Day of Atonement. Remember O Lord, the feast of mercies and the time of return (?) . . . Thou hast established it for us as a feast of fasting, and everlas[ting] precept . . . Thou knowest the hidden things and the things reveal[ed] . . .

Fr. 3

. . . Thou didst establish [Thy Covenant] with Noah . . .

Fr. 3 [cf. 1Q34bis]

For Thou hast caused us to rejoice, removing our grief, and hast assembled our banished ones for a feast of . . . Thou shalt gather our dispersed women for the season of . . . Thy [me]rcies on our congregation like ra[in-drops on the earth in the season of sowing . . . and like showers on the gr]ass in the seasons of sprouting and . . . We shall recount Thy marvels from generation to generation. Blessed be the Lord who has caused us to rejoice . . .

Fr. 132

II [Prayer for the Day of the] Firstfruits. Remember O Lord the feast of . . . and the pleasing free-will offerings which Thou hast commanded . . . [to br]ing before Thee the firstfruits of [Thy] works . . .

15. DAILY PRAYERS (4Q503)

A manuscript from cave 4 (4Q503) consisting of 225 papyrus fragments, edited by M. Baillet (*DJD* VII, Oxford, 1982, pp. 105–36), lists evening and morning benedictions for each day of a month. The calendar followed appears to be lunar since evening precedes morning. The editor places the writing in the first quarter of the first century B.C.

III And when the sun rises . . . the firmament of heaven, they shall bless. Answer[ing they shall say:] Blessed be the Go[d of Israel . . .] Today . . . in the fourt[h of the gates of light . . .] On the fifth [of the month in the eve]ning, they shall bless. Answering, they shall say: Blessed be the God [of Israel] who hides . . . before him in every division of his glory . . . today the fourte[enth] . . . light of the day. Peace be on you, Israel . . . [When the sun] rise[s] to illumine the earth, they shall bless, and again the numbe[r shall be] ele[ven days] to the feasts of joy and the appointed times of g[lory] for [this d]ay is in the fifteenth of the gate[s of light] . . . [Peace be on you,] Israel. On the sixth of the month in the evening, they shall bless. Answering, they shall [say]: Bles[sed be the God] of Isreal . . . And when [the sun rises to illumine the earth, they shall bless. Answering, they shall say]

Frs. 7–9

IV . . . Peace [be on you, Israel] . . . On the seventh of [the month in the evening, they shall bless. Answering, they shall say:] Blessed be the God of Is[rael] . . .

Fr. 11

[On the t]welfth of the month in the evening [they shall bless] . . . [This continues up to probably the 26th of the month.]

16. THE BLESSINGS (1QSb)

◦—◦

These fragments from a collection of blessings were originally attached
to the Scroll of the Community Rule and the Messianic Rule. They have
been skilfully pieced together by J. T. Milik (*DJD* 1, Oxford, 1955,
pp. 118–29), who dates them to around 100 B.C.

The Blessings were to be recited by the Master or Guardian, and
were, as it seems, intended for the Messianic age, and perhaps for the
ceremony of the institution of the new Community. It is however possible
that they were actually used during the course of some liturgy anticipat-
ing and symbolizing the coming of the Messianic era. All the members
of the Covenant are blessed first, followed by someone who seems to be
the priestly head of the Community, the Messiah of Aaron. The next
blessing is addressed to the sons of Zadok, the Priests (and Levites?), and
finally the Prince of the Congregation, the Messiah of Israel, is blessed.
The rest of the document is lost.

The Blessing of the Faithful

I   Words of blessing. The Master shall bless them that fear [God
and do] His will, that keep His commandments, and hold fast to
His holy [Covenant], and walk perfectly [in all the ways of] His
[truth]; whom He has chosen for an eternal Covenant which shall
endure for ever.

May the [Lord bless you from the Abode of His holiness]; may
  He open for you from heaven an eternal fountain which [shall
  not fail]!
  . . .

May He [favour] you with every [heavenly] blessing; [may He
  teach you] the knowledge of the Holy Ones!
[May He unlock for you the] everlasting [fountain; may He not
  withhold the waters of life from] them that thirst!
  . . .

The Blessing of the High Priest

II   . . .

III   May the Lord lift His countenance towards you; [may He delight in the] sweet odour [of your sacrifices]!

May He choose [all] them that sit in your pries[tly college]; may He store up all your sacred offerings, and in the [season of] . . . all your seed!

May He [lift] His countenance towards all your congregation!

May He place upon your head [a diadem] . . . in [everlasting] glory; may He sanctify your seed in glory without end!

May He grant you everlasting [peace] . . .

May He fight [at the head of] your Thousands [until the generation of falsehood is ended] . . . [to bend] many peoples before you . . . all the riches of the world . . .

For God has established all the foundations of . . . may He lay the foundation of your peace for ever!

The Blessing of the Priests

Words of blessing. The M[aster shall bless] the sons of Zadok the Priests, whom God has chosen to confirm His Covenant for [ever, and to inquire] into all His precepts in the midst of His people, and to instruct them as He commanded; who have established [His Covenant] on truth and watched over all His laws with righteousness and walked according to the way of His choice.

May the Lord bless you from His holy [Abode]; may He set you as a splendid jewel in the midst of the congregation of the saints!

May He [renew] for you the Covenant of the [everlasting] priesthood; may He sanctify you [for the House] of Holiness!

May He [judge all] the leaders by your works, and all [the princes] of the peoples by the words from out of your lips!

May He give you as your portion the first-fruits of [all delectable things]; may He bless by your hand the counsel of all flesh!

IV   . . . may everlasting blessings be the crown upon your head! . . .

[For] He has chosen you [to] . . . and to number the saints and to [bless] your people . . . the men of the Council of God by your hand, and not by the hand of a prince . . .

. . . May you be as an Angel of the Presence in the Abode of Holiness to the glory of the God of [hosts] . . .

May you attend upon the service in the Temple of the Kingdom and decree destiny in company with the Angels of the Presence, in common council [with the Holy Ones] for everlasting ages and time without end; for [all] His judgements are [truth]!

May He make you holy among His people, and an [eternal] light [to illumine] the world with knowledge and to enlighten the face of the Congregation [with wisdom]!

[May He] consecrate you to the Holy of Holies! For [you are made] holy for Him and you shall glorify His Name and His holiness . . .

V . . .

The Blessing of the Prince of the Congregation

The Master shall bless the Prince of the Congregation . . . and shall renew for him the Covenant of the Community that he may establish the kingdom of His people for ever, [that he may judge the poor with righteousness and] dispense justice with [equity to the oppressed] of the land, and that he may walk perfectly before Him in all the ways [of truth], and that he may establish His holy Covenant at the time of the affliction of those who seek God.

May the Lord raise you up to everlasting heights, and as a fortified tower upon a high wall!

[May you smite the peoples] with the might of your hand and ravage the earth with your sceptre; may you bring death to the ungodly with the breath of your lips!

[May He shed upon you the spirit of counsel] and everlasting might, the spirit of knowledge and of the fear of God; may righteousness be the girdle [of your loins] and may your reins be girdled [with faithfulness]!

May He make your horns of iron and your hooves of bronze; may you toss like a young bull [and trample the peoples] like the mire of the streets!

For God has established you as the sceptre. The rulers . . . [and all the kings of the] nations shall serve you. He shall strengthen you with His holy Name and you shall be as a [lion; and you shall not lie down until you have devoured the] prey which nought shall deliver . . .

17. PURIFICATION RITUAL (4Q512)

⟨∘⟩

Badly worn papyrus fragments from cave 4 (4Q512) contain prayers recited to obtain purification from various kinds of ritual uncleanness. M. Baillet (*DJD* VII, pp. 263–86) suggests an early first century B.C. date for the script.

Frs. 29–32

VII And he will bless there [the God of Israel. Answering, he will say: Blessed art Thou, God of Israel. And I stand] before Thee on the feas[t] . . . Thou hast . . . me for purity . . . and his burnt offering and he will bless. Answering he will say: Blessed art Thou, [God of Israel, who hast delivered me from al]l my sins and purified me from impure indecency and hast atoned so that I come . . . purification and the blood of the burnt offering of Thy good-will and the pleasing memorial . . .

Fr. 11

X [And on completin]g [his] seven days of puri[fication] . . . and he shall wash his clothes with w[ater and cleanse his body] and he shall put on his garments and shall bless ag[ain] . . . the God of Isra[e]l . . .

18. THE TRIUMPH OF RIGHTEOUSNESS (1Q27)

Originally entitled *The Book of Mysteries* by J. T. Milik (*DJD* I, pp. 102–5), these fragments expound the familiar theme of the struggle between good and evil, but their nature is difficult to determine. Perhaps they derive from a sermon, or from an apocalyptical writing. Fragments pertaining to this work, found in cave 4, still await publication.

I . . . the mysteries of sin . . . They know not the mystery to come, nor do they understand the things of the past. They know not that which shall befall them, nor do they save their soul from the mystery to come.

And this shall be the sign for you that these things shall come to pass.

When the breed of iniquity is shut up, wickedness shall then be banished by righteousness as darkness is banished by the light. As smoke clears and is no more, so shall wickedness perish for ever and righteousness be revealed like a sun governing the world. All who cleave to the mysteries of sin shall be no more; knowledge shall fill the world and folly shall exist no longer.

This word shall surely come to pass; this prophecy is true. And by this may it be known to you that it shall not be taken back.

Do not all the peoples loathe iniquity? And yet it is spread by them all. Does not the fame of truth issue from the mouth of all the nations? Yet is there a lip or tongue which holds to it? Which nation likes to be oppressed by another stronger than itself, or likes its wealth to be wickedly seized? And yet which nation has not oppressed another, and where is there a people which has not seized [another]'s wealth?

19. THE SEDUCTRESS (4Q184)

A long and relatively well-preserved Wisdom poem from cave 4 (4Q184) depicts, by means of the metaphor of the harlot, the dangers and attraction of false doctrine. See J. M. Allegro, A. A. Anderson, *DJD* v, pp. 82–5; J. Strugnell, *Revue de Qumrân*, 1970, pp. 263–8. Palaeographically, the text is dated to the first century B.C., but the work may be much older, possibly antedating the Qumran sect.

. . . speaks vanity
   and . . . errors.
She is ever prompt to oil her words,
   and she flatters with irony,
     deriding with iniquitous l[ips].
Her heart is set up as a snare,
   and her kidneys as a fowler's nets.
Her eyes are defiled with iniquity,
   her hands have seized hold of the Pit.
Her legs go down to work wickedness,
   and to walk in wrong-doings.
Her . . . are foundations of darkness,
   and a multitude of sins is in her skirts.
Her . . . are darkness of night,
   and her garments . . .
Her clothes are shades of twilight,
   and her ornaments plagues of corruption.
Her couches are beds of corruption,
   and her . . . depths of the pit.
Her inns are couches of darkness,
   and her dominions in the midst of the night.
She pitches her dwelling on the foundations of darkness,
   she abides in the tents of silence.
Amid everlasting fire is her inheritance,
   not among those who shine brightly.
She is the beginning of all the ways of iniquity.
Woe (and) disaster to all who possess her!
   And desolation to all who hold her!
For her ways are ways of death,

    and her paths are roads of sin,
    and her tracks are pathways to iniquity,
    and her bye-ways are rebellious wrong-doings.
Her gates are gates of death,
and from the entrance of the house
    she sets out toward the underworld.
None of those who enter there will ever return,
    and all who possess her will descend to the Pit.
She lies in wait in secret places,
. . .

In the city's squares she veils herself,
    and she stands at the gates of towns.
She will never re[st] from wh[orin]g,
    her eyes glance hither and thither.
She lifts her eyelids naughtily
    to stare at a virtuous one and join him,
    and an important one to trip him up,
    at upright men to pervert their way,
    and the righteous elect to keep them from the commandment,
    at the firmly established to bring them down wantonly,
    and those who walk in uprightness to alter the statute.
To cause the humble to rebel against God,
    and turn their steps away from the ways of justice,
    to bring insolence to their heart,
    so that they march no more in the paths of uprightness;
    to lead men astray to the ways of the Pit,
    and seduce with flatteries every son of man.

20. EXHORTATION TO SEEK WISDOM (4Q185)

❦

Large fragments of a Wisdom poem in which a teacher encourages his 'people', his 'sons', the 'Simple', to search for Wisdom have been preserved in cave 4 (4Q185). The script is believed to be late Hasmonaean, i.e. from the first half of the first century B.C. As is often the case in Wisdom literature, events of the patriarchal and Mosaic past are used for didactic purposes. See J. M. Allegro, A. A. Anderson, *DJD* v, pp. 85–7; cf. J. Strugnell, *Revue de Qumrân*, 1970, pp. 269–73.

I   . . .
And you, sons of men, woe to you!
For he (man) sprouts from his ground like grass,
  and his grace blossoms like a flower.
His [gl]ory blows away and his . . . dries up,
  and the wind carries away its flower
. . .
so that it is found no more . . .
They shall seek him but shall not find him,
  and there is no hope (for him);
  and his days are like a shadow over the ea[rth].
Now pray hearken to me, my people;
  heed me, o you Simple;
  become wise through the might of God.
Remember His miracles which He did in Egypt,
  and His marvels in the land of Ham.
Let your heart shake because of His fear,
II   and do His will . . .
  . . . your souls according to His good graces,
  and search for yourself a way towards life,
  a highway [towards . . .]
  a remnant for your sons after you.
And why have you given up your soul to vanity,
  . . . judgement?
Hearken to me, o my sons,
  and do not rebel against the words of Y H W H.
Do not walk . . .
  [but in the way He established] for Jacob,

and in the path which He decreed for Israel.
Is one day not better . . .
. . . His fear,
   and not to be afflicted (?) by dread and the fowler's net.
. . . to be set apart from His angels,
   for there is no darkness, nor gloom . . .
And you, what do you understand . . .
   before Him evil shall go towards every people.
Happy is the man to whom it (Wisdom) has been given thus,
   . . . the evil,
   nor let the wicked boast, saying:
It has not been given me, nor . . .
   . . . to Israel,
   and with a good measure He measures it;
   and He will redeem His people,
   and He will put to death those who hate His Wisdom.

Seek it and find it, grasp it and possess it!
With it is length of days and fatness of bone,
   the joy of the heart and . . .
Happy is the man who works it
. . .
   who does not seek it . . . of deceit,
   nor holds to it with flatteries.
As it has belonged to his fathers,
   so will he inherit it,
   and hold fast to it with all the strength of his might,
   and all his immeasurable . . .
   and he shall cause his offspring to inherit it.

I know how to labour for good . . .

21. SONGS OF THE SAGE (4Q510–11)

Scraps from two manuscripts from cave 4 (4Q510–11) represent a mixture of sapiential psalms and poems of exorcism. Their editor, M. Baillet (*DJD* VII, pp. 215–62), assigns the script to the end of the first century B.C. or the turning of the era. The first fragment preserves an interesting list of names of demons.

4Q510

. . . praises. Ben[edictions for the K]ing of glory. Words of thanksgiving in psalms of . . . to the God of knowledge, the Splendour of power, the God of gods, Lord of all the holy. [His] domini[on] is over all the powerful mighty ones and by the power of his might all shall be terrified and shall scatter and be put to flight away by the splendour of the dwel[ling] of his kingly glory. And I, the Master, proclaim the majesty of his beauty to frighten and ter[rify] all the spirits of the destroying angels and the spirits of the bastards, the demons, Lilith, the howlers (?) and [the yelpers . . .] they who strike suddenly to lead astray the spirit of understanding and to appal their heart and their . . . in the age of the domination of wickedness and the appointed times for the humiliation of the sons of ligh[t], in the guilt of the ages of those smitten by iniquity, not for eternal destruction but for the humiliation of sin. Exalt, O just, the God of marvels. My psalms are for the upright. . . . May all whose way is perfect exalt him.

4Q511

Fr. 1

. . . [on the ea]rth and in all the spirits of his dominion always. Let the seas b[le]ss him in their turn and all the creatures living in them. May they proclaim the . . . of beauty all of them. Let them rejoice before the God of justice with shouts of salvation, for there shall be no destroyer in their territories, and no spirit of wickedness shall walk in there. For the glory of the God of knowledge has shone forth in his words, and none of the sons of iniquity shall endure.

Fr. 2

I For the Master. [First] Song. Praise the name of his holiness; all who know [justice], exalt him . . . He put an end to the chief of the dominations without . . . eternal [joy] and everlasting life, to cause light to shine . . . his [l]ot is the best of Jacob and the inheritance of G[o]d . . . of Israel . . . they who guard the way of God and the pat[h] of his [hol]iness for the saints of his people. By the discerning knowledge [of Go]d, he placed Israel in twelve camps . . . the lot of God with the ange[ls] of the luminaries of his glory. In his name the praises . . . he has established for the feast of the year and for a common government that they may walk [in] the lot of [God] according to [his] glory [and] serve him in the lot of the people of his throne. For the God of . . .

Fr. 8

[For the Master]. Second [S]ong to frighten those who terrify him . . .

Fr. 18

II I have hated all the works of impurity. For God has caused the knowledge of understanding to shine in my heart. Just chastisers (deal) with my perversity, and faithful judges with all my sinful guilt. For God is my judge and by the hand of a stranger [He] shall not . . .

Frs. 28–9

. . . [they shall] rejoice in God with jubilation. And I [will thank Th]ee for, because of Thy glory, Thou hast [s]et knowledge on my foundations of dust to pr[aise Thee]. . . . of a shape [of clay] was I moulded and from darkness was I kneaded . . . and iniquity is in the limbs of my flesh . . .

Fr. 30

Thou hast sealed . . . the [e]arth . . . and they are deep. [The heavens and the heavens of the] heavens, and the abysses and the dar[k places of the earth] . . . Thou, O my God, hast sealed them all and there is none to open (them) . . . Does one measure by the hollow of a human hand the waters of the great (ocean)? Are [the heavens estimated by the span (of fingers)? In one third (of a measure)] can any contain the dust of the earth, and weigh the mountains in a balance, or the hills in scal[es]? Man did not make these. How can he measure the spirit of [God]?

Fr. 35

God in all flesh, and an avenging judgement to destroy wickedness, and for the raging anger of God towards those seven times refined. God shall sancti[fy] (some) of the holy as an everlasting sanctuary for himself, and purity shall endure among the cleansed. They shall be priests, his righteous people, his host, servants, the angels of his glory. They shall praise him with marvellous prodigies. I, I spread the fear of God in the ages of my generations to exalt the name . . . [to terrify] by his might al[l] the spirits of the 'bastards', subduing them by [his] fear . . .

Frs. 63–4

II   . . . I will bless Thy name and in my appointed periods I will recount Thy marvels and I will engrave them as precepts of Thy glory's praises. At the beginning of every thought of a knowing heart and (with) the offering of that which flows from the righteous lips when ready for all true worship and with all . . .

Fr. 63

III   As for me, my tongue shall extol Thy righteousness, for Thou hast released it. Thou hast placed on my lips a fount of praise and in my heart the secret of the commencement of all human actions and the completion of the deeds of the perfect of way, and the judgements regarding all the service done by them, justifying the just by Thy truth and condemning the wicked for their guilt. To announce peace to all the men of the Covenant and to utter a dreadful cry of woe for all those who breach it . . .

IV   May they bless all Thy works always and blessed be Thy name for ever and ever. Amen, amen.

C. BIBLE INTERPRETATION

Three types of biblical Commentary have been recovered from the Qumran caves.

The first, represented by Genesis Apocryphon, sets out to render the Bible story more intelligible and attractive by giving it more substance, by reconciling conflicting statements, and also by reinterpreting in the light of contemporary standards and beliefs any passages which might seem to give offence.

The second type of Commentary departs from the biblical text and, relying on one or several passages, creates a new story. The Words of Moses and the Prayer of Nabonidus, inspired by Deuteronomy and Daniel, come into this category.

The third and most characteristic form of exegesis applies prophetic texts to the past, present, and future of the sect. Normally the commentator expounds a biblical book verse by verse, but some works – A Midrash on the Last Days, The Heavenly Prince Melchizedek, etc. – follow the traditional Jewish example and assemble passages from different parts of Scripture in order to develop a common theme.

22. THE GENESIS APOCRYPHON (1QapGen)

❧

Found in cave 1, and published by N. Avigad and Y. Yadin (*A Genesis Apocryphon*, Jerusalem, 1956), 1QapGen is an incomplete manuscript with twenty-two surviving columns of Aramaic text. Only the translated five columns are reasonably well preserved. Column II narrates the miraculous birth of Noah, whose father, Lamech, suspects that his wife has conceived by one of the fallen angels. Her denials fail to convince him and he asks his father, Methuselah, to travel to Paradise and obtain reassurance from his own father, Enoch.

Columns XIX–XXII, corresponding to Gen. xii–xv, deal with Abraham's journey to Egypt, his return to Canaan, the war against the invading Mesopotamian kings, and the renewal to him of a divine promise of a son. This lively and delightful narrative, largely devoid of sectarian bias, throws valuable light on inter-Testamental Bible interpretation. It is a mixture of Targum, Midrash, re-written Bible and autobiography.

Most scholars assign the manuscript to the late first century B.C. or the first half of the first century A.D. The composition itself is generally thought to originate from the second century B.C. Its relationship to the mid-second-century book of Jubilees is generally accepted, but views differ on whether it depends on Jubilees or vice versa. I slightly prefer the theory that in its pre-Qumran version the Genesis Apocryphon precedes Jubilees, which would postulate for the former a date at least as early as the first half of the second century B.C.

. . . **II** Behold, I thought then within my heart that conception was (due) to the Watchers and the Holy Ones . . . and to the Giants . . . and my heart was troubled within me because of this child. Then I, Lamech, approached Bathenosh [my] wife in haste and said to her, '. . . by the Most High, the Great Lord, the King of all the worlds and Ruler of the Sons of Heaven, until you tell me all things truthfully, if . . . Tell me [this truthfully] and not falsely . . . by the King of all the worlds until you tell me truthfully and not falsely.'

Then Bathenosh my wife spoke to me with much heat [and] . . . said, 'O my brother, O my lord, remember my pleasure . . .

the lying together and my soul within its body. [And I tell you] all things truthfully.'

My heart was then greatly troubled within me, and when Bathenosh my wife saw that my countenance had changed . . . Then she mastered her anger and spoke to me saying 'O my lord, O my [brother, remember] my pleasure! I swear to you by the Holy Great One, the King of [the heavens] . . . that this seed is yours and that [this] conception is from you. This fruit was planted by you . . . and by no stranger or Watcher or Son of Heaven . . . [Why] is your countenance thus changed and dismayed, and why is your spirit thus distressed . . . I speak to you truthfully.'

Then I, Lamech, ran to Methuselah my father, and [I told] him all these things. [And I asked him to go to Enoch] his father for he would surely learn all things from him. For he was beloved, and he shared the lot [of the angels], who taught him all things. And when Methuselah heard [my words . . . he went to] Enoch his father to learn all things truthfully from him . . . his will.

He went at once to Parwain and he found him there . . . [and] he said to Enoch his father, 'O my father, O my lord, to whom I . . . And I say to you, lest you be angry with me because I come here . . .

XIX   . . . And I said, 'Thou art . . .' . . . '. . . until now you have not come to the Holy Mountain.'

And I (Abraham) departed . . . and I travelled towards the south . . . until I came to Hebron [at the time when Hebron] was being built; and I dwelt there [two years].

Now there was famine in all this land, and hearing that there was prosperity in Egypt I went . . . to the land of Egypt . . . I [came to] the river Karmon, one of the branches of the River (Nile) . . . and I crossed the seven branches of the River . . . We passed through our land and entered the land of the sons of Ham, the land of Egypt.

And on the night of our entry into Egypt, I, Abram, dreamt a dream; [and behold], I saw in my dream a cedar tree and a palm tree . . . men came and they sought to cut down the cedar tree and to pull up its roots, leaving the palm tree (standing) alone. But the palm tree cried out saying, 'Do not cut down this cedar tree, for cursed be he who shall fell [it].' And the cedar tree was spared because of the palm tree and [was] not felled.

And during the night I woke from my dream, and I said to Sarai my wife, 'I have dreamt a dream . . . [and I am] fearful [because of] this dream.' She said to me, 'Tell me your dream that I may know it.' So I began to tell her this dream . . . [the interpretation] of the dream . . . '. . . that they will seek to kill me, but will spare you . . . [Say to them] of me, he is my brother, and because of you I shall live, and because of you my life shall be saved . . .'

And Sarai wept that night on account of my words . . .

Then we journeyed towards Zoan, I and Sarai . . . by her life that none should see her . . .

And when those five years had passed, three men from among the princes of Egypt [came at the command] of Pharaoh of Zoan to inquire after [my] business and after my wife and they gave . . . goodness, wisdom, and truth. And I exclaimed before them . . . because of the famine . . . And they came to ascertain . . . with much food and drink . . . the wine . . .

(During the party, the Egyptians must have seen Sarai, and on their return they praised her to the king.)

XX . . . '. . . and beautiful is her face! How . . . fine are the hairs of her head! How lovely are her eyes! How desirable her nose and all the radiance of her countenance . . . How fair are her breasts and how beautiful all her whiteness! How pleasing are her arms and how perfect her hands, and how [desirable] all the appearance of her hands! How fair are her palms and how long and slender are her fingers! How comely are her feet, how perfect her thighs! No virgin or bride led into the marriage chamber is more beautiful than she; she is fairer than all other women. Truly, her beauty is greater than theirs. Yet together with all this grace she possesses abundant wisdom, so that whatever she does is perfect (?).'

When the king heard the words of Harkenosh and his two companions, for all three spoke as with one voice, he desired her greatly and sent out at once to take her. And seeing her, he was amazed by all her beauty and took her to be his wife, but me he sought to kill. Sarai said to the king, 'He is my brother,' that I might benefit from her, and I, Abram, was spared because of her and I was not slain.

And I, Abram, wept aloud that night, I and my nephew Lot, because Sarai had been taken from me by force. I prayed that night and I begged and implored, and I said in my sorrow while my tears ran down: 'Blessed art Thou, O Most High God, Lord of all the worlds, Thou who art Lord and king of all things and who rulest over all the kings of the earth and judgest them all! I cry now before Thee, my Lord, against Pharaoh of Zoan the king of Egypt, because of my wife who has been taken from me by force. Judge him for me that I may see Thy mighty hand raised against him and against all his household, and that he may not be able to defile my wife this night (separating her) from me, and that they may know Thee, my Lord, that Thou art Lord of all the kings of the earth.' And I wept and was sorrowful.

And during that night the Most High God sent a spirit to scourge him, an evil spirit to all his household; and it scourged him and all his household. And he was unable to approach her, and although he was with her for two years, he knew her not.

At the end of those two years the scourges and afflictions grew greater and more grievous upon him and all his household, so he sent for all [the sages] of Egypt, for all the magicians, together with all the healers of Egypt, that they might heal him and all his household of this scourge. But not one healer or magician or sage could stay to cure him, for the spirit scourged them all and they fled.

Then Harkenosh came to me, beseeching me to go to the king and to pray for him and to lay my hands upon him that he might live, for the king had dreamt a dream . . . But Lot said to him, 'Abram my uncle cannot pray for the king while Sarai his wife is with him. Go, therefore, and tell the king to restore his wife to her husband; then he will pray for him and he shall live.'

When Harkenosh had heard the words of Lot, he went to the king and said, 'All these scourges and afflictions with which my lord the king is scourged and afflicted are because of Sarai the wife of Abram. Let Sarai be restored to Abram her husband, and this scourge and the spirit of festering shall vanish from you.'

And he called me and said, 'What have you done to me with regard to [Sarai]? You said to me, She is my sister, whereas she is your wife; and I took her to be my wife. Behold your wife who is with me; depart and go hence from all the land of Egypt! And now pray for me and my house that this evil spirit may be expelled from it.'

So I prayed [for him] . . . and I laid my hands on his [head]; and the scourge departed from him and the evil [spirit] was expelled [from him], and he lived. And the king rose to tell me . . . and the king swore an oath to me that . . . and the king gave her much [silver and gold] and much raiment of fine linen and purple . . . And Hagar also . . . and he appointed men to lead [me] out [of all the land of Egypt]. And I, Abram, departed with very great flocks and with silver and gold, and I went up from [Egypt] together with my nephew [Lot]. Lot had great flocks also, and he took a wife for himself from among [the daughters of Egypt.

I pitched my camp] **XXI** [in] every place in which I had formerly camped until I came to Bethel, the place where I had built an altar. And I built a second altar and laid on it a sacrifice, and an offering to the Most High God. And there I called on the name of the Lord of worlds and praised the Name of God and blessed God, and I gave thanks before God for all the riches and favours which He had bestowed on me. For He had dealt kindly towards me and had led me back in peace into this land.

After that day, Lot departed from me on account of the deeds of our shepherds. He went away and settled in the valley of the Jordan, together with all his flocks; and I myself added more to them. He kept his sheep and journeyed as far as Sodom, and he bought a house for himself in Sodom and dwelt in it. But I dwelt on the mountain of Bethel and it grieved me that my nephew Lot had departed from me.

And God appeared to me in a vision at night and said to me, 'Go to Ramath Hazor which is north of Bethel, the place where you dwell, and lift up your eyes and look to the east and to the west and to the south and to the north; and behold all this land which I give to you and your seed for ever.'

The next morning, I went up to Ramath Hazor and from that high place I beheld the land from the River of Egypt to Lebanon and Senir, and from the Great Sea to Hauran, and all the land of Gebal as far as Kadesh, and all the Great Desert to the east of Hauran and Senir as far as Euphrates. And He said to me, 'I will give all this land to your seed and they shall possess it for ever. And I will multiply your seed like the dust of the earth which no man can number; neither shall any man number your seed. Rise and go! Behold the length and breadth of the land for it is yours; and after you, I will give it to your seed for ever.'

And I, Abram, departed to travel about and see the land. I began my journey at the river Gihon and travelled along the coast of the Sea until I came to the Mountain of the Bull (Taurus). Then I travelled from the coast of the Great Salt Sea and journeyed towards the east by the Mountain of the Bull, across the breadth of the land, until I came to the river Euphrates. I journeyed along the Euphrates until I came to the Red Sea (Persian Gulf) in the east, and I travelled along the coast of the Red Sea until I came to the tongue of the Sea of Reeds (the modern Red

Sea) which flows out from the Red Sea. Then I pursued my way in the south until I came to the river Gihon, and returning, I came to my house in peace and found all things prosperous there. I went to dwell at the Oaks of Mamre, which is at Hebron, north-east of Hebron; and I built an altar there, and laid on it a sacrifice and an oblation to the Most High God. I ate and drank there, I and all the men of my household, and I sent for Mamre, Ornam and Eshkol, the three Amorite brothers, my friends, and they ate and drank with me.

Before these days, Kedorlaomer king of Elam had set out with Amrafel king of Babylon, Ariok king of Kaptok, and Tidal king of the nations which lie between the rivers; and they had waged war against Bera king of Sodom, Birsha king of Gomorrah, Shinab king of Admah, Shemiabad king of Zeboim, and against the king of Bela. All these had made ready for battle in the valley of Siddim, and the king of Elam and the other kings with him had prevailed over the king of Sodom and his companions and had imposed a tribute upon them.

For twelve years they had paid their tribute to the king of Elam, but in the thirteenth year they rebelled against him. And in the fourteenth year, the king of Elam placed himself at the head of all his allies and went up by the Way of the Wilderness; and they smote and pillaged from the river Euphrates onward. They smote the Refaim who were at Ashteroth Karnaim, the Zumza-mim who were at Ammon, the Emim [who were at] Shaveh ha-Keriyyoth, and the Horites who were in the mountains of Gebal, until they came to El Paran which is in the Wilderness. And they returned . . . at Hazazon Tamar.

The king of Sodom went out to meet them, together with the king [of Gomorrah], the king of Admah, the king of Zeboim, and the king of Bela, [and they fought] a battle in the valley [of Sid-dim] against Kedorlaomer [king of Elam and the kings] who were with him. But the king of Sodom was vanquished and fled, and the king of Gomorrah fell into the pits . . . [And] the king of Elam [carried off] all the riches of Sodom and [Gomorrah] . . . and they took Lot the nephew **XXII** of Abram who dwelt with them in Sodom, together with all his possessions.

Now one of the shepherds of the flocks which Abram had given to Lot escaped from captivity and came to Abram: at that time Abram dwelt in Hebron. He told him that Lot his nephew had been taken, together with all his possessions, and that he had not been slain, and that the kings had gone by the Way of the Great

Valley (of the Jordan) in the direction of their land, taking captives and plundering and smiting and slaying, and that they were journeying towards the land of Damascus.

Abram wept because of Lot his nephew. Then he braced himself; he rose up and chose from among his servants three hundred and eighteen fighting men trained for war, and Ornam and Eshkol and Mamre went with him also. He pursued them until he came to Dan, and came on them while they were camped in the valley of Dan. He fell on them at night from four sides and during the night he slew them; he crushed them and put them to flight, and all of them fled before him until they came to Helbon which is north of Damascus. He rescued from them all their captives, and all their booty and possessions. He also delivered Lot his nephew, together with all his possessions, and he brought back all the captives which they had taken.

When the king of Sodom learned that Abram had brought back all the captives and all the booty, he came out to meet him; and he went to Salem, which is Jerusalem.

Abram camped in the valley of Shaveh, which is the valley of the king, the valley of Beth-ha-Kerem; and Melchizedek king of Salem brought out food and drink to Abram and to all the men who were with him. He was the Priest of the Most High God. And he blessed Abram and said, 'Blessed be Abram by the Most High God, Lord of heaven and earth! And blessed be the most High God who has delivered your enemies into your hand!' And Abram gave him the tithe of all the possessions of the king of Elam and his companions.

Then the king of Sodom approached and said to Abram, 'My lord Abram, give me the souls which are mine, which you have delivered from the king of Elam and taken captive, and you may have all the possessions.'

Then said Abram to the king of Sodom, 'I raise my hand this day to the most High God, Lord of heaven and earth! I will take nothing of yours, not even a shoe-lace or shoe-strap, lest you say, Abram's riches come from my possessions! I will take nothing but that which the young men with me have eaten already, and the portion of the three men who have come with me. They shall decide whether they will give you their portion.' And Abram returned all the possessions and all the captives and gave them to the king of Sodom; he freed all the captives from this land who were with him, and sent them all back.

After these things, God appeared to Abram in a vision and said to him, 'Behold, ten years have passed since you departed from Haran. For two years you dwelt here and you spent seven years in Egypt, and one year has passed since you returned from Egypt. And now examine and count all you have, and see how it has grown to be double that which came out with you from Haran. And now do not fear, I am with you; I am your help and your strength. I am a shield above you and a mighty safeguard round about you. Your wealth and possessions shall multiply greatly.' But Abram said, 'My Lord God, I have great wealth and possessions but what good shall they do to me? I shall die naked, childless shall I go hence. A child from my household shall inherit from me. Eliezer son . . . shall inherit from me.' And He said to him, 'He shall not be your heir, but one who shall spring [from your body shall inherit from you].' . . .

23. THE BLESSINGS OF JACOB (4QPBless)

❦

The subject of this interpretation is the blessing of Judah, i.e. of the tribe from which David was born. The commentator emphasizes that the royal power will belong for ever to the descendants of David, thereby implying that all non-Davidic rulers, such as the contemporary Hasmonean priest-kings, occupy the throne unlawfully. If so, the composition best fits into the first half of the first century B.C. For the text, see J. M. Allegro, 'Further Messianic References in Qumran Literature', *Journal of Biblical Literature*, 1956, pp. 174–6.

The sceptre shall not depart from the tribe of Judah, nor the ruler's staff from between his feet, until he comes to whom it belongs. And the peoples shall be in obedience to him (Gen. xlix, 10)

Whenever Israel rules there shall [not] fail to be a descendant of David upon the throne. For the *ruler's staff* is the Covenant of kingship, [and the clans] of Israel are the *feet*, until the Messiah of Righteousness comes, the Branch of David. For to him and to his seed was granted the Covenant of kingship over his people for everlasting generations . . .

24. THE AGES OF THE CREATION (4Q180)

❦

A badly worn manuscript from cave 4 (4Q180) has been published under this title by J. M. Allegro. Its decipherment and interpretation have been further improved by J. Strugnell and J. T. Milik. The only section yielding coherent sense deals with the myth of the fallen angels and the daughters of men, which is based on Genesis vi, 1–4, and fully developed in I Enoch. If Milik's reconstruction is correct, the work presents human history as divided into seventy weeks of years (70 × 7 years), the first ten of which cover the period from Noah to Abraham. The manuscript is claimed by Strugnell to belong to the first century A.D. See J. M. Allegro, A. A. Anderson, *DJD* v, pp. 77–9; cf. J. Strugnell, *Revue de Qumrân*, 1970, pp. 252–4; J. T. Milik, *Journal of Jewish Studies*, 1972, pp. 110–24.

Interpretation concerning the ages made by God, all the ages for the accomplishment [of all the events, past] and future. Before ever He created them. He determined the works of . . . age by age. And it was engraved on [heavenly] tablets . . . the ages of their domination. This is the order of the cre[ation of man from Noah to Abraham, un]til he begot Isaac: ten [weeks (of years)].

And the interpretation concerns Azazel and the angels who [came to the daughters of men; and] they bore to them giants. And concerning Azazel . . . and iniquity, and to cause them all to inherit wickedness . . . judgements and judgement of the congregation . . .

25. THE TESTAMENT OF AMRAM (4QAmram)

◦−◦

An Aramaic document surviving in five fragmentary copies in cave 4 contains an admonition by Amram, the father of Moses, to his children. The context is that of the Book of Exodus, but the visions and teachings are the author's free compositions. Amram's age at his death (137 years) is borrowed from Exod. vi, 20, but its dating to the 152nd year of the captivity reflects the tradition according to which the Israelites remained in Egypt, not for 430 years (Exod. xii, 40), nor 400 years (Gen. xv, 13), but 210 years. Cf. J. Heinemann, '210 Years of Egyptian Exile', *Journal of Jewish Studies*, 1971, pp. 19–30.

In the gravely damaged text of the vision, Amram sees the chief Angel of Darkness, Melkiresha', already mentioned in the *Curses of Satan and his lot* (p. 160–61). He also addresses the leader of the Army of Light, whose name has disappeared in one of the many lacunae. But it is highly probable that one of his 'three names' is Melchizedek, as will appear presently from the reading of the Melchizedek document from cave 11 (pp. 298–300 below). See J. T. Milik '4Q visions de 'Amram et une citation d'Origène', *Revue Biblique*, 1972, pp. 77–97.

Copy of the book of the words of the vision of Amram, son of Kehat, son of Levi, al[l that] he explained to his sons and enjoined on them on the day of [his] death, in his one-hundred-and-thirty-seventh year, which was the year of his death, [in] the one-hundred-and-fifty-second year of Israel's exile in Egypt.

(I saw Watchers) in my vision, a dream vision, and behold two (of them) argued about me and said . . . and they were engaged in a great quarrel concerning me. I asked them: 'You, what are you . . . thus . . . [about me?'] They answered and [said to me: 'We have been made m]asters and rule over all the sons of men.' And they said to me: 'Which of us do you [choose. . .]

I raised my eyes and saw one of them. His looks were frightening [like those of a vi]per, and his [ga]rm[en]ts were multi-coloured and he was extremely dark . . .

And afterwards I looked and behold . . . by his appearance

and his face was like that of an adder, and he was covered with . . . together, and his eyes . . .

. . . this [Watcher]: 'Who is he? He said to me: 'This Wa[tcher] . . . [and his three names are . . .] and Melkiresha'.'

And I said: 'My Lord, what . . .' [And he said to me] . . . [and all his paths are dark]ness, and all his work is darkness, and he is . . . in darkness . . . you see. And he rules over all darkness and I [rule over all light] . . .

. . . [the order] of the Most High as far as 'the Lands' (beyond the Ocean). I rule over all Light, and over al[l that is God's], and I rule over the men of His grace and p[eace. And I] rule [over all the Sons of Lig]ht.'

And I asked and said to him: 'What are [your names?] . . . [He answered and sa]id to me: '[My] three names are . . .

I an[nou]nce (this) to you [and al]so I will indeed inform y[ou . . . For all the Sons of Light] will shine, [and all the Sons] of Darkness will be dark. [For all the Sons of Light] . . . and by all their knowledge they will . . . and the Sons of Darkness will be burnt . . . For all folly and wicked[ness are dar]k, and all [pea]ce and truth are brigh[t. For all the Sons of Light g]o towards the light, towards [eternal] jo[y and rej]oicin[g], and all the Sons of Dar[kness go towards death] and perdition . . . The people shall have brightness . . . and they will cause them to live . . .

And now to you, Amram my son, [I] enjo[in] . . . and [to] your [son]s, and to their sons I enjoin . . ., and they gave them to Levi my father, and Levi my father [gave them] to me . . . and my books in testimony that they might be warned by them . . .

26. THE WORDS OF MOSES (1Q22)

Fragments of four very mutilated columns of a manuscript from cave 1 have been skilfully reconstructed by J. T. Milik (*DJD* I, pp. 91–7). They form a farewell discourse of Moses which takes its inspiration from various passages of Deuteronomy and is chiefly remarkable for the emphasis laid on the appointment of special teachers, or interpreters, of the Law (Levites and Priests).

[God spoke] to Moses in the [fortieth] year after [the children of] Israel had come [out of the land of] Egypt, in the eleventh month, on the first day of the month, saying:

'[Gather together] all the congregation and go up to [Mount Nebo] and stand [there], you and Eleazar son of Aaron. Inter-[pret to the heads] of family of the Levites and to all the [Priests], and proclaim to the children of Israel the words of the law which I proclaimed [to you] on Mount Sinai. Proclaim care[fully] into their ears all that I [require] of them. And [call] heaven and [earth to witness against] them; for they will not love what I have commanded [them to do], neither [they] nor their children, [during all] the days they shall [live upon the earth].

[For] I say that they will abandon [me, and will choose the abominations of the nations,] their horrors [and their idols. They will serve] false gods which shall be for them a snare and a pitfall. [They will sin against the] holy [days], and against the Sabbath and the Covenant, [and against the commandments] which I command you to keep this day.

[Therefore I will smite] them with a mighty [blow] in the midst of the land [which they] cross the Jordan [to possess]. And when all the curses come upon them and catch up with them to destroy them and [blot] them out, then shall they know that the truth has been [fulfilled] with regard to them.'

Then Moses called Eleazar son of [Aaron] and Joshua [son of Nun and said to them,] 'Speak [all these words to the people] . . .:

[Be still] **II** O Israel, and hear! This [day shall you become the people] of God, your [God. You shall keep my laws] and my testimonies [and my commandments which I] command you to [keep this] day. [And when you] cross the [Jordan so that I may give] you great [and good cities], and houses filled with all [pleasant things, and vines and olives] which [you have not planted, and] wells which you have not dug, [beware,] when you have eaten and are full, that your hearts be not lifted up, and that [you do not forget what I have commanded you to do this day. For] it is this that will bring you life and length of [days].'

And Moses [spoke to the children] of Israel [and said to them]:

'[Behold,] forty [years have passed since] the day we came out of the land [of Egypt, and today has God], our God, [uttered these words] from out of His mouth: [all] His [precepts and] all [His] precepts.

'[But how shall I carry] your loads [and burdens and disputes alone]? When I have [established] the Covenant and commanded [the way] in which you shall walk, [appoint wise men whose] work it shall be to expound [to you and your children] all these words of the Law. [Watch carefully] for your own sakes [that you keep them, lest] the wrath [of your God] kindle and burn against you, and He stop the heavens above from shedding rain [upon you], and [the water beneath the earth from] giving you [harvest].'

And Moses [spoke further] to the children of Israel.

'Behold the commandments [which God has] commanded you to keep . . .'

27. THE SAMUEL APOCRYPHON (4Q160)

❧

Fragments of an account of the story of Samuel from cave 4 (4Q160), said to pertain to the second century B.C., were published by J. M. Allegro and A. A. Anderson, *DJD* v, Oxford, 1968, pp. 9–11. They follow the first book of Samuel and include a narrative passage, a dialogue between Samuel and Eli, a prayer and an autobiographical discourse.

Fr. 1

[F]or [I have s]worn [to] the house [of Eli that the iniquity of the house of Eli relating to sacrifices and offerings shall never be expiated. And] Samue[l] heard the words of the Lord . . . [and] Samuel lay down before Eli. And he rose and opened the ga[tes of the house of the Lord. And Samuel was afraid] to report to Eli the oracle. Answering, Eli said [to Samuel: Samuel, my son, let] me know the vision of God. Do not [hide it from me, pray! May God do to you thus and may he add to it] if you hide from me anything of the words that he spoke to you. [And] Samuel [reported all and hid nothing] . . .

Frs. 3–5

. . . Thy servant. I have not restrained my strength until this, for . . . [let them] be gathered, O my God, to Thy people and be a help to it and raise it . . . [and deliver] their [fe]e[t] from muddy clay [and] establish for them a rock from of old, for Thy praise [is over all the peo]ples. Thy people shall take refuge [in Thy house] . . . Amid the rage of the enemies of Thy people, Thou shalt verify Thy glory [and] over the lands and seas . . . and Thy fear is over [al]l. . and kingdom. And all the peoples of Thy lands shall know [that] Thou hast created them . . . and the multitudes shall understand that this is Thy people . . . Thy holy ones whom Thou hast sanctified.

☙

Translatable fragments of four commentaries on Isaiah were discovered in cave 4 (4QpIsa^a-d = 4Q161–4). A fifth (4QpIsa^f = 4Q165) is too mutilated to be rendered into English. The first document alludes to the defeat of the Kittim and expounds the renowned Messianic prophecy of Isa. xi. The second and the third deal with the Jewish opponents of the sect. The fourth, relying on Isa. liv, identifies the Community as the new Jerusalem. They all may be assigned to the first century B.C.(Cf. *DJD* v, pp. 11–30.)

4Q161

Frs. 5–6

. . . when they return from the desert of the peo[ples] . . . the Prince of the Congregation and afterwards . . . will depart from them . . . *He has come to Aiath; he has passed through [Migron]. At Mikhmash [he has left his baggage; they have passed by] Maabarah; Geba is their night camp; [Ramah] trem[bles; Gibea of Saul has fled]; Bath Gallim, [cry out a shrill] note; [Laish,] hear it; [answer her, Anathoth;] Madmenah [flees]; the inhabitants of Gebim take refuge. [Today he is to stop in Nob. He shakes] his hand towards the mountain of the daughter of Zion, the hills of Jerusalem* (x, 28–32).

[The interpretation of the] decree concerns the coming end of days . . . [trem]bles when he ascends from the Vale of Accho to wage war against . . . and none is like him and in all the cities of . . . and as far as the frontier of Jerusalem. . . .

Frs. 8–10

. . . *[and the tallest tre]es [shall be cut down and] the lofty [shall be felled] with the axe, and Lebanon through a powerful one shall fall* (x, 33–34).

[Its interpretation concerns the Kit]tim who shall crush the house of Israel and the humble . . . all the nations and the valiant shall be dismayed and [their] he[arts] shall melt. [And that which he said, *The tallest] trees shall be cut down*, these are the valiant of the Kit[tim] . . . [And that which he sa]id. *The heart of the forest shall be felled with the axe*, th[ey] . . . for the war of the Kittim. *And Lebanon through a po[werful one shall fall* (x, 34). Its interpretation concerns the] Kittim who will be given into the hand of his great one . . . when he flees from be[fore Is]rael . . .

[*And there shall come forth a rod from the stem of Jesse and a Branch shall grow out of its roots. And the spirit of the Lord shall rest upon him, the spirit of wisdom and understanding, the spirit of counsel and might, the spirit of knowledge and of the fear of the Lord. And his delight shall be in the fear of the Lord. He shall not judge by what his eyes see, or pass sentence by what his ears hear; he shall judge the poor righteously and shall pass sentence justly on the humble of the earth]* (xi, 1–3).

[Interpreted, this concerns the Branch] of David who shall arise at the end [of days] . . . God will uphold him with [the spirit of might, and will give him] a throne of glory and a crown of [holiness] and many-coloured garments . . . [He will put a sceptre] in his hand and he shall rule over all the [nations]. And Magog . . . and his sword shall judge [all] the peoples.

And as for that which He said, *He shall not [judge by what his eyes see] or pass sentence by what his ears hear*: interpreted, this means that . . . [the Priests] . . . As they teach him, so will he judge; and as they order, [so will he pass sentence]. One of the Priests of renown shall go out, and garments of . . . shall be in his hands . . .

4Q162

[*For ten acres of vineyard shall produce only one* bath, *and an* omer *of seed shall yield but one* ephah] (v, 10).

Interpreted, this saying concerns the last days, the devastation of the land by sword and famine. At the time of the Visitation of the land there shall be *Woe to those who rise early in the morning to run after strong drink, to those who linger in the evening until wine inflames them. They have zither and harp and timbrel and flute and wine at their feasts, but they do not regard the work of the Lord or see the deeds of His hand. Therefore my people go into exile for want of knowledge, and their noblemen die of hunger and their multitude is parched with thirst. Therefore Hell has widened its gullet and opened its mouth beyond measure, and the nobility of Jerusalem and her multitude go down, her tumult and he who rejoices in her* (v, 11–14).

These are the Scoffers in Jerusalem who have *despised the Law of the Lord and scorned the word of the Holy One of Israel. Therefore the wrath of the Lord was kindled against His people. He stretched out His hand against them and smote them; the mountains trembled and their corpses were like sweepings in the middle of the streets. And [His wrath] has not relented for all these things [and His hand is stretched and still]* (v, 24–25).

This is the congregation of Scoffers in Jerusalem . . .

4Q163

Thus said the Lord, the Holy One of Israel, 'You shall be saved by returning and resting; your strength shall be in silence and trust.' But you would not. You [said], 'No. We will flee upon horses and will ride on swift steeds.' Therefore your pursuers shall be speedy also. A thousand shall flee (before) the threat of one; at the threat of five you shall flee [till] you are left like a flagstaff on top of a mountain and like a signal on top of a hill. Therefore the Lord waits to be [gracious to] you; therefore He exalts Himself to have mercy on you. For the Lord is a God of justice. How blessed are all those who wait for him! (xxx, 15–18)

This saying, referring to the last days, concerns the congregation of those who seek smooth things in Jerusalem . . . [who despise the] Law and do not [trust in God] . . . As robbers lie in wait for a man . . . they have despised [the words of] the law . . .

O people of Zion [who live in Jerusalem, you shall weep no more. At the sound of] your crying [He will be gracious to you; He will answer you] when He [hears it. Although the Lord give you bread of oppression and water of distress, your Teacher] shall be hidden [no more and your eyes shall see your Teacher] . . . (xxx, 19–20).

4Q164

Behold, I will set your stones in antimony (liv, 11b).

[Interpreted, this saying concerns] . . . all Israel is like antimony surrounding the eye.

And I will lay your foundations with sapphires (liv, 11c).

Interpreted, this concerns the Priests and the people who laid the foundations of the Council of the Community . . . the congregation of His elect (shall sparkle) like a sapphire among stones.

[And I will make] all your pinnacles [of agate] (liv, 12a).

Interpreted, this concerns the twelve [chief Priests] who shall enlighten by judgement of the Urim and Tummim . . . which are absent from them, like the sun with all its light, and like the moon . . .

[And all your gates of carbuncles] (liv, 12b).

Interpreted, this concerns the chiefs of the tribes of Israel . . .

29. THE NEW JERUSALEM (5Q15)

Fragments belonging to an Aramaic writing describing the Jerusalem of the eschatological age have been identified in caves 1 (1Q32), 2 (2Q24), 4, 5 (5Q15) and 11. They are inspired by Ezekiel xl-xlviii (cf. also Revelation xxi). Among the edited manuscripts, only the text found in cave 5, completed by J. T. Milik with the help of two large unpublished parallel fragments from cave 4, provides an intelligible portion. On palaeographical considerations, 5Q15 is thought to date to around the turn of the era.

The visionary responsible for this work accompanies an angelic 'surveyor' who measures everything in the New Jerusalem, from the size of the blocks of houses, the avenues and the streets, to the detailed dimensions of rooms, stairs and windows. A full picture of the city, including also the measurements of the walls, will be available only after the publication of the document from cave 4.

The dimensions are given in 'reeds', each of which consists of seven 'cubits'. But there seem to be two cubits among ancient Jewish measures, one approximately 20 inches (521 mm), the other 18 inches (446 mm) long.

The translation is based on Milik's edition and interpretation of 5Q15 in *DJD* III, Oxford, 1962, pp. 184–93. (For smaller fragments, see Milik, *DJD* I, Oxford, 1955, pp. 134–5; M. Baillet, *DJD* III, Oxford, 1962, pp. 84–90; B. Jongeling, 'Publication provisoire d'un fragment provenant de la grotte 11 de Qumrân (11Q Jér nouv ar)', *Journal for the Study of Judaism*, 1970, pp. 58–64).

I And he led me into the city, and he measured each block of houses for its length and width, fifty-one reeds by fifty-one, in a square a[ll round] = 357 cubits to each side. A passage surrounds the block of houses, a street gallery, three reeds, = 21 cubits, (wide).

[He] then [showed me the di]mensions of [all] the blo[cks of houses. Between each block there is a street], six reeds, = 42 cubits, wide. And the width of the avenues running from east to west: two of them are ten reeds, = 70 cubits, wide. And the third, that to the [lef]t (i.e. north) of the Temple, measures eighteen reeds, = 126 cubits in width. And the wid[th of the streets] running from south [to north: t]wo of [them] have nine reeds and four cubits, = 67 cubits, each street.

[And the] mid[dle street passing through the mid]dle of the city, its [width measures] thirt[een] ree[ds] and one cubit, = 92 cubits. And all [the streets of the city] are paved with white stone . . . marble and jasper.

[And he showed me the dimensions of the ei]ghty [side-doors]. The wid[th of the] side-doors is two reeds, [= 14 cubits, . . . Each door has tw]o wings of stone. The width of the w[ing] is [one] reed, [= 7 cubits.]

And he showed me [the dimensions] of the twelve [entranc]es. The width of their doors are three reeds, [= 21] cubits. [Each door has tw]o [wings]. The width of the wing is one reed and a half, = 10 ½ cubits . . . [And beside each door there are two tow]ers, one to [the r]ight and one to the l[ef]t. Its width [is of the same dimension as] its length, [five reeds by five, = 35 cubits. The stairs beside] the inside door, on the [righ]t side of the towers, [rise] to the top of the to[wers. Their width is five cubits. The towers and the stairs are five reeds by five and] five cubits, = 40 [cubits], on each side of the door.

[And he showed me the dimensions of the doors of the blocks of houses. Their width] is two reeds, = 14 cub[its. And the wi]d[th]. . . [And he measured] the wid[th of each th]reshold: two reeds, = 14 cubits, [and the lintel: one cubit. And he measured above each] threshold i[ts win]gs. And he measured beyond the threshold. Its length is [thirteen] cubits [and its width ten cubits.]

[And he] le[d m]e [be]yond the threshold. [And behold] another threshold, and a door next to the inner wall [on the right side, of the same dimensions as the outer door. Its width] is four [cu]bits, [its] height seven [cubits], and it has two wings. And in front of this door there is [an entrance threshold. Its width is one reed] **II** 7 [cubits]. And the l[eng]th of the entrance is two reeds, = 14 cubits, and its height is two reeds, = 14 cubits. [And the door] fa[cing the other do]or opening into the block of houses has the same dimensions as the outer door. On the left of this entrance, he showed [me] a round [stair-case]. Its length is of the same dimension as its width: two reeds by two, = 14 cubits. The do[ors (of the stair-case) facing] the other doors are of the same dimensions. And a pillar is inside the stair-case around which the stairs ri[se]; its width and d[epth are six cubits by six], square. And the stairs which rise beside it, their width is four cubits, and they rise in a spiral [to] a height of [two] r[eeds] to [the roof].

And he led me [into] the block of houses, and he showed me the houses there. From one door to the oth[er, there are fifteen: eigh]t on one side as far as the corner, and sev]en from the corner to the other door. The length of the house[s is three reed]s, = 2 [1 cubits, and their width], two [reed]s, = 14 cubits. Likewise, for all the chambers; [and their height is t]wo [reeds], = 1[4] cu[bit]s, [and their doors are in the middle.] (Their) width is t[w]o reeds, = 1[4] cubits. [And he measured the width (of the rooms) in the middle of the house, and inside the upper floor: four [cubits]. Length and height: one reed, = 7 cubits.

[And he showed me the dimensions of the dining-[halls]. Each has [a length] of ninete[en] cubits [and a width] of twelve [cubits]. Each contains twenty-two couche[s and ele]ven windows of lattice-work (?) above [the couches]. And next to the hall is an outer conduit. [And he measured] the . . . of the window: its height, two cubits; [its width: . . . cubits;] and its depth is that of the width of the wall. [The height of the inner (aspect of the window) is . . . cubits, and that of the outer (aspect), . . . cubits.]

[And he measured the l]im[it]s of the . . . [Their length] is nineteen [cubits] and [their] width, [twelve cubits] . . .

30. THE PRAYER OF NABONIDUS (4QprNab)

◦⚬◦

Whilst the book of Daniel (iv) writes of the miraculous recovery of Nebuchadnezzar after an illness which lasted seven years, this interesting Aramaic composition tells a similar story about the last king of Babylon, Nabonidus. The principal difference between the two is that Nebuchadnezzar was cured by God Himself when he recognized His sovereignty, whereas a Jewish exorcist healed Nabonidus by teaching him the truth and forgiving his sins. J. T. Milik considers the work to be older than Daniel, but a late second or early first century B.C. dating seems to be less adventurous (cf. *Revue Biblique*, 1956, pp. 407–11).

The words of the prayer uttered by Nabunai king of Babylon, [the great] king, [when he was afflicted] with an evil ulcer in Teiman by decree of the [Most High God].

I was afflicted [with an evil ulcer] for seven years . . . and an exorcist pardoned my sins. He was a Jew from among the [children of the exile of Judah, and he said], 'Recount this in writing to [glorify and exalt] the name of the [Most High God'. And I wrote this]:

'I was afflicted with an [evil] ulcer in Teiman [by decree of the Most High God]. For seven years [I] prayed to the gods of silver and gold, [bronze and iron], wood and stone and clay, because [I believed] that they were gods . . .'

31. PSEUDO-DANIELIC WRITINGS (4QpsDan and 4Q246)

◇

In addition to the Prayer of Nabonidus, cave 4 has revealed further Aramaic remains of a composition akin to the biblical book of Daniel. The first of these (4QpsDan, fr. C) was published by J. T. Milik (*Revue Biblique*, 1956, pp. 411–15). The second (4Q246), a document containing the phrases 'son of God' and 'son of the Most High', was the subject of a lecture given by the same scholar in 1972 and reported by J. A. Fitzmyer (*A Wandering Aramean*, 1979, pp. 90–93). Milik supposes that the composition is historical, but its precise nature must for the time being be left undecided.

4QpsDan, fr. C

. . . The children of Israel chose themselves rather than [God and they sacri]ficed their sons to the demons of idolatry. God was enraged against them and determined to surrender them to Nebu[chadnezzar, king of Ba]bel and to devastate their land . . .

*4QpsDan A*ᵃ = *4Q246*

II He shall be called son of God, and they shall designate him son of the Most High. Like the appearance of comets, so shall be their kingdom. For (brief) years they shall reign over the earth and shall trample on all; one people shall trample on another and one province on another until the people of God shall rise and all shall rest from the sword.

32. COMMENTARIES ON HOSEA (4Q166–7)

∞

Two fragmentary manuscripts (4Q166–7) include exegeses of Hosea. In the first, the unfaithful wife is the Jewish people led astray by her lovers, the Gentiles. The second refers cryptically to 'the furious young lion', mentioned also in the Commentary on Nahum, and to 'the last Priest who shall . . . strike Ephraim' (cf. *DJD* V, pp. 31–2).

Commentary A

[She knew not that] it was I who gave her [the new wine and oil], who lavished [upon her silver] and gold which they [used for Baal] (ii, 8).

Interpreted, this means that [they ate and] were filled, but they forgot God who . . . They cast His commandments behind them which he had sent [by the hand of] His servants the Prophets, and they listened to those who led them astray. They revered them, and in their blindness they feared them as though they were gods.

Therefore I will take back my corn in its time and my wine [in its season]. I will take away my wool and my flax lest they cover [her nakedness]. I will uncover her shame before the eyes of [her] lovers [and] no man shall deliver her from out of my hand (ii, 9–10).

Interpreted, this means that He smote them with hunger and nakedness that they might be shamed and disgraced in the sight of the nations on which they relied. They will not deliver them from their miseries.

I will put an end to her rejoicing, [her feasts], her [new] moons, her Sabbaths, and all her festivals (ii, 11).

Interpreted, this means that [they have rejected the ruling of the law, and have] followed the festivals of the nations. But [their rejoicing shall come to an end and] shall be changed into mourning.

I will ravage [her vines and her fig trees], of which she said, 'They are my wage [which my lovers have given me'.] I will make of them a thicket and the [wild beasts] shall eat them . . . (ii, 12).

Commentary B

Fr. 2

. . . and your wound shall not be healed (v, 13).
[Its] in[terpretation concerns] . . . the furious young lion . . .

For I will be like a lion [to E]ph[ra]im [and like a young lion to the house of Judah (v, 14a).
Its interpretation con]cerns the last Priest who shall stretch out his hand to strike Ephraim . . .

[I will go and come back to my place un]til they [will] feel guilty and seek my face; in their distress they will seek me eagerly (v, 15).
Its interpretation is that God [has hid]den his face from . . . and they did not listen . . .

Frs. 7–9

[But they, like Adam, have b]roken the Covenant (vi, 7).
[Its] interpretation . . . they have forsaken God and walked according to the decrees [of the Gentiles] . . .

33. COMMENTARY ON MICAH (1Q14)

❧

Tiny fragments from cave 1 (1Q14) represent an exposition of Micah (DJD 1, pp. 77–80)Although the prophet's words are intended to castigate both Samaria and Jerusalem, the Qumran commentator interprets Samaria as alluding to the 'Spouter of Lies', the enemy of the sect, but relates Judah and Jerusalem to the Teacher of Righteousness and his Community.

[All this is] for the transgression [of Jacob and for the sins of the House of Israel. What is the transgression of Jacob?] Is it not [Samaria? And what is the high place of Judah? Is it not Jerusalem? I will make of Samaria a ruin in the fields, and of Jerusalem a plantation of vines] (i, 5–6).

Interpreted, this concerns the Spouter of Lies [who led the] Simple [astray.].

And what is the high place of Judah? [Is it not Jerusalem?] (i, 5).

[Interpreted, this concerns] the Teacher of Righteousness who [expounded the law to] his [Council] and to all who freely pledged themselves to join the elect of [God to keep the Law] in the Council of the Community; who shall be saved on the Day [of Judgement] . . .

34. COMMENTARY ON NAHUM (4Q169)

∽◦∾

Substantial remains of a Nahum interpretation were retrieved from cave 4 (4Q169) and published in *DJD* v, pp. 37–42. They cover parts of chapters i and ii, and the first fourteen verses of chapter iii. Their historical significance has been discussed in Chapter II (pp. 25–31). It is worthy of notice that the commentator employs not only cryptograms (Kittim, furious young lion, etc.), but actually names two Greek kings (Demetrius and Antiochus). Reference to 'the furious young lion' as one who 'hangs men alive' shows that 'hanging', a probable synonym for crucifixion, was practised as a form of execution. It is legislated on also in the Temple Scroll (LXIV, 6–13), where it is the capital punishment reserved for traitors. In biblical law, by contrast, only the dead body of an executed criminal is to be hanged, that is, displayed in public as an example (Deut. xxi, 21).

On palaeographical grounds the manuscript is dated to the second half of the first century B.C.

[In whirlwind and storm is his way and] cloud is the d[ust of his feet *(i, 3).*

Its interpretation] ... The [whirlwinds and the storm]s are (from) the fir[mam]ents of his heaven and of his earth which he has cre[ated].

He rebu[kes] the sea and dri[es it up] (i, 4a).

Its [int]erpretation: the sea is all the K[ittim who are] ... to execut[e] judgement against them and destroy them from the face [of the earth] together with [all] their [com]manders whose dominion shall be finished.

[Bashan and] Carmel have withered and the sprout of Lebanon withers (i, 4b).

Its interpretation ... [will per]ish in it, the summit of wickedness for the ... Carmel and to his commanders. Lebanon and the sprout of Lebanon are [the priests, the sons of Zadok and the men of] their [counc]il and they shall perish from before ... the elect ... [a]ll the inhabitants of the world.

The mo[untains quake before him and the hills heave and the earth [is lifted up] before him, and [the world and all that dwell in it. Who can stand before his wrath? And who can arise] against his furious anger? (i, 5–6a).

[Its] in[terpretation] . . .

[*Where is the lions' den and the cave of the young lions?*] (ii, 11).

[Interpreted, this concerns] . . . a dwelling-place for the ungodly of the nations.

Whither the lion goes, there is the lion's cub, [with none to disturb it] (ii, 11b).

[Interpreted, this concerns Deme]trius king of Greece who sought, on the counsel of those who seek smooth things, to enter Jerusalem. [But God did not permit the city to be delivered] into the hands of the kings of Greece, from the time of Antiochus until the coming of the rulers of the Kittim. But then she shall be trampled under their feet . . .

The lion tears enough for its cubs and it chokes prey for its lionesses (ii, 12a).

[Interpreted, this] concerns the furious young lion who strikes by means of his great men, and by means of the men of his council.

[*And chokes prey for its lionesses; and it fills*] *its caves [with prey] and its dens with victims* (ii, 12a–b).

Interpreted, this concerns the furious young lion [who executes revenge] on those who seek smooth things and hangs men alive, . . . formerly in Israel. Because of a man hanged alive on [the] tree, He proclaims, '*Behold I am against [you, says the Lord of Hosts*'].

[*I will burn up your multitude in smoke*], *and the sword shall devour your young lions. I will [cut off] your prey [from the earth]* (ii, 13).

[Interpreted] . . . *your multitude* is the bands of his army . . . and his *young lions* are . . . his *prey* is the wealth which [the priests] of Jerusalem have [amassed], which . . . Israel shall be delivered . . .

[*And the voice of your messengers shall no more be heard*] (ii, 13b).

[Interpreted] **II** . . . his *messengers* are his envoys whose voice shall no more be heard among the nations.

Woe to the city of blood; it is full of lies and rapine (iii, 1ab).

Interpreted, this is the city of Ephraim, those who seek smooth things during the last days, who walk in lies and falsehood.

The prowler is not wanting, noise of whip and noise of rattling wheel, prancing horse and jolting chariot, charging horsemen, flame and glittering spear, a multitude of slain and a heap of carcasses. There is no end to the corpses; they stumble upon their corpses (iii, 1c–3).

Interpreted, this concerns the dominion of those who seek smooth things, from the midst of whose assembly the sword of the nations shall never be wanting. Captivity, looting, and burning shall be among them, and exile from dread of the enemy. A multitude of guilty corpses shall fall in their days; there shall be no end to the sum of their slain. They shall also stumble upon their body of flesh because of their guilty counsel.

Because of the many harlotries of the well-favoured harlot, the mistress of seduction, she who sells nations through her harlotries and families through her seductions (iii, 4).

Interpreted, this concerns those who lead Ephraim astray, who lead many astray through their false teaching, their lying tongue, and deceitful lips – kings, princes, priests, and people, together with the stranger who joins them. Cities and families shall perish through their counsel; honourable men and rulers shall fall through their tongue's [decision].

Behold, I am against you – oracle of the Lord of hosts – and you will lift up your skirts to your face and expose your nakedness to the nations and your shame to the kingdoms (iii, 5).

Interpreted . . . cities of the east. For the *skirts* are . . . **III** and the nations shall . . . among them their filthy idols.

I will cast filth upon you and treat you with contempt and render you despicable, so that all who look upon you shall flee from you (iii, 6–7a).

Interpreted, this concerns those who seek smooth things, whose evil deeds shall be uncovered to all Israel at the end of time. Many shall understand their iniquity and treat them with contempt because of their guilty presumption. When the glory of Judah shall arise, the simple of Ephraim shall flee from their assembly; they shall abandon those who lead them astray and shall join Israel.

They shall say, Niniveh is laid waste; who shall grieve over her? Whence shall I seek comforters for you? (iii, 7b.).

Interpreted, this concerns those who seek smooth things,

whose counsel shall perish and whose congregation shall be dispersed. They shall lead the assembly astray no more, and the simple shall support their counsel no more.

Are you better than Amon which lay among the rivers? (iii, 8a).
Interpreted, *Amon* is Manasseh, and the *rivers* are the great men of Manasseh, the honourable men of . . .

Which was surrounded by waters, whose rampart was the sea and whose walls were waters? (iii, 8b).
Interpreted, these are her valiant men, her almighty warriors.

Ethiopia [and Egypt] were her [limitless] strength (iii, 9a).
[Interpreted] . . .

[Put and the Lybians were your helpers] (iii, 9b.)
IV   Interpreted, these are the wicked of [Judah], the House of Separation, who joined Manasseh.

Yet she was exiled; she went into captivity. Her children were crushed at the top of all the streets. They cast lots for her honourable men, and all her great men were bound with chains (iii, 10).
Interpreted, this concerns Manasseh in the final age, whose kingdom shall be brought low by [Israel . . .] his wives, his children, and his little ones shall go into captivity. His mighty men and honourable men [shall perish] by the sword.

[You shall be drunk] and shall be stupified (iii, 11a).
Interpreted, this concerns the wicked of E[phraim . . .] whose cup shall come after Manasseh . . .

[You shall also seek] refuge in the city because of the enemy (iii, 11b).
Inter[preted, this concerns . . .] their enemies in the city . . .

[All your strongholds shall be] like fig trees with newly-ripe figs (iii, 12a).

35. COMMENTARY ON HABAKKUK (1QpHab)

⟨∞⟩

This well-preserved and detailed exposition of the first two chapters of the book of Habakkuk comes from cave 1 and was published in 1950 (M. Burrows, The DSS of St Mark's Monastery pls. LV-LXI)

The copy dates probably to the late first century B.C. The Habakkuk Commentary is one of the main sources for the study of Qumran origins as well as Essene Bible exegesis and the sect's theology regarding prophecy. The historical and doctrinal aspects of the document are analysed in Chapters II and III.

I [*Oracle of Habakkuk the prophet. How long, O Lord, shall I cry*] *for help and Thou wilt not* [*hear*]? (i, 1–2).

[Interpreted, this concerns the beginning] of the [final] generation . . .

[*Or shout to Thee 'Violence', and Thou wilt not deliver?*] (i, 2b)
. . .

[*Why dost Thou cause me to see iniquity and to look upon trouble? Desolation and violence are before me*] (i, 3).

. . . God with oppression and unfaithfulness . . . they rob riches.

[*There is quarrelling and contention*] (i, 3b).
. . .

So the law is weak [*and justice never goes forth*] (i, 4a–b).
[Interpreted] this concerns those who have despised the Law of God . . .

[*For the wicked encompasses*] *the righteous* (i, 4c).
[*The wicked* is the Wicked Priest, and *the righteous*] is the Teacher of Righteousness . . .

[*So*] *justice goes forth* [*perverted*] (i, 4d).
. . .

[*Behold the nations and see, marvel and be astonished; for I accomplish a deed in your days, but you will not believe it when*] **II** *told* (i, 5).

[Interpreted, this concerns] those who were unfaithful together with the Liar, in that they [did] not [listen to the word received by] the Teacher of Righteousness from the mouth of God. And it concerns the unfaithful of the New [Covenant] in that they have not believed in the Covenant of God [and have profaned] His holy Name. And likewise, this saying is to be interpreted [as concerning those who] will be unfaithful at the end of days. They, the men of violence and the breakers of the Covenant, will not believe when they hear all that [is to happen to] the final generation from the Priest [in whose heart] God set [understanding] that he might interpret all the words of His servants the Prophets, through whom He foretold all that would happen to His people and [His land].

For behold, I rouse the Chaldeans, that [*bitter and hasty*] *nation* (i, 6a).
Interpreted, this concerns the Kittim [who are] quick and valiant in war, causing many to perish. [All the world shall fall] under the dominion of the Kittim, and the [wicked . . .] they shall not believe in the laws of [God . . .]

[*Who march through the breadth of the earth to take possession of dwellings which are not their own*] (i, 6b).
. . .   **III**   they shall march across the plain, smiting and plundering the cities of the earth. For it is as He said, *To take possession of dwellings which are not their own.*

They are fearsome and terrible; their justice and grandeur proceed from themselves (i, 7).
Interpreted, this concerns the Kittim who inspire all the nations with fear [and dread]. All their evil plotting is done with intention and they deal with all the nations in cunning and guile.

Their horses are swifter than leopards and fleeter than evening wolves. Their horses step forward proudly and spread their wings; they fly from afar like an eagle avid to devour. All of them come for violence; the look on their faces is like the east wind (i, 8–9a).
[Interpreted, this] concerns the Kittim who trample the earth with their horses and beasts. They come *from afar*, from the islands of the sea, to devour all the peoples *like an eagle* which cannot be satisfied, and they address [all the peoples] with anger and [wrath and fury] and indignation. For it is as He said, *The look on their faces is like the east wind.*

[*They heap up*] *captives* [*like sand*] (i, 9b).

. . .

IV *They scoff* [*at kings*], *and princes are their laughing-stock* (i, 10a).

Interpreted, this means that they mock the great and despise the venerable; they ridicule kings and princes and scoff at the mighty host.

They laugh at every fortress; they pile up earth and take it (i, 10b).

Interpreted, this concerns the commanders of the Kittim who despise the fortresses of the peoples and laugh at them in derision. To capture them, they encircle them with a mighty host, and out of fear and terror they deliver themselves into their hands. They destroy them because of the sins of their inhabitants.

The wind then sweeps on and passes; and they make of their strength their god (i, 11).

Interpreted, [this concerns] the commanders of the Kittim who, on the counsel of [the] House of Guilt, pass one in front of the other; one after another [their] commanders come to lay waste the earth. [*And they make*] *of their strength their god*: interpreted, this concerns [. . . all] the peoples . . .

[*Art Thou not from everlasting, O Lord, my God, my Holy One? We shall not die.*] *Thou hast ordained them,* [*O Lord*], **V** *for judgement; Thou hast established them, O Rock, for chastisement. Their eyes are too pure to behold evil; and Thou canst not look on distress* (i, 12–13a).

Interpreted, this saying means that God will not destroy His people by the hand of the nations; God will execute the judgement of the nations by the hand of His elect. And through their chastisement all the wicked of His people shall expiate their guilt who keep His commandments in their distress. For it is as he said, *Too pure of eyes to behold evil:* interpreted, this means that they have not lusted after their eyes during the age of wickedness.

O traitors, why do you stare and stay silent when the wicked swallows up one more righteous than he? (i, 13b).

Interpreted, this concerns the House of Absalom and the members of its council who were silent at the time of the chastisement of the Teacher of Righteousness and gave him no help against the Liar who flouted the Law in the midst of their whole [congregation].

Thou dealest with men like the fish of the sea, like creeping things, to

*rule over them. They draw [them all up with a fish-hook], and drag them
out with their net, and gather them in [their seine. Therefore they sacrifice]
to their net. Therefore they rejoice [and exult and burn incense to their
seine; for by them] their portion is fat [and their sustenance rich]* (i,
14–16).

. . .   **VI**   the Kittim. And they shall gather in their riches,
together with all their booty, *like the fish of the sea.* And as for that
which He said, *Therefore they sacrifice to their net and burn incense
to their seine:* interpreted, this means that they sacrifice to their
standards and worship their weapons of war. *For through them
their portion is fat and their sustenance rich:* interpreted, this means
that they divide their yoke and their tribute – *their sustenance* –
over all the peoples year by year, ravaging many lands.

Therefore their sword is ever drawn to massacre nations mercilessly (i,
17).
Interpreted, this concerns the Kittim who cause many to perish
by the sword – youths, grown men, the aged, women and children
– and who even take no pity on the fruit of the womb.

*I will take my stand to watch and will station myself upon my fortress.
I will watch to see what He will say to me and how [He will answer] my
complaint. And the Lord answered [and said to me, 'Write down the vision
and make it plain] upon the tablets, that [he who reads] may read it
speedily* (ii, 1–2).
. . .   **VII**   and God told Habakkuk to write down that which
would happen to the final generation, but He did not make
known to him when time would come to an end. And as for that
which He said, *That he who reads may read it speedily*: interpreted
this concerns the Teacher of Righteousness, to whom God made
known all the mysteries of the words of His servants the Prophets.

*For there shall be yet another vision concerning the appointed time. It
shall tell of the end and shall not lie* (ii, 3a).
Interpreted, this means that the final age shall be prolonged,
and shall exceed all that the Prophets have said; for the mysteries
of God are astounding.

If it tarries, wait for it, for it shall surely come and shall not be late (ii,
3b).
Interpreted, this concerns the men of truth who keep the Law,
whose hands shall not slacken in the service of truth when the
final age is prolonged. For all the ages of God reach their

appointed end as he determines for them in the mysteries of His wisdom.

Behold, [his soul] is puffed up and is not upright (ii, 4a).

Interpreted, this means that [the wicked] shall double their guilt upon themselves [and it shall not be forgiven] when they are judged . . .

[But the righteous shall live by his faith] (ii, 4b).

VIII Interpreted, this concerns all those who observe the Law in the House of Judah, whom God will deliver from the House of Judgement because of their suffering and because of their faith in the Teacher of Righteousness.

Moreover, the arrogant man seizes wealth without halting. He widens his gullet like Hell and like Death he has never enough. All the nations are gathered to him and all the peoples are assembled to him. Will they not all of them taunt him and jeer at him saying, 'Woe to him who amasses that which is not his! How long will he load himself up with pledges?' (ii, 5–6).

Interpreted, this concerns the Wicked Priest who was called by the name of truth when he first arose. But when he ruled over Israel his heart became proud, and he forsook God and betrayed the precepts for the sake of riches. He robbed and amassed the riches of the men of violence who rebelled against God, and he took the wealth of the peoples, heaping sinful iniquity upon himself. And he lived in the ways of abominations amidst every unclean defilement.

Shall not your oppressors suddenly arise and your torturers awaken; and shall you not become their prey? Because you have plundered many nations, all the remnant of the peoples shall plunder you (ii, 7–8a).

[Interpreted, this concerns] the Priest who rebelled [and violated] the precepts [of God . . . to command] **IX** his chastisement by means of the judgements of wickedness. And they inflicted horrors of evil diseases and took vengeance upon his body of flesh. And as for that which He said, *Because you have plundered many nations, all the remnant of the peoples shall plunder you*: interpreted this concerns the last Priests of Jerusalem, who shall amass money and wealth by plundering the peoples. But in the last days, their riches and booty shall be delivered into the hands of the army of the Kittim, for it is they who shall be the *remnant of the peoples*.

Because of the blood of men and the violence done to the land, to the city, and to all its inhabitants (ii, 8b).

Interpreted, this concerns the Wicked Priest whom God delivered into the hands of his enemies because of the iniquity committed against the Teacher of Righteousness and the men of his Council, that he might be humbled by means of a destroying scourge, in bitterness of soul, because he had done wickedly to His elect.

Woe to him who gets evil profit for his house; who perches his nest high to be safe from the hand of evil! You have devised shame to your house: by cutting off many peoples you have forfeited your own soul. For the [stone] cries out [from] the wall [and] the beam from the woodwork replies (ii, 9–11).

[Interpreted, this] concerns the [Priest] who ... **X** that its stones might be laid in oppression and the beam of its woodwork in robbery. And as for that which He said, *By cutting off many peoples you have forfeited your own soul*: interpreted this concerns the condemned House whose judgement God will pronounce in the midst of many peoples. He will bring him thence for judgement and will declare him guilty in the midst of them, and will chastise him with fire of brimstone.

Woe to him who builds a city with blood and founds a town upon falsehood! Behold, is it not from the Lord of Hosts that the peoples shall labour for fire and the nations shall strive for naught? (ii, 12–13).

Interpreted, this concerns the Spouter of Lies who led many astray that he might build his city of vanity with blood and raise a congregation on deceit, causing many thereby to perform a service of vanity for the sake of its glory, and to be pregnant with [works] of deceit, that their labour might be for nothing and that they might be punished with fire who vilified and outraged the elect of God.

For as the waters cover the sea, so shall the earth be filled with the knowledge of the glory of the Lord (ii, 14).

Interpreted, [this means that] when they return ... **XI** the lies. And afterwards, knowledge shall be revealed to them abundantly, like the waters of the sea.

Woe to him who causes his neighbours to drink; who pours out his venom to make them drunk that he may gaze on their feasts! (ii, 15).

Interpreted, this concerns the Wicked Priest who pursued the

Teacher of Righteousness to the house of his exile that he might confuse him with his venomous fury. And at the time appointed for rest, for the Day of Atonement, he appeared before them to confuse them, and to cause them to stumble on the Day of Fasting, their Sabbath of repose.

You have filled yourself with ignominy more than with glory. Drink also, and stagger! The cup of the Lord's right hand shall come round to you and shame shall come on your glory (ii, 16).

Interpreted, this concerns the Priest whose ignominy was greater than his glory. For he did not circumcise the foreskin of his heart, and he walked in the ways of drunkenness that he might quench his thirst. But the cup of the wrath of God shall confuse him, multiplying his . . . and the pain of . . .

[For the violence done to Lebanon shall overwhelm you, and the destruction of the beasts] **XII** *shall terrify you, because of the blood of men and the violence done to the land, the city, and all its inhabitants* (ii, 17).

Interpreted, this saying concerns the Wicked Priest, inasmuch as he shall be paid the reward which he himself tendered to the Poor. For *Lebanon* is the Council of the Community; and the *beasts* are the Simple of Judah who keep the Law. As he himself plotted the destruction of the Poor, so will God condemn him to destruction. And as for that which He said, *Because of the blood of the city and the violence done to the land:* interpreted, *the city is* Jerusalem where the Wicked Priest committed abominable deeds and defiled the Temple of God. *The violence done to the land:* these are the cities of Judah where he robbed the Poor of their possessions.

Of what use is an idol that its maker should shape it, a molten image, a fatling of lies? For the craftsman puts his trust in his own creation when he makes dumb idols (ii, 18).

Interpreted, this saying concerns all the idols of the nations which they make so that they may serve and worship them. But they shall not deliver them on the Day of Judgement.

Woe [to him who says] to wood, 'Awake', and to dumb [stone, 'Arise'! Can such a thing give guidance? Behold, it is covered with gold and silver but there is no spirit within it. But the Lord is in His holy Temple]: **XIII** *let all the earth be silent before Him!* (ii, 19–20).

Interpreted, this concerns all the nations which serve stone and wood. But on the Day of Judgement, God will destroy from the earth all idolatrous and wicked men.

◦◦◦

Two manuscripts with 'Herodian' script from cave 4 (4Q171, 4Q173) include interpretations of Psalms (*DJD* v, pp. 42–53). The bulk of the text is devoted to Psalm xxxvii, in which the destiny of the just and the wicked is expounded in connection with the story of the sect and its opponents, and in particular, the struggle between the Teacher of Righteousness and the Wicked Priest.

Recognizable remains of Psalms xlv and cxxvii also survive.

4Q171

I *[Be sil]ent before [the Lord and] long for him, and be not heated against the successful, the man who [achi]eves his plans* (xxxvii, 7a).

Its interpretation concerns the Liar who has led astray many by his lying words so that they chose frivolous things and heeded not the interpreter of knowledge in order to . . . **II** they shall perish by the sword and famine and plague.

Relent from anger and abandon wrath. Do not be angry, it tends only to evil; for the wicked shall be cut off (8–9a).

Interpreted, this concerns all those who return to the Law, to those who do not refuse to turn away from their evil. For all those who are stubborn in turning away from their iniquity shall be cut off.

But those who wait for the Lord shall possess the land (9b).

Interpreted, this is the congregation of His elect who do His will.

A little while and the wicked shall be no more; I will look towards his place but he shall not be there (10).

Interpreted, this concerns all the wicked. At the end of the forty years they shall be blotted out and not an [evil] man shall be found on the earth.

But the humble shall possess the land and delight in abundant peace (11).

Interpreted, this concerns [the congregation of the] Poor who shall accept the season of penance and shall be delivered from all the snares of Satan. Afterwards, all who possess the earth shall delight and prosper on exquisite food.

The wicked draw the sword and bend their bow to bring down the poor and needy and to slay the upright of way. Their sword shall enter their own heart and their bows shall be broken (14–15).

Interpreted, this concerns the wicked of Ephraim and Manasseh, who shall seek to lay hands on the Priest and the men of his Council at the time of trial which shall come upon them. But God will redeem them from out of their hand. And afterwards, they shall be delivered into the hand of the violent among the nations for judgement.

[The Lord knows the days of the perfect and their portion shall be for ever. In evil times they shall not be shamed] (18–19a).

III to the penitents of the desert who, saved, shall live for a thousand generations and to whom all the glory of Adam shall belong, as also to their seed for ever.

And in the days of famine they shall be [satisfi]ed, but the wicked shall perish (19b–20a).

Interpreted, this [means that] He will keep them alive during the famine and the time of humiliation, whereas many shall perish from famine and plague, all those who have not departed [from there] to be with the congregation of His elect.

And those who love the Lord shall be like the pride of pastures (20b).

Interpreted, [this concerns] the congregation of His elect, who shall be leaders and princes . . . of the flock among their herds.

Like smoke they shall all of them vanish away (20c).

Interpreted, [this] concerns the princes [of wickedness] who have oppressed His holy people, and who shall perish like smoke [blown away by the wind].

The wicked borrows and does not repay, but the righteous is generous and gives. Truly, those whom He [blesses shall possess] the land, but those whom He curses [shall be cut off] (21–22).

Interpreted, this concerns the congregation of the Poor, who [shall possess] the whole world as an inheritance. They shall possess the High Mountain of Israel [for ever], and shall enjoy [everlasting] delights in His Sanctuary. [But those who] shall be *cut off,*

they are the violent [of the nations and] the wicked of Israel; they
shall be cut off and blotted out for ever.

*The steps of the man are confirmed by the Lord and He delights in all
his ways; though [he stumble, he shall not fall, for the Lord shall support
his hand] (23–24).*
Interpreted, this concerns the Priest, the Teacher of
[Righteousness whom] God chose to stand before Him, for He
established him to build for Himself the congregation of . . .

IV   *The wicked watches out for the righteous and seeks [to slay him. The
Lord will not abandon him into his hand or] let him be condemned when
he is tried (32–33).*
Interpreted, this concerns the Wicked [Priest] who [watched
the Teacher of Righteousness] that he might put him to death
[because of the ordinance] and the law which he sent to him. But
God will not *aban[don him and will not let him be condemned when he
is] tried.* And [God] will pay him his reward by delivering him into
the hand of the violent of the nations, that they may execute upon
him [judgement].

*For the choirmaster: according to [the lili]es. [for the sons of Korah.
Maskil A song of love.*
Th]ey are the seven divisions of the penitents of Is[rael . . .].

My he[art] is astir with a good word. I speak of my work to the King
(XLV, 1).
[Its interpretation . . . spir]it of holiness for . . . books of . . .

And my tongue is the pen of [a speedy scribe (xlv, 1).
Its interpretation] concerns the Teacher of [Righteous-
ness] . . . God with an answering tongue . . .

4Q173

*[. . . Vai]n is it for you to rise early and lie down late. You shall eat the
bread of toil; [he shall feed those who love him in (their) sleep* (cxxvii, 2).
Its interpretation is th]at they shall seek . . . Teacher of
Righteousness . . . [pri]est at the end of the a[ge] . . .

37. A MIDRASH ON THE LAST DAYS (4Q174)

◦━◦

This collection of texts assembled from 2 Samuel and the Psalter, and combined with other scriptural passages, serves to present the sectarian doctrine identifying the Community with the Temple, and to announce the coming of the two Messiahs, the 'Branch of David' and the 'Interpreter of the Law'. Originating from cave 4 (4Q174), and known also as 'Florilegium' (*DJD* v, pp. 53–7), the composition probably belongs to the late first century B.C.

I . . .*[I will appoint a place for my people Israel and will plant them that they may dwell there and be troubled no more by their] enemies. No son of iniquity [shall afflict them again] as formerly, from the day that [I set judges] over my people Israel* (2 Sam. vii, 10).

This is the House which [He will build for them in the] last days, as it is written in the book of Moses, *In the sanctuary which Thy hands have established, O Lord, the Lord shall reign for ever and ever* (Exod. xv, 17–18). This is the House into which [the unclean shall] never [enter, nor the uncircumcised,] nor the Ammonite, nor the Moabite, nor the half-breed, nor the foreigner, nor the stranger, ever; for there shall My Holy Ones be. [Its glory shall endure] forever; it shall appear above it perpetually. And strangers shall lay it waste no more, as they formerly laid waste the Sanctuary of Israel because of its sin. He has commanded that a Sanctuary of men be built for Himself, that there they may send up, like the smoke of incense, the works of the Law.

And concerning His words to David, *And I [will give] you [rest] from all your enemies* (2 Sam. vii, 11), this means that He will give them rest from all the children of Satan who cause them to stumble so that they may be destroyed [by their errors,] just as they came with a [devilish] plan to cause the [sons] of light to stumble and to devise against them a wicked plot, that [they might become subject] to Satan in their [wicked] straying.

The Lord declares to you that He will build you a House (2 Sam. vii, 11C). *I will raise up your seed after you* (2 Sam. vii, 12). *I will establish the throne of his kingdom [for ever]* (2 Sam. vii, 13). *I [will be] his father and he shall be my son* (2 Sam. vii, 14). He is the Branch of David who shall arise with the Interpreter of the Law [to rule] in Zion [at the end] of time. As it is written, *I will raise up the tent of David that is fallen* (Amos ix, 11). That is to say, the fallen *tent of David* is he who shall arise to save Israel.

Explanation of *How blessed is the man who does not walk in the counsel of the wicked* (Ps. i, 1). Interpreted, this saying [concerns] those who turn aside from the way [of the people] as it is written in the book of Isaiah the Prophet concerning the last days, *It came to pass that [the Lord turned me aside, as with a mighty hand, from walking in the way of] this people* (Isa. viii, 11). They are those of whom it is written in the book of Ezekiel the Prophet, *The Levites [strayed far from me, following] their idols* (Ezek. xliv, 10). They are the sons of Zadok who [seek their own] counsel and follow [their own inclination] apart from the Council of the Community.

[Why] do the nations [rage] and the peoples meditate [vanity, the kings of the earth] rise up, [and the] princes take counsel together against the Lord and against [His Messiah]? (Ps. ii, 1). Interpreted, this saying concerns [the kings of the nations] who shall [rage against] the elect of Israel in the last days. **II** This shall be the time of the trial to co[me over the house of Judah to perfect . . . Belial, and a remnant of the people shall be left according to the lot (assigned to them), and they shall practise the whole Law . . . Moses. This is the time of which it is written in the book of Daniel, the prophet: *But the wicked shall do wickedly and shall not understand, but the righteous shall purify themselves and make themselves white* (Dan. xii, 10). The people who know God shall be strong. They are the masters who understand . . .

38. A MESSIANIC ANTHOLOGY OR TESTIMONIA
(4Q175)

⋘⋙

This short document from cave 4 (4Q175), dating to the early first century B.C., similar in literary style to the Christian *Testimonia*, or collection of Messianic proof-texts, includes five quotations arranged in four groups, the last being followed by a particular interpretation (*DJD* v, pp. 57–60).

The first group consists of two texts from Deuteronomy referring to the Prophet similar to Moses; the second is an extract from a prophecy of Balaam about the royal Messiah; the third is a blessing of the Levites and, implicitly, of the Priest-Messiah.

The last group opens with a verse from Joshua which is then expounded by means of a quotation from the sectarian Psalms of Joshua. Most experts hold that the commentator, bearing in mind the biblical passage, is alluding to three characters, a father ('an accursed man') and his two sons. However, the verb 'arose' in the second sentence is in the singular, and it would seem correct to interpret this text as referring to the two brothers only.

The Lord spoke to Moses saying:

You have heard the words which this people have spoken to you; all they have said is right. O that their heart were always like this, to fear me and to keep my commandments always, that it might be well with them and their children for ever! (Deut. v, 28–9). *I will raise up for them a Prophet like you from among their brethren. I will put my words into his mouth and he shall tell them all that I command him. And I will require a reckoning of whoever will not listen to the words which the Prophet shall speak in my Name* (Deut. xviii, 18–19).

He took up his discourse and said:

Oracle of Balaam son of Beor. Oracle of the man whose eye is penetrating. Oracle of him who has heard the words of God, who knows the wisdom of the Most High and sees the vision of the Almighty, who falls and his eyes are opened. I see him but not now. I behold him but not near. A star shall come out of Jacob and a sceptre shall rise out of Israel; he shall crush the temples of Moab and destroy all the children of Sheth (Num. xxiv, 15–17).

And of Levi he said:

Give Thy Tummim to Levi, and Thy Urim to Thy pious one whom Thou didst test at Massah, and with whom Thou didst quarrel at the waters of Meribah; who said to his father and mother, 'I know you not', and who did not acknowledge his brother, or know his sons. For they observed Thy word and kept Thy Covenant. They shall cause Thy precepts to shine before Jacob and Thy Law before Israel. They shall send up incense towards Thy nostrils and place a burnt offering upon Thine altar. Bless his power, O Lord, and delight in the work of his hands. Smite the loins of his adversaries and let his enemies rise no more (Deut. xxxiii, 8–11).

When Joshua had finished offering praise and thanksgiving, he said:

Cursed be the man who rebuilds this city! May he lay its foundation on his first-born, and set its gate upon his youngest son (Josh. vi, 26). Behold, an accursed man, a man of Satan, has risen to become a fowler's net to his people, and a cause of destruction to all his neighbours. And [his brother] arose [and ruled], both being instruments of violence. They have rebuilt [Jerusalem and have set up] a wall and towers to make of it a stronghold of ungodliness . . . in Israel, and a horror in Ephraim and in Judah . . . They have committed an abomination in the land, and a great blasphemy among the children [of Israel. They have shed blood] like water upon the ramparts of the daughter of Zion and within the precincts of Jerusalem.

39. ORDINANCES OR COMMENTARIES ON BIBLICAL LAWS (4Q159, 4Q513-4)

◦◦◦

Three manuscripts from cave 4 (4Q159, 4Q513-4), published respectively in *DJD* v, pp. 6-9, and vii, pp. 287-98, and probably belonging to the turn of the era, include re-interpretations of various biblical laws.

In the first statute, the interpreter deduces from Deut. xxiii, 25-6, that a poor man may eat ears of corn in the field of another person, but is not allowed to take any home. On a threshing floor, however, he may both eat and gather provisions for his family.

Next follows a statute referring to the tax of half a shekel to be contributed to the upkeep of the place of worship by every Israelite aged twenty. Later Jewish tradition interpreted this passage as instituting a yearly tax to be paid by every male Israelite (cf. Neh. x, 32; Matt. xvii, 24-7; see also the treatise *Shekalim* or *Shekel Dues* in the Mishnah). The Qumran ordinance, however, insists on one single payment, thereby complying with the scriptural rule and at the same time refusing regular support to the Temple of Jerusalem. Here 4Q159 and 4Q513, frs. 1-2, partly overlap.

The third statute (4Q159, frs. 2-4) deals with the prohibition on selling an Israelite as a slave (cf. Lev. xxv, 39-46); with a case to be judged by a court of twelve magistrates; with the forbidden interchange of garments between men and women (cf. Deut. xxii, 5); and with the charge laid by a husband against his wife that she was not a virgin when he married her (Deut. xxii, 13-21).

Finally, 4Q513, frs. 2-4, and 4Q514 legislate on purity rules.

4Q159

II . . .   Any destitute [Israelite] who goes into a threshing floor may eat there and gather for himself and for [his] hou[sehold. But should he walk among corn standing in] the field, he may eat but may not bring it to his house to store it.

Concerning . . . the money of valuation that a man gives as ransom for his life, it shall be half [a shekel . . .] He shall give it only once in his life. Twenty gerahs make one shekel according to [the shekel of the Temple (cf. Exod. xxx, 12–13) . . .] For the 600,000, one hundred talents; for the 3,000, half a talent = 30 minahs); [for the 500, five minahs;] and for the 50, half a minah, (which is) twenty-five shekels (cf. Exod. xxxviii, 25–6) . . .

4Q159, *frs* 2–4

. . . before Isra[el] shall [n]ot serve Gentiles among foreign[ers, for I have brought them out from the land of] Egypt, and I have commanded concerning them that none shall be sold as a slave . . .

. . . [t]en men and two priests, and they shall be judged before these twelve . . . spoke in Israel against a person, they shall inquire in accordance with them. Whosoever shall rebel . . . , shall be put to death for he has acted wilfully.

Let no man's garment be on a woman all [the days of her life]. Let him [not] be covered with a woman's mantle, nor wear a woman's tunic, for this is an abomination.

If a man slanders a virgin of Israel, if in . . . when he married her, let him say so. And they shall examine her [concerning her] trustworthiness, and if he has not lied concerning her, she shall be put to death. But if he has humiliated her [false]ly, he shall be fined two minahs, and shall not divorce her all his life.

4Q513

. . . [Tw]enty [gerahs] make a shekel according to the she[kel of the sanctuary . . .] The half-[shekel consists of twe]lv[e me'ahs, [two] zuzim . . . also sources of uncleanness. The ephah and the bath, also sources of uncleanness, have the same capacity, (viz.) ten 'issarons (=tenths). A bath of wine corresponds to an ephah of corn. The seah consists of three and one-third of 'issarons, sources of uncleanness, and the tithe of the ephah [is the 'issaron].

4Q514

I He shall not eat . . . for all the unclean . . . to count for [him seven days of wa]shing and he shall wash and cleanse on the d[a]y of [his] purification. Whoever has not begun his purification from his 'fo[un]t' [shall not eat]. [Neither shall he eat] in his first (degree of) uncleanness. All those temporarily unclean shall wash on the day of their [pu]rification, and cleanse (their garments) with water and shall become clean. Afterwards they may eat their bread according to the law of purity. Whoever has not begun his purification from his 'fount' shall not eat [and be arrogant] in his first (degree of) uncleanness. Whoever is still in his first (degree of) uncleanness shall not eat. All those temporarily [un]clean on the day of their pu[rification] shall wash and cleanse (their garments) with water and they shall be clean. Afterwards they may eat their bread according to the l[aw. None] shall e[at] or drink with whomsoev[er] prepares . . .

40. THE HEAVENLY PRINCE MELCHIZEDEK
(11Q Melch)

◦⌁◦

A striking first-century-B.C. document, composed of thirteen fragments from cave 11 and centred on the mysterious figure of Melchizedek, was first published by A. S. van der Woude in 1965. It takes the form of an eschatological midrash in which the proclamation of liberty to the captives at the end of days (Isa. lxi, 1) is understood as being part of the general restoration of property during the year of Jubilee (Lev. xxv, 13), seen in the Bible (Deut. xv, 2) as a remission of debts.

The heavenly deliverer is Melchizedek. Identical with the archangel Michael, he is the head of the 'sons of Heaven' or 'gods of Justice' and is referred to as *elohim* and *el*. The same terminology occurs in the Songs for the Holocaust of the Sabbath. These Hebrew words normally mean 'God', but in certain specific contexts Jewish tradition also explains *elohim* as primarily designating a 'judge'. Here Melchizedek is portrayed as presiding over the final Judgement and condemnation of his demonic counterpart, Belial/Satan, the Prince of Darkness, elsewhere also called Melkiresha' (cf. above pp. 161, 263). The great act of deliverance is expected to occur on the Day of Atonement at the end of the tenth Jubilee cycle.

This manuscript sheds valuable light not only on the Melchizedek figure of the Epistle to the Hebrews vii, but also on the development of the messianic concept in the New Testament and early Christianity.

For the text, see A. S. van der Woude, 'Melchizedek als himmlische Erlösergestalt . . .'. *Oudtestamentische Studien*, Leiden, 1965, pp. 354–73; M. de Jonge, A. S. van der Woude, '11Q Melchizedek and the New Testament', *New Testament Studies*, 1966, pp. 301–26; J. T. Milik, *Journal of Jewish Studies*, 1972, pp. 96–109.

. . . And concerning that which He said, *In [this] year of Jubilee [each of you shall return to his property* (Lev. xxv, 13); and likewise, *And this is the manner of release:] every creditor shall release that which he has lent [to his neighbour. He shall not exact it of his neighbour and his brother], for God's release [has been proclaimed]* (Deut. xv, 2). [And it will be proclaimed at] the end of days concerning the captives as [He said, *To proclaim liberty to the captives* (Isa. lxi, 1). Its interpretation is that He] will assign them to the Sons of Heaven and to the inheritance of

Melchizedek; f[or He will cast] their [lot] amid the po[rtions of Melch-ize]dek, who will return them there and will proclaim to them liberty, forgiving them [the wrong-doings] of all their iniquities.

And this thing will [occur] in the first week of the Jubilee that follows the nine Jubilees. And the Day of Atonement is the e[nd of the] tenth [Ju]bilee, when all the Sons of [Light] and the men of the lot of Mel[chi]zedek will be atoned for. [And] a statute concerns them [to prov]ide them with their rewards. For this is the moment of the Year of Grace for Melchizedek. [And h]e will, by his strength, judge the holy ones of God, executing judgement as it is written concerning him in the Songs of David, who said, ELOHIM *has taken his place in the divine council; in the midst of the gods he holds judgement* (Psalms lxxxii, 1). And it was concerning him that he said, (Let the assembly of the peoples) *return to the height above them;* EL (*god*) *will judge the peoples* (Psalms vii, 7–8). As for that which he s[aid, *How long will you] judge unjustly and show partiality to the wicked? Selah* (Psalms lxxxii, 2), its interpretation concerns Satan and the spirits of his lot [who] rebelled by turning away from the precepts of God to . . . And Melchizedek will avenge the vengeance of the judge-ments of God . . . and he will drag [them from the hand of] Satan and from the hand of all the sp[irits of] his [lot]. And all the 'gods [of Justice'] will come to his aid [to] attend to the de[struction] of Satan. And *the height* is . . . all the sons of God . . . this . . . This is the day of [Peace/Salvation] concerning which [God] spoke [through Isa]iah the prophet, who said, *[How] beautiful upon the moun-tains are the feet of the messenger who proclaims peace, who brings good news, who proclaims salvation, who says to Zion: Your* ELOHIM [*reigns*] (Isa. lii. 7). Its interpretation; *the mountains* are the prophets . . . and *the messenger* is the Anointed one of the spirit, concerning whom Dan [iel] said, *[Until an anointed one, a prince* (Dan. ix, 25)] . . . [And he *who brings] good [news], who proclaims [salvation]: it is concerning him that it is written* . . .*[To comfort all who mourn, to grant to those who mourn in Zion]* (Isa. lxi, 2–3). *To comfort [those who mourn:* its interpretation], to make them understand all the ages of t[ime] . . . In truth . . . will turn away from Satan . . . by the judgement[s] of God, as it is written concerning him, [*who says to Zion; your* ELOHIM *reigns. Zion* is . . ., those who uphold the Covenant, who turn from walking [in] the way of the people. And *your* ELOHIM is [Melchizedek, who will save them from] the hand of Satan.

As for that which He said, *Then you shall send abroad [the loud] trum-p[et] in the [seventh] m[on]th* (Lev. xxv, 9) . . .

41. CONSOLATIONS OR TANHUMIM (4Q176)

❦

A large number of small fragments of a cave 4 manuscript (4Q176), edited by J. M. Allegro in 1968 (*DJD*, v, 60–67) represent a scriptural anthology centred on the theme of divine consolation. Originally, each citation was accompanied by a sectarian exegesis, but only a few examples of the latter survive. The majority of the extant remains belong to Isaiah xl–lv. The translated passage is based on Psalm lxxix, 2–3, and is followed by a new title – From the Book of Isaiah: Consolations – and the quotation of the opening verses of Isa. xl. The four asterisks symbolize the Tetragram indicated simply by dots.

I   And he shall accomplish Thy miracles and Thy righteousness among Thy people. And they shall . . . Thy sanctuary, and shall dispute with the kingdoms over the blood of . . . Jerusalem and shall see the bodies of Thy priests . . . *and none to bury them* (Ps. lxxix, 3). From the Book of Isaiah: Consolations [*Comfort, comfort, my people] – says your God – speak to the heart of Jerusalem and c[ry to her that] her [bondage is completed], that her punishment is accepted, that she has received from the hand of **** double for all her sins . . .* (Isa. xl, 1–3).

D. MISCELLANEA

42. 'HOROSCOPES' (4Q186, 4QMessAr)

◦◦◦

Two documents from cave 4, one in Hebrew, the other in Aramaic, both dating probably to the end of the first century B.C., contain fragments of 'horoscopes', or more precisely, astrological physiognomies claiming a correspondence between a person's features and destiny and the configuration of the stars at the time of his birth.

The Hebrew text, published by J. M. Allegro, is written in a childish cypher. The text runs from left to right instead of the normal right to left and uses, in addition to the current Hebrew 'square' alphabet, letters borrowed from the archaic Hebrew (or Phoenician) and Greek scripts. The spiritual qualities of three individuals described there are reflected in their share of Light and Darkness. The first man is very wicked: eight parts of Darkness to a single part of Light. The second man is largely good: six parts of Light against three parts of Darkness. The last is almost perfect: eight portions of Light and only one of Darkness.

As far as physical characteristics are concerned, shortness, fatness, and irregularity of the features are associated with wickedness, and their opposites reflect virtue.

In the astrological terminology of the document, the 'second Column' doubtless means the 'second House'; and a birthday 'in the foot of the Bull' should probably be interpreted as the presence, at that moment, of the sun in the lower part of the constellation Taurus.

The Aramaic 'horoscope' is, according to its editor J. Starcky, that of the final Prince of the Congregation, or Royal Messiah. It is just as likely, however, that the text alludes to the miraculous birth of Noah (cf. pp. 252–3 above).

Whether the sectaries forecast the future by means of astrology, or merely used horoscope-like compositions as literary devices, it is impossible to decide at present, though I am inclined towards the latter alternative. That such texts are found among the Scrolls should not, however, surprise anyone. For if many Jews frowned on astrology, others, such as the Hellenistic Jewish writer Eupolemus, credited its invention to Abraham! (Cf. G. Vermes, *Scripture and Tradition in Judaism*, Leiden, 1973, pp. 80–82.)

For the texts see J. M. Allegro, A. A. Anderson, *DJD* v, pp. 88–91; J. Strugnell, *Revue de Qumrân*, 1970, pp. 274–6; J. Starcky, 'Un texte

messianique araméen de la grotte 4 de Qumrân', *Mémorial du cinquan-
tenaire de L'École des langues orientales anciennes de l'Institut Catholique de
Paris*, Paris, 1964, pp. 51–66.

'Horoscopes' 4Q186(1)

II . . . and his thighs are long and lean, and his toes are thin
and long. He is of the second Column. His spirit consists of six
(parts) in the House of Light and three in the Pit of Darkness.
And this is his birthday on which he (is to be/was?) born: in the
foot of the Bull. He will be meek. And his animal is the bull.
III . . . and his head . . . [and his cheeks are] fat. His teeth are
of uneven length (?). His fingers are thick, and his thighs are
thick and very hairy, each one. His toes are thick and short. His
spirit consists of eight (parts) in the House of Darkness and one
from the House of Light . . .

'Horoscopes' 4Q186(2)

I . . . order. His eyes are black and glowing. His beard is . . .
and it is . . . His voice is gentle. His teeth are fine and well aligned.
He is neither tall, nor short. And he . . . And his fingers are thin
and long. And his thighs are smooth. And the soles of his feet . . .
[And his toes] are well aligned. His spirit consists of eight (parts)
[in the House of Light, of] the second Column, and one [in the
House of Darkness. And this is] his birthday on which he (is to
be/was) born: . . . And his animal is . . .

'Horoscope' of the Messiah or an Account of the Birth of Noah
(4QMessAr)

I . . . of his hand: two . . . a birthmark. And the hair will be red.
And there will be lentils on . . . and small birthmarks on his thigh.
[And after t]wo years he will know (how to distinguish) one thing
from another. In his youth, he will be like . . . [like a m]an who
knows nothing until the time when he knows the three Books.
    And then he will acquire wisdom and learn und[erstand-
ing] . . . vision to come to him on his knees. And with his father
and his ancestors . . . life and old age. Counsel and prudence will
be with him, and he will know the secrets of man. His wisdom
will reach all the peoples, and he will know the secrets of all the
living. And all their designs against him will come to nothing, and

(his) rule over all the living will be great. His designs [will succeed] for he is the Elect of God. His birth and the breath of his spirit . . . and his designs shall be for ever . . .

APPENDICES

❧

The Copper Scroll (3Q15)

Strictly speaking, The Copper Scroll (3Q15) does not fall within the scope of the present book since it is a non-religious document, but it has stimulated so much curiosity and speculation that the reader may appreciate a brief summary of its discovery and contents, and of the argument surrounding it.

It was found by archaeologists in cave 3 during the excavations of 1952, but the metal had become so badly oxidized during the course of the centuries that the scroll could not be unfolded. It was therefore sent to Professor H. Wright Baker of the Manchester College of Science and Technology who, in 1956, carefully divided it into longitudinal strips and, in the same year, returned it to Jordan. The Hebrew text, representing twelve columns of script, was published by J. T. Milik in *DJD* III, Oxford, 1962, pp. 199–302.

The inscription lists sixty-four hiding-places, in Jerusalem and in various districts of Palestine, where gold, silver, aromatics, scrolls, etc., are said to have been deposited. Allegro reckons that the treasure must have amounted to over three thousand talents of silver, nearly one thousand three hundred talents of gold, sixty-five bars of gold, six hundred and eight pitchers containing silver, and six hundred and nineteen gold and silver vessels. In other words, using the post-biblical value of the talent as a yardstick, the total weight of precious metal must have added up to sixty-five tons of silver and twenty-six tons of gold.

Who could have possessed such a fortune? Was there ever any truth in it?

J. T. Milik thinks not. He believes that the exaggerated sums indicate that the scroll is a work of fiction and that its chief interest to scholars lies in the fields of linguistics and topography. He dates it from about A.D. 100, thus ruling out any connection with the rest of the Qumran writings since the latter were placed in the caves not later than A.D. 68.

Other scholars hold that the treasure was a real one. A. Dupont-Sommer maintains that it represented the fortune of the Essene sect, while K. G. Kuhn, Chaim Rabin, and J. M. Allegro believe that it belonged to the Temple of Jerusalem, Allegro adding to this hypothesis the theory that the Zealots were responsible for the concealment of the gold and silver and for the writing of the scroll. It has also been suggested that we are dealing here with funds collected for the rebuilding of the Temple after A.D. 70, or with the hidden treasure of Bar Kokhba, leader of the second Jewish revolution against Rome in A.D. 132–5.

Milik's argument would certainly seem to account for the vast quantities of treasure mentioned. It does not, however, explain two of the document's most striking characteristics, namely, the dry realism of its style, very different from that of ancient legends, and the fact that it is recorded on copper instead of on the less expensive leather or papyrus. For if it is, in fact, a sort of fairy-story, the present text can only represent the outline of such a tale, and who in their senses would have engraved their literary notes on valuable metal?

It goes without saying that the contention that the treasure was a real one is supported by the very arguments which undermine Milik's. From the business-like approach, and the enduring material on which the catalogue is inscribed, it might sensibly be supposed that the writer was not indulging some frivolous dream. Again, in view of the fact that the Copper Scroll was found among writings known to come from Qumran, Dupont-Sommer would appear justified in allocating the fortune to the Essenes. It requires, by comparison, a strong feat of the imagination to accept that all this wealth belonged originally to the treasure chambers of the Temple, and that it was placed in hiding, in a hostile environment, in A.D. 68: before, that is to say, there was any immediate danger to the capital city of Jerusalem. Allegro bypasses this objection by presuming that, as Qumran was by then in the hands of the Zealots, it was no longer unfriendly to the Jerusalem authorities. But it has not yet been explained why the sack of the Temple and city should have been foreseen, and provided for, so early.

In favour of Kuhn, Rabin and Allegro, it is nevertheless possible to envisage that the Temple possessed such riches as these, whereas, despite Dupont-Sommer's undoubtedly true remarks concerning the apparent compatibility of religious poverty and fat revenues, it is still hard to accept that the Essenes, a relatively small community, should have amassed such disproportionate wealth.

This is all that can safely be said of the Copper Scroll at the present time. Access to the original document, now housed in Amman in Jordan, will allow scholars to improve their reading of the extremely difficult text – the published reproductions are of little use in this respect – but even so, it will probably be some time before a convincing answer is given to the many puzzles confronting us.

B.C.

197   Judaea became a province of the Seleucid Empire ruled by the Syrian successors of ALEXANDER THE GREAT.

187–175   SELEUCUS IV. Beginning of Hellenistic infiltration, resisted by the Zadokite High Priest ONIAS III.

175–164   ANTIOCHUS IV (EPIPHANES). ONIAS deposed and replaced by his Hellenophile brother JASON.

172   JASON expelled from office in favour of MENELAUS, Hellenizing High Priest from 172–162 B.C.

171   ONIAS III murdered at the instigation of MENELAUS. Forced Hellenization.

169   ANTIOCHUS led by MENELAUS profaned and plundered the Temple of Jerusalem.

168   ANTIOCHUS thwarted by the Romans in his second campaign against Egypt.

167   Persecution of those Jews who opposed the unification of the Seleucid Empire on the basis of Greek culture and religion. Official abolition of Jewish religion and practice under threat of death. The Temple transformed into a sanctuary of Olympian Zeus.

166   Rising of the Maccabees supported by all the traditional parties under the leadership of JUDAS MACCABEE.

164   Truce. Cleansing of the Temple, still held by MENELAUS.

162–150   DEMETRIUS I. MENELAUS executed by the Syrians. ALCIMUS appointed High Priest by the king.

161   JUDAS killed in battle. JONATHAN assumed leadership of the rebels (161–152 B.C.).

160   ALCIMUS, the last Hellenizing High Priest, died of a stroke. End of Syrian military intervention.

152–145   ALEXANDER BALAS usurped the Seleucid throne and appointed JONATHAN High Priest (152–143/2 B.C.).

145–142   ANTIOCHUS VI, son of ALEXANDER, raised to the throne by TRYPHON, his father's general. JONATHAN named governor of Syria. SIMON, his brother, made military governor of the Palestinian littoral.

143	JONATHAN arrested by TRYPHON.
143/2–135/4	SIMON High Priest and ethnarch.
142	JONATHAN executed in prison.
140	SIMON's titles confirmed as hereditary. Foundation of the Maccabean, or Hasmonean, dynasty.
135/4	SIMON murdered by his son-in-law.
135/4–104	JOHN HYRCANUS I High Priest and ethnarch. Opposed by the Pharisees.
104–103	ARISTOBULUS I High Priest and king.
103–76	ALEXANDER JANNAEUS High Priest, king, and conqueror. Resisted by the Pharisees.
76–67	ALEXANDRA, widow of JANNAEUS, queen. Friend of the Pharisees. HYRCANUS II High Priest.
67	HYRCANUS II king and High Priest. Deposed by his brother ARISTOBULUS.
67-63	ARISTOBULUS II king and High Priest. Taken prisoner by POMPEY in 63 B.C. after the fall of Jerusalem. Judaea became a Roman province.
63–40	HYRCANUS II reinstated as High Priest without the royal title.
40–37	ANTIGONUS, son of ARISTOBULUS II, occupied the throne and pontificate with Parthian support. HYRCANUS maimed and exiled.
37–4	HEROD THE GREAT. End of Hasmonean dynasty. HYRCANUS executed in 30 B.C.
27–A.D. 14	AUGUSTUS emperor.
6 B.C. (?)	Birth of JESUS OF NAZARETH.
4 B.C.-A.D. 6	ARCHELAUS ethnarch of Judaea and Samaria.

A.D.

14–37	TIBERIUS emperor.
26–36	PONTIUS PILATE prefect of Judaea.
27–30 (?)	Ministry and crucifixion of JESUS.
66–70	First Jewish War ending with the capture of Jerusalem and the destruction of the Temple by TITUS.
74	Fall of Masada.

MAJOR EDITIONS OF QUMRAN MANUSCRIPTS

❧

Cave 1

M. Burrows, J. C. Trever, W. H. Brownlee, *The Dead Sea Scrolls of St. Mark's Monastery* I (New Haven, 1950): contains Isaiah[a], Habakkuk Commentary; II/2 (New Haven, 1951): Manual of Discipline=1QS. There is no II/1.

E. L. Sukenik, *The Dead Sea Scrolls of the Hebrew University* (Jerusalem, 1954–5): contains Isaiah[b], War Rule, Thanksgiving Hymns.

D. Barthélemy, J. T. Milik, *Discoveries in the Judaean Desert I: Qumran Cave I* (Oxford, 1955): contains all the fragments from 1Q.

N. Avigad, Y. Yadin, *A Genesis Apocryphon* (Jerusalem, 1956).

Caves 2–3 and 5–10

M. Baillet, J. T. Milik, R. de Vaux, *Discoveries in the Judaean Desert of Jordan III: Les petites grottes de Qumrân* (Oxford, 1962): contains fragments and the Copper Scroll.

Cave 4

J. M. Allegro, A. A. Anderson, *Discoveries in the Judaean Desert of Jordan V: I (4Q158–4Q186)* (Oxford, 1968): contains mostly exegetical fragments. For editorial improvements, see J. Strugnell, 'Notes en marge du volume V des *Discoveries in the Judaean Desert of Jordan*', *Revue de Qumrân* 7 (1970), pp. 163–276.

J. T. Milik, *The Books of Enoch: Aramaic Fragments of Qumran Cave 4* (Oxford, 1976).

R. de Vaux, J. T. Milik, *Discoveries in the Judaean Desert VII: Qumran Grotte 4 II: I. Archéologie. II. Tefillin, Mezuzot et Targums (4Q128–4Q157)* (Oxford, 1977).

M. Baillet, *Discoveries in the Judaean Desert VII: Qumran Grotte 4 III (4Q482–4Q520)* (Oxford, 1982): contains fragments of the War Rule and remains of liturgical and sapiential compositions.

314

Carol Newsom, *Songs of the Sabbath Sacrifice: A Critical Edition* (Atlanta, 1985).

Judith E. Sanderson, *An Exodus Scroll from Qumran: 4QpaleoExod^m and the Samaritan Tradition* (Atlanta, 1986).

Eileen M. Schuller, *Non-Canonical Psalms from Qumran: A Pseudepigraphic Collection* (Atlanta, 1987).

Cave 11

J. A. Sanders, *Discoveries in the Judaean Desert of Jordan IV: The Psalm Scroll of Qumran Cave 11 (11QPs^a)* (Oxford, 1965).

J. P. M. van der Ploeg, A. S. van der Woude, B. Jongeling, *Le Targum de Job de la grotte XI de Qumrân* (Leiden 1971).

Y. Yadin, *M^egillat ha-Miqdash* I–III (Jerusalem, 1977)=*The Temple Scroll* I–III (Jerusalem, 1983).

D. N. Freedman, K. A. Matthews, *The Paleo-Hebrew Leviticus Scroll (11QpaleoLev)* (Winona Lake, 1985).

Unidentified Cave

Y. Yadin, *Tefillin from Qumran (XQPhyl 1–4)* (Jerusalem, 1969).

GENERAL BIBLIOGRAPHY

❦

The following list contains standard introductory material to the Dead Sea Scrolls, published in English, both for the general reader and for college and university students.

1. Qumran Bibliographies

B. Jongeling, *A Classified Bibliography of the Finds in the Desert of Judah: 1958–1969* (Leiden, 1971).

J. A. Fitzmyer, *The Dead Sea Scrolls: Major Publications and Tools for Study* (Missoula, 1975; 2nd edn, 1977).

2. General Studies

M. Burrows, *The Dead Sea Scrolls* (New York, 1955).

T. H. Gaster, *The Dead Sea Scriptures in English Translation* (Garden City, New York, 1956; 3rd edn, 1976).

M. Burrows, *More Light on the Dead Sea Scrolls* (New York, 1958).

F. M. Cross, *The Ancient Library of Qumran and Modern Biblical Studies* (New York, 1958; Grand Rapids, 2nd edn, 1980).

J. T. Milik, *Ten Years of Discovery in the Wilderness of Judaea* (London, 1959).

A. Dupont-Sommer, *The Essene Writings from Qumran* (Oxford, 1961).

G. R. Driver, *The Judaean Scrolls* (Oxford, 1965).

Edmund Wilson, *The Dead Sea Scrolls 1947–1969* (London, 1969).

R. de Vaux, *The Archaeology of the Dead Sea Scrolls* (London, 1973).

G. Vermes, *The Dead Sea Scrolls: Qumran in Perspective* (London, 1977; Philadelphia, 1981; 2nd edn, London, 1982).

G. W. E. Nickelsburg, *Jewish Literature Between the Bible and the Mishnah* (Philadelphia and London, 1981).

P. R. Davies, *Qumran* (Guildford, 1982).

B. Z. Wacholder, *The Dawn of Qumran: The Sectarian Torah and the Teacher of Righteousness* (Cincinnati, 1983).

D. Dimant, 'Qumran Sectarian Literature' in M. Stone (ed.), *Jewish Writings of the Second Temple Period* (Assen and Philadelphia, 1984).

3. Vocalized Hebrew Text and Qumran Hebrew

E. Lohse, *Die Texte aus Qumran hebräisch und deutsch* (Munich, 1964; 2nd edn, 1971).

E. Qimron, *The Hebrew of the Dead Sea Scrolls* (Atlanta, 1986).

M. A. Knibb, *The Qumran Community* (Cambridge, 1987)

4. Advanced Introduction

E. Schürer, G. Vermes, F. Millar, M. Goodman, *The History of the Jewish People in the Age of Jesus Christ* III, part 1–2 (Edinburgh, 1986). (Contains detailed classified bibliographies.)

5. The Scrolls and the New Testament

K. Stendahl (ed.), *The Scrolls and the New Testament* (London, 1958).

M. Black, *The Scrolls and Christian Origins* (London, 1961).

J. Murphy-O'Connor (ed.), *Paul and Qumran* (London, 1968).

M. Black (ed.). *The Scrolls and Christianity* (London, 1969).

J. H. Charlesworth (ed.), *John and Qumran* (London, 1972).

G. Vermes, *Jesus and the World of Judaism* (London, 1983; Philadelphia, 1984).

M. Newton, *The Concept of Purity at Qumran and in the Letters of Paul* (Cambridge, 1985).

N. S. Fujita, *A Crack in the Jar: What Ancient Jewish Documents Tell us about the New Testament* (New York, 1986).

INDEX